ADVANCE PRAISE

"Timely, relevant, and necessary. In these unprecedented times, Patricia Jennings provides readers with a valuable resource steeped in history, research, powerful anecdotes, and illuminating frameworks that help to support teachers. *Teacher Burnout Turnaround* is an important read for those who want to disrupt the chronic burnout that plagues too many of our teachers."

—**Tyrone C. Howard,** Pritzker Family Endowed Chair of
Education, University of California, Los Angeles

"Dig deeper into the lives of people who eventually 'beat the odds,' and you'll likely find human relationships that helped. And quite possibly, one of those relationships will have been with a teacher: one who helped them believe in themselves, whatever their life circumstances—a teacher like Patricia Jennings. After reading Patricia's new book, *Teacher Burnout Turnaround*, I'm reminded that our greatest source of strength may actually be each other."

—**Mark Katz, Ph.D.,** author of *Children Who Fail at School
but Succeed at Life* and *On Playing a Poor Hand Well*

"*Teacher Burnout Turnaround* empowers teachers to change the education system from within in ways that will improve both their own and their students' well-being. Readers will find helpful classroom examples throughout. Jennings—a leader in creating caring and prosocial classrooms—speaks directly to teachers, But anyone concerned with education, including professors, professional development providers, administrators, and policy makers, will find it richly thought provoking."

—**Christi Bergin, Ph.D.,** Associate Dean of Research & Innovation,
College of Education, University of Missouri, and
author of *Designing a Prosocial Classroom*

"Dr. Jennings has embraced and shared the research on mindfulness practices, showing educators how contagious feelings are in our classrooms, schools, and districts. Her new book is a critically important read for all educators and staff in this time of unpredictable chronic adversities; it can help alleviate the pain and fear many of our children and adults will carry into our buildings!"

—**Lori Desautels, Ph.D.,** Assistant Professor, Butler University

TEACHER BURNOUT
TURNAROUND

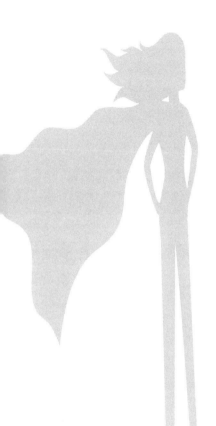

TEACHER BURNOUT TURNAROUND

STRATEGIES FOR EMPOWERED EDUCATORS

Patricia A. Jennings

Foreword by Chad Ratliff

W. W. NORTON & COMPANY

Independent Publishers Since 1923

Note to Readers: Models and/or techniques described in this volume are illustrative or are included for general informational purposes only; neither the publisher nor the author(s) can guarantee the efficacy or appropriateness of any particular recommendation in every circumstance. As of press time, the URLs displayed in this book link or refer to existing sites. The publisher and author are not responsible for any content that appears on third-party websites.

For information about permission to reproduce selections from this book, write to
Permissions, W. W. Norton & Company, Inc., 500 Fifth Avenue, New York, NY 10110

For information about special discounts for bulk purchases, please contact
W. W. Norton Special Sales at specialsales@wwnorton.com or 800-233-4830

Manufacturing by Sheridan Books
Production manager: Katelyn MacKenzie

Library of Congress Cataloging-in-Publication Data

Names: Jennings, Patricia A., author.
Title: Teacher burnout turnaround : strategies for empowered educators / Patricia A. Jennings.
Description: First edition. | New York : W. W. Norton & Company, [2021] |
    Series: Norton Books in education | Includes bibliographical references and index.
Identifiers: LCCN 2020019905 | ISBN 9780393714258 (paperback) |
    ISBN 9780393714265 (epub)
Subjects: LCSH: Teachers—Job stress. | Burn out (Psychology)—Prevention. |
    Stress management. | Affective education.
Classification: LCC LB2840.2 .J46 2021 | DDC 371.1001/9—dc23
LC record available at https://lccn.loc.gov/2020019905

W. W. Norton & Company, Inc., 500 Fifth Avenue, New York, N.Y. 10110
www.wwnorton.com

W. W. Norton & Company Ltd., 15 Carlisle Street, London W1D 3BS

1 2 3 4 5 6 7 8 9 0

This book is dedicated to the teachers of the world who devote their lives to the optimal development of our children and youths. It is time for society to recognize our important work, and to shift societal priorities to transforming our schools and our communities to tackle the current and future challenges before us with courage, mindfulness, compassion, and creativity. My hope is that this book ushers in the decade of the teacher.

Contents

Foreword

On Liberating Teachers

by Chad Ratliff

"Leaders who do not act dialogically, but insist on imposing their decisions, do not organize the people—they manipulate them. They do not liberate, nor are they liberated: they oppress."

Paolo Freire, Pedagogy of the Oppressed

Today teachers are faced with unprecedented demands resulting in extremely high levels of burnout and attrition. A matrix of pressures bears down on the profession, many stemming from the antiquated system we have inherited from the industrial revolution. We are now well into the twenty-first century; however, our school systems have been left far behind. Fortunately, there is hope that these systems can be transformed from within by applying systems and design thinking to this problem.

Educators are finding themselves uniquely positioned to be the agents of this change. However, in order to do this, educators need a toolbox of skills that will help us build inner resilience, change the way we think about school, and empower our students. *Teacher Burnout Turnaround* provides such a toolbox and comes at a particularly critical juncture in education. As we try to change our teaching and learning to adapt to the challenges of living in a pandemic, these skills are more essential than ever. Those of us who are committed to this transformational process will find this an essential guide.

Educational dialogue takes place on three levels: philosophy, policy, and practice. Policy is the political manifestation of a philosophy that defines the purpose of schooling. Practice is rooted in and driven by one's own philosophy within the context of policy. Too often, teachers give little thought to the cultivation of a philosophical foundation, so their practice defaults to prior educational experiences. This means the vast majority of public school teachers are traditionalists without even knowing it.

Liberating teachers—adult learners—begins by exposing them to how schooling can be different, and how that difference can change our calculus of winners and losers. But this isn't done by projecting slides on a screen; it requires that one person who, in the face of dissonance, will change and then bring others along. One person at a time, the fundamental philosophical shift essential to deep change becomes practice. A leader can't mandate agency. Leaders first have to know educators as individuals, then give them the autonomy to reflect on challenges to their beliefs. That begins with understanding how the tightly-held beliefs about schooling were formed, as well as how they became part of DNA of education.

Essentially, two types of schooling exist: that which seeks to assimilate and oppress and that which seeks to enlighten and empower. This book speaks to those of us committed to the latter. Incremental shifts in practice are not the focus of our work. We are committed to significant transformation of the teaching and learning culture in our schools. We have learned that for educators to change pedagogies, they must commit to learning *how to learn* in today's world. This means reflection, inquiry, and study in collaboration with colleagues and mentors. Provocation of thought and processing drives professional growth beyond superficial change to deep change, that which results in substantively different learning experiences for young people. We see this occur when professional learning opportunities shift from normative learning (top-down and program-driven) to experiential learning that gets educators out of the box. When our educators own their learning, seeing themselves as designers, creators, and makers, they shift their approach to working with learners.

Tish Jennings trusts teachers. She believes many problems in schools can be solved through an authentic emancipation of the energy, commitment, imagination, and potential of teachers and principals. This accessible guide for school change keeps students and teachers at the center of the work to ensure deep, meaningful, sustainable, and long overdue shifts in traditional schooling. As the education sector and indeed, society as a whole, undergoes a period of great historical change, the timing is perfect for *Teacher Burnout Turnaround: Strategies for Empowered Educators.*

Acknowledgments

This book was inspired by the work of many education reformers who focused on student-centered, inquiry based, experiential education and the ongoing work of teaching as learning. My study of the work of Maria Montessori and subsequent years applying her methods and philosophy in both private and public-school settings inspired me to extend my work beyond the single classroom. My work is also inspired by the Reggio Emilia approach, the creative aspects of the Waldorf approach, and Vygotsky. Finally, I must thank the many developmental scholars who have contributed to our understanding of how children learn and develop and how best to optimize this process in school settings. Now is the time to apply this knowledge to truly fulfilling the promise of the public school system: to prepare our youngest for the challenges and opportunities to come.

TEACHER BURNOUT

TURNAROUND

Introduction

For the past twenty years, I have been carefully following the teacher burnout crisis and watching as each year the attrition rate increases. We have now reached a crossroads; the exodus of teachers from the profession is real and growing, and the problem is threatening to unravel our education systems across the country and around the world. As a teacher, teacher educator, and researcher studying teacher stress, the causes of teacher burnout became clear: untenable working conditions and completely misguided reform efforts. To address this crisis, educators must be actively engaged in school transformation. As teachers, we understand what our students need more than anyone. Furthermore, the growing teacher shortage gives us new leverage in a rapidly failing system. I wrote this book to guide teachers through the process of effecting change by learning how to apply systems and design thinking, as well as how to use their leverage to make sustainable change from the ground up. Finally, I hope to inspire teachers to empower their students to engage in meaningful, self-directed learning that will prepare them for the coming decades of uncertainty.

The Evolution of My Thinking

I began my teaching career as a Montessori teacher, first working with preschoolers, and then students grades 1–5. Creating completely student-centered learning environments, I had the inspiring opportunity to witness the power of children's innate drive to learn. When students are guided towards directing their own learning, the teacher's job is much easier. I created and maintained the rich environment full of autodidactic materials, showed students how to use them, and created norms and procedures to facilitate ongoing assessment and cooperation. Most important of all, together we created a strong community bond by engaging in cooperative learning projects and sharing the thrill of discovery. While working under these conditions was truly rewarding, I saw a greater need among the many children and youths who did not have the opportunity to access such innovative educational environments. I felt driven to discover a way to contribute and help transform the public school system.

As I began working in the public schools as a teacher and as a teacher educator, the contrasts were striking. In a small, independent school, you can create your own schedule. You are not harnessed to an oppressive time structure managed by harsh bells (which always made me jump, because I was so immersed in my teaching that they took me by surprise). This inflexible schedule is in some ways the hallmark of the public school system because it controls so much of what we can do during the school day. It is also a remnant of the factory system that early policy-makers applied to the challenge of scaling a school system for a growing population.

I witnessed and experienced for myself how oppressive the system can be, especially in contrast to the student-centered, cooperative learning model. I also worked as the internship director for a teacher education program and taught classroom management. These roles gave me the opportunity to spend many hours observing classrooms and the student teachers in my classes. I noticed how stressful the public school classroom can be, and how this stress can interfere with classroom management, exacerbating the stress. However, I didn't have the skills or knowledge to understand why it is stressful and how to help teachers manage this stress, so I went back to graduate school and earned a doctorate in human development, with a focus on adult social and emotional development, stress, and coping. Applying this learning to my previous experience, it became crystal clear why teaching is stressful. As I began to scour the research literature on teacher stress, I was surprised to find that very little research had addressed this issue.

I led the development of a mindfulness-based intervention called Cultivating Awareness and Resilience in Education (CARE) designed to address teacher stress, and I conducted extensive research to prove its efficacy. However, throughout this research there was always a question nudging me from the background. While CARE was helping teachers manage emotional reactivity and reduce some of the stressful conditions in their classrooms, it wasn't addressing the oppressive system weighing them down. It became clear that the context needed to be addressed as well. As I accumulated more knowledge about the nature of the system and its impact on teachers and students, I began to see opportunities for change. As greater numbers of teachers were leaving the profession for retirement or more lucrative professions, and fewer young people were seeing teaching as a viable professional option, it dawned on me that the shortage itself could be a point of leverage for teachers to change the system from within. I began to study the systems themselves to understand the primary drivers of teacher stress and identify the leverage points that teachers could use to effect change. It became clear that teachers are best positioned to understand how to transform the system because we have the most direct contact with our students, who, after all, are the primary reason we have an education system. I also saw how the system had disempowered teachers from the beginning, and how we would need to reconceptualize our profession to empower ourselves to become such change agents.

At the same time, I was aware of the increasing rate of change in our society and how, more than ever, we need to harness all of our diversity to tackle the problems we collectively face. It became clear that without a school system that honors and cultivates this diversity, we may be putting our collective resilience at risk. Like the factory farm model designed to produce uniform ears of corn, our schools are designed to produce uniform students, assessed by a standard that stigmatizes, rather than celebrates, differences. Grown like this, the corn is much more susceptible to blight. Similarly, our factory model schools are making us more susceptible to the multiple risks we face today, from climate security to unusual pathogens such as COVID-19, by strangling the creativity of our future workforce. At a time when we need the diversity of human perspectives, skills, and innate abilities more than ever, teachers have the opportunity to turn this situation around, supporting the much-needed transformation of our schools and our profession.

The Structure of This Book

This book addresses these challenges and opportunities in three parts intended to take the reader through a process of discovering how the problem of teacher burnout developed and how changing the way we think about our schools and our profession can help us effect change from within.

In Part I: Addressing Teacher Stress & Burnout, I provide an overview of the problem. While our societies have changed dramatically over the years, our schools have not caught up. Teachers are now expected to teach twenty-first century skills in a nineteenth century system. In Chapter 1: How Did We Get Here? Where Can We Go? we learn that we are operating in an archaic system that was developed to scale education to a growing population. Originally intended to teach the very basic skills of reading, writing, and arithmetic, it has never caught up with the current needs to cultivate citizens who can collaborate on creative problem-solving with systems and design thinking. This old factory model has imposed oppressive systems on teachers and their students resulting in the teacher burnout crisis. In Chapter 2: The Stress Matrix, we explore teacher work contexts and the multitude of stressors that impact us each day, highlighting potential leverage points to change the system and improve opportunities for our students to learn. To conclude Part I, Chapter 3: Building Inner Resilience explains why teaching itself can be stressful and what skills teachers need to successfully meet these demands.

With this background, Part II: Preparing for Transformative Change guides readers towards new ways of thinking about school and our work as teachers. We are in a unique position to effect change because of the burnout crisis. But first we need to reimagine the teaching profession. In Chapter 4: Changing the Way We Think About School I introduce systems thinking and apply it to our school systems to see opportunities for change. But to do this, we need to overcome archaic mental habits that evolved in a world that was much more stable and predictable. Chapter 5: Mind Traps examines common ways these mental habits interfere with systems thinking. This leads to an introduction to design thinking and how to apply it in the innovative process of transforming our learning environments in Chapter 6: Design Thinking.

Finally, Part III: Empowering Teachers is the book's launching pad. Here's where I address new ways to distribute leadership in schools that empower teachers and improve working conditions. In Chapter 7: Taking the Lead I describe these new models of leadership that are empowering teachers to make the changes they identify to improve our learning environments. With this understanding, Chapter 8: Teacher Professionalism introduces readers to models of professionalism that can empower us and raise our professional status as knowledge workers. Finally, Chapter 9: Empowering Students addresses how we can empower our students to take charge of their own learning and in doing so, enhance student outcomes and better prepare them for the twenty-first century. When our students are empowered, they require less of our control and more of what we love about teaching: helping our students thrive.

It is my sincere wish that this book contributes to the grassroots movement of teacher empowerment and leadership so that our profession can take the lead on building the education system we wish to see in the world. I present this book with deep gratitude for the dedication and commitment you have to preparing our children and youth for an uncertain future.

PART I

ADDRESSING TEACHER STRESS AND BURNOUT

Ms. Cummings has been teaching for 15 years at Jefferson Elementary school in a mid-sized city in the southeastern part of the United States. Over the years, she has developed her skills, and she is now one of the most talented teachers at Jefferson. She has a particular knack for building supportive relationships with her fifth graders, often the toughest grade of students in the school. She is a valuable asset to the school and to her colleagues; the students and their parents appreciate her work. However, she is becoming discouraged. "I know how to teach. I've been doing this for over a decade. I don't need a scripted lesson plan and a pacing chart. I feel like these new mandates treat me like an amateur who needs them to teach a lesson like I use a cookbook to make a meal." As I listened to her, I noticed her face fall into deep sadness. "I love teaching, but I hate this way of teaching," she said. "I'm afraid I'm not going to make it; I'm burning out."

Each day over 6 million U.S. teachers like Ms. Cummings manage learning environments, build community, cultivate relationships, manage behavior, and promote academic and social–emotional learning with the most diverse student population in human history. Most choose the profession with the noble intention of making a positive difference in children's lives, and most are highly skilled professionals with years of experience. Yet, teachers are precious, under-recognized human capital. During this time of rapid social and technological change, we will see how teachers are becoming ever more valuable.

Most of us enter the teaching profession motivated to do our best to support our students' growth and development, and given the appropriate preparation and opportunity, teachers can do this very well. After all, on average we spend over a thousand hours a year with our students. We get to know who they are, how they learn, and what they need to thrive. Given these thousands of hours per year of classroom experience, teachers have the potential to make the most significant impact in transforming our schools to better prepare our students for the twenty-first century. However, teacher stress and burnout are a growing problem worldwide, and even the most dedicated educators are leaving the profession in droves.

Burnout occurs when a teacher experiences overwhelming stressors and lacks the means to manage these stressors. When the demands of the situation overwhelm the available resources, teachers become emotionally exhausted and give up. The burnout crisis has led to a teacher shortage. New teachers burnout at unprecedented levels: nearly 50% leave within their first five years, and first-year teacher attrition rates have increased by one-third in recent decades (Ingersoll, 2012). Teacher preparation programs are experiencing declining enrollments and graduation rates in almost every U.S. state (Partelow, 2019). Particularly worrisome is that this decline is marked by a demographic shift in new teachers. Fewer people of color and men see teaching as a viable option, resulting in a higher proportion of white women in the teaching workforce during a time when our student demographics are the most diverse ever and research has shown that a diverse workforce of teachers benefits children of color (Miller, 2018). Younger generations have many more lucrative career options of higher social status. This generation is not saddled with the same gender-based career choices that earlier generations of women faced and that attracted them to teaching in the first place.

How do we prevent burnout and rebuild a thriving education workforce? To address this question, we need to consider the current demands and resources and how we, as teachers, can leverage them to improve our schools and working conditions. In this book we will examine how we can take incremental steps to increase personal and systemic resources for teachers while also transforming their work in a way that relieves outmoded and unrealistic demands and improves student outcomes, which are tied to twenty-first-century learner needs.

CHAPTER 1

How Did We Get Here? Where Can We Go?

Today, teacher stress and burnout are the "canary in the coal mine"—a warning sign of massive school system failure. Stress and burnout are eroding teachers' motivation and performance and the quality of their classroom interactions, their relationships with students, and their commitment to the profession. Most concerning is that this burnout crisis is impacting the quality of our children's education (Carver-Thomas & Darling-Hammond, 2017).

Why Teachers Are Stressed Out

Ms. Cummings expressed her frustration about her salary. "After 15 years of teaching, I've seen my salary rise only about 5%. In our state, we understood that the recession of 2008 put pressure on the state budget, but since the economy has recovered, the state never made up our losses. It's like the state leaders would rather look the other way. We feel angry and abandoned, especially after the state assembly voted raises for themselves but voted down our pay raise."

Teachers like Ms. Cummings form the backbone of the education workforce.

Though the demands of teaching have increased, compensation has not kept up. Not only are teachers paid less than other professionals with the same levels of education, but over the past two decades, teaching salaries also have not kept up with inflation, adding pressure to teachers' lives as they struggle to make ends meet. The pay and benefits no longer provide a livable wage, especially in large metropolitan areas. The rising costs of a university degree leave teachers with huge student debt. These factors make the teaching profession not only unattractive but also impractical for most. The combination of antiquated systems, lack of institutional support, stressful work environments, and lack of adequate compensation has led education systems to a point of crisis (Allegretto & Mishel, 2018).

At the same time, in the global knowledge economy, a high-quality education is more important than ever. Without educated citizens, modern nations cannot tackle the challenges that are hitting us now and will continue to loom large in our collective futures. However, it has also become more difficult than ever to predict what our young people will need to know and will need to be able to do. Rapid social and technological changes make it virtually impossible to predict what life will be like even a decade from now, putting extreme pressure on parents and schools to quickly adapt to this changing reality. As I make final edits to this book, I am in quarantine working and teaching from home. During a typical year, my students would be looking forward to celebrating their graduation from college. But now they too are stuck at home, far away from friends, no way to share their joy, except virtually. As the year 2020 began, none of us could have imagined how quickly our world would change as a result of the COVID-19 pandemic.

Our school systems were designed during the Industrial Revolution when, for the first time in human history, masses of children needed to be efficiently taught basic skills to facilitate their entry into an industrial workforce. The skills identified as necessary for the twenty-first century job market, such as creativity, systems thinking, perspective taking, abstract reasoning, awareness, empathy, and technological literacy, are difficult to teach in the traditional factory-model classroom. As our culture develops new technologies, the disparity that already exists between urban and rural schools and poorly- and well-resourced schools is growing even wider—COVID-19 laid these disparities bare for all to see as schools had to move instruction online. These rapid changes are creating major challenges for teachers and educational systems. Neoliberal approaches of applying theories of human capital and market-driven improvement have not only failed to improve schools but have also added pressure to teachers by overloading them with unrealistic accountability measures, such as students' standardized test scores, while at the same time taking away teachers' autonomy to teach in ways that they know are best for their students (Hursh & Martina, 2016).

Asked to rely on teaching methods that extract knowledge from context so they focus on test items, teachers are finding students passive, disengaged, and struggling to see any relevance between what they are learning and their actual lives. While there have always been small pockets of innovation in the United States, overall this archaic system imposes a nineteenth-century structure onto twenty-first-century teachers and learners, causing extreme stress in both. Our schools are becoming warehouses of untapped potential that is being crushed by an outmoded system. The history of teachers and teaching in the United States provides us with a better understanding of how we came to a place where some of our most valuable human capital is so underappreciated and under-resourced, and how, as a society, we have left education behind.

The Factory Model

Dramatic social changes during the middle of the nineteenth century and the beginning of the twentieth century resulted in huge increases in enrollment in American schools. These increases were the result of compulsory attendance laws, immigration, and mass movements from rural areas to cities as industry grew. These social changes drove the need for more teachers and more centralized administration systems. A whole new system of hierarchy and control emerged: the beginning of our modern district system (Urban et al., 2019).

As the school systems grew, the number of women in the teaching workforce grew in response to the need for more teachers. Women teachers were paid less and were perceived as more compliant to top-down control systems. To justify this feminization process, female teachers were touted as better caregivers: "God seems to have made woman peculiarly suited to guide and develop the infant mind, and it seems... very poor policy to pay a man 20 or 22 dollars a month, for teaching children the ABCs, when a female could do the work more successfully at one third of the price" (Littleton School Committee, Littleton, Massachusetts, 1849, as cited by Hess, 2010, p. 136). This quote epitomizes one of the primary issues underlying the ongoing challenges leading us to the present crisis. The teaching profession, poorly paid and female-dominated, has never been recognized as the important profession it is. This is true in the United States and many other developed nations.

Early school systems were designed to efficiently move students through a standardized learning process to develop basic skills and inculcate values of good citizenship. There was very little science to guide the process, and given the task to scale and the industrial mindset of the time, the factory model made sense. Students were organized into cohorts by age, based on the assumption that learning processes are standard and age-related. Subject areas were siloed into separate and arbitrarily delineated learning periods, and students were passed from one grade to the next, like cars in an assembly line. Most teaching was didactic; most learning was rote.

Over time, a standard curriculum of what to teach and when became the norm. The school day was regulated by the clock and a series of harsh-sounding bells, just like those in the nearby factory. Teachers and students were expected to regulate their activities in alignment with the bells. The year was divided into semesters and the summer was left open so children could help their parents, although at this point there were populations of city children who were no longer involved in agriculture. Learning was structured and graded based on a universal standard that assumed developmental uniformity. Teachers were expected to control students and make them achieve this standard, and students were expected to do whatever the teacher said. Disciple was meted with judgment and punishment. Some students found it easy to fit into this factory system; however, many did not. Those who deviated from the standard, for whatever reason, often failed. Just like Henry Ford's assembly lines, the educational system was designed to promote uniformity, compliance, and standardization.

If you compare educating children to growing crops, the factory model is like monoculture. The same strain of plant is grown in rows to expedite efficient planting, pruning, and harvesting. The aim is a standardized product—the perfectly shaped red apple, a bright yellow cob of corn, grapes with the perfect taste or sweetness for making wine. The standardized product fits into a factory system for efficient harvesting, processing, packaging, and delivery. Only the perfect or near-perfect products make it to the grocery shelves. Apples that don't make the grade end up as apple juice or applesauce.

While this system has dramatically increased food production, it is also risky because monoculture farming is susceptible to pests and disease wiping out a whole harvest. When farmers plant the exact same strain across vast acres of farmland, when one plant becomes infected, all the crops are more likely to become infected. For example, in 1970 a blight destroyed corn crops in North America, ruining 15% of the harvest (Bruns, 2017). More than 85% of the corn planted in the United States was of the same variety, making the all the corn planted that year more susceptible to the fungus. In contrast, a biodynamic farm employing permaculture intentionally promotes biodiversity by planting a wide range of crops together and by encouraging animal diversity, which promotes a strong ecosystem of various plants and animals working together and creating a more fertile, thriving land.

I believe that today our school systems need to transition from the monocultural factory system, designed to promote standardization, to a permaculture model that values and promotes all forms of diversity, such as race, culture, behavior, learning, thinking, health, appearance, abilities, perceptions, and gender. It is this vast human diversity that is most needed for solving our problems today. Just as monoculture puts our food supply at risk, our monoculturally-oriented school systems put our survival at risk by pathologizing and rejecting students who do not easily conform to the standards being imposed on them. To build social and cultural resilience, as well as resistance to the various blights that may arise during these challenging times, we need to cultivate human diversity rather than strive for conformity. Let's examine human strengths and adaptive "superpowers" to see how we can leverage them to transform education to meet twenty-first-century educational needs for an ever more diverse student population.

Human Superpowers

Humans have an incredible ability to adapt to change. In fact, that's what we're really good at, what we've evolved to do very well. Just look at human history. Our ancestors, a small population of no more than 10,000, began to migrate from East Africa roughly 70,000 years ago, eventually spreading along the southern coast of Asia and to Oceania and then across Europe about 40,000 years ago (Henn et al., 2012). After the last glacial era, north Eurasian populations migrated across the Bering Strait to the Americas about 20,000 years ago. Then 12,000 years ago, northern Eurasia was inhabited, and around 4,000 years ago Arctic Canada and Greenland were reached by the Paleo-Eskimo expansion. Humans inhabited the Polynesian Islands about 2,000 years ago. New Zealand has only been inhabited by humans for about 750 years (Matisoo-Smith, 2017)! Seven and a half billion of us now cover the globe, and our growing population is threatening life on this planet. Consider what it took for us to spread across the entire globe and create the diverse cultures we have today. We are a hardy and creative species. We survive and thrive because we have evolved the ability to cooperate, to defend ourselves, and to invent stuff.

Three primary superpowers give us this edge. We can call them the three Cs: connection, communication, and cognition. Our most primal superpower is human connection: love, sharing positive feelings with one another. Human connection power is the glue that holds us together. Early human communities would have never survived and thrived without love and the bonds of affiliation. Scientists who study altruism argue that affective bonds were required for the next generation to survive (Keltner, 2012). Human infants are extremely underdeveloped. As our ancestors' bodies evolved to stand upright and our brains grew in size, our hips narrowed, and babies had to come out earlier in their development, while they still fit through the birth canal. This adaptation lead to further adaptations, such as the need to care for and love our babies until they could take care of themselves, which took many years. But prematurity and plasticity gave us another edge: the ability to adapt to whatever environment we were born into. Because human infants' development was incomplete when they were born, we were able to broaden our horizons and survive under all kinds of conditions, from steamy jungles to the frigid arctic. This parent–child connection superpower extended to other humans, building communities that provided us with the strong bonds we needed to survive. Indeed, the strongest human motive is to belong to a supportive, loving community and to be valued as a contributing member of that community. In this prehistoric world, banishment was the worst punishment because it meant death.

Another human superpower is our advanced ability to communicate through language, music, complex gestures, and refined facial expressions. Through language we can share ideas, plan together, communicate feelings, and create new ways of thinking about the world. Spoken language likely changed our brains in ways we still do not understand. However, given the evolution of the brain, it is likely that language and cognition, the third superpower, evolved together (Berwick & Chomsky, 2016).

Our large brain distinguishes us from the early hominins giving us cognitive abilities not found in any other animal species. We have the capacity to remember the past and imagine a possible future. Building on the memories of past experience, we can create new worlds from our imagination. Eventually, cognitive and language powers together allowed us to create written language, which developed into history and formalized culture, religion, and governments.

Our human superpowers are critical to education. Immature humans require care and preparation to join the ranks of adults in human societies. In modern education systems, we have focused a great deal of attention on language and cognition, but until recently we have ignored the most primal superpower: connection. Indeed, as we will see, this superpower may hold the key to bottom-up school transformation.

Throughout most of human history children learned by observing the adults around them and by playing with their peers. Education was a natural process that took place within small communities to prepare the next generation. Hunter–gatherer children played with miniature hunting and gathering tools. They learned the lore of the land from the adults in their community, which foods are safe to gather and eat and which might make you sick, where certain animals tend to gather and how to approach them unnoticed (Bennett & Reynolds, 2018).

With the advent of agriculture, children learned by helping their parents with chores. They learned how to plant and care for crops and farm animals. Children of craftspeople learned the same way, as apprentices to their parents or other elders. In this way, children refined the knowledge and skills they needed to succeed as an adult in the world. This observational method of learning served the general population until the advent of the industrial revolution.

The Evolution of Formal Education

During these early stages of human cultural development, formal schooling was unnecessary because everything was learned at home, in the fields, or at the workshop. Over time, as more complex cultures evolved, there grew a need for higher learning to manage and transmit culture, laws, and other critical bases of knowledge, such as engineering and medicine, from one generation to the next. In most cases, only the privileged elite had access to this higher education—the young men of the upper classes who first learned at home from tutors and then attended boarding schools and universities.

Each stage of cultural development resulted in ever greater hierarchic structures: classes of people from the ruling elites to the poorest surfs. As city states developed, specialized occupations became a necessity. Rules in the form of laws were established to maintain order. Art and discovery were expensive and dependent on patronage. Love was controlled by rules of marriage and family.

The demand for workers stimulated migration from rural to urban areas. It was around this time that universal education was recognized as important, primarily as a means to prepare citizens of a democracy. Given the huge demands of educating the masses, early school systems were created with the intention of making basic education available to everyone, basic being equivalent to a third-grade education today (e.g., basic reading, writing, and arithmetic, and basic citizenship).

Even though most teachers in early schools were men, the teaching profession never was respected in the United States. Educated men would become teachers temporarily, teaching until they could attend university and find a more acceptable profession. As the need for workers with a basic education grew, the need for education at a massive scale increased. At the time, the factory was the ideal model of production at scale. Thus, early policy makers turned to the factory as a model for building education systems, with subservient women as workers and men as managers (Goldstein, 2015).

This archaic factory model is mostly still in place throughout the United States and other developed countries. In recent years, a more modern business model has been layered on, but both assume uniformity in child development, the teaching process (inputs), and desired student learning outcomes (outputs). Granted, there have been some successful movements to reform this model over the years; however, they have never made it to scale. These movements are like a pendulum swinging back and forth between two polarities: whole language versus phonics, standards-based assessments versus portfolios, open versus closed classrooms, etc. All of these reform movements are simply tweaks, replacing parts in the machine but not changing the nature of the system itself. More recently, the competitive business model has been applied to top-down education reform. Rather than transforming the system, it simply adds competitive pressure to an already broken system. Charter schools, school choice, and school competition were viewed as ways to put free market pressure on schools and teachers and force them to improve. Unfortunately, this approach has been a miserable failure (Ravitch, 2016).

The Power of Young People

Today our young people spend hours in buildings being asked to engage in activities that seem mostly irrelevant to them. Families with resources have a great advantage because they can purchase homes in desirable neighborhoods with high property tax rates that fund excellent schools. The affluent can send their children to excellent private schools that have the freedom experiment with new ways to teach and learn while children from families with less resources suffer in under-resourced schools bogged down by government regulations and top-heavy bureaucracies. As teachers struggle with this antiquated system, their students are becoming ever more resistant to the compliance that the system requires. Students recognize that the system is broken, and they are no longer willing to go along with it. A new generation of students is beginning to insist we pay attention to what is important to their future. Educators, students, and parents are poised to transform our antiquated system from the inside out. There are so many topics today that ignite kids' passion and that can form an excellent basis for all kinds of learning. When students are engaged, it can be dramatic. Below I recount some recent, striking examples of students who have great influence, not because I expect all students to have these particular abilities but to present the potential our students hold. Young people have tremendous power when they speak out and organize, and their savvy use of new technologies is amplifying this power.

One example is Malala Yousafzai, a Pakistani activist who received the Nobel Prize at age 17, the youngest laureate ever. In opposition to the local Taliban's banning of education for girls, her family opened a chain of schools in the Swat Valley in Khyber Pakhtunkhwa, northwest Pakistan. Inspired by her father's humanitarian work and role models Muhammad Ali Jinnah and Benazir Bhutto, she, at age 11, began writing a blog for the *BBC* (British Broadcasting Corporation) *Urdu* under a pseudonym, documenting her life under Taliban occupation. Her work became more visible when the New York Times made a documentary about her life (Ellick & Ashraf, 2009). She began giving interviews and was nominated for the International Children's Peace Prize by activist Desmond Tutu. On October 9, 2012, Yousafzai and two other girls were shot by a Taliban gunman. The assassination attempt was intended to stop her activism, but fortunately she survived. The attempt on her life sparked an international outpouring of support for Yousafzai and her work to extend educational opportunities to women and girls worldwide.

Greta Thunberg is a young Swedish activist. At age 15 she began protesting outside the Swedish parliament to bring attention to the urgency of the climate change crisis. She initiated the school strike for climate movement that has been growing around the world since the United Nations Climate Change Conference (COP24) in December 2018. During the spring and fall of 2019, millions of students in hundreds of countries around the world joined her in striking and protesting. That spring three deputies of the Norwegian parliament nominated Thunberg, age 16, for the Nobel Peace Prize, and she was featured on the cover of *Time* magazine. To top it off, *Time* made her "person of the year" in 2019, the youngest ever, naming her a "next generation leader." Her impact has been described as the "Greta Thunberg effect," now perceived by OPEC (the Organization of the Petroleum Exporting Countries) as the greatest threat to the fossil fuel industry. Greta was diagnosed with Asperger's syndrome, which she claims is her superpower because it gives her the capacity to view climate crisis in stark terms (Rourke, 2019).

On February 14, 2018, a gunman killed seventeen students and staff members and injured seventeen others at Marjory Stoneman Douglas High School in Parkland, Florida. While the community mourned, many of the students felt compelled do something to prevent the continued threats to students in schools across the United States. Twenty students founded *Never Again MSD*, a gun control advocacy group. Two of the students, David Hogg and Emma González, have had a particularly strong impact. On February 17, 2018 Emma gave a speech against gun violence that went viral, proclaiming "We call B.S." on the inaction by NRA-funded politicians. Subsequently, González has continued to be an outspoken activist on gun control, making high profile media appearances and helping organize the March for Our Lives. Speaking at the demonstration, González led six minutes of silence for the victims of the Parkland massacre, which, she explained, was the length of the shooting spree. David Hogg, too, became a gun control advocate and an activist against gun violence. In conjunction with his gun control advocacy, he has helped lead several high-profile protests, marches, and boycotts. He and his sister Lauren wrote #*NeverAgain: A New Generation Draws the Line* (Hogg & Hogg, 2018), a

New York Times bestseller. He also initiated a successful voter registration drive, getting tens of thousands of new young voters to the polls in 2018.

While young people are showing strength and courage to speak out during these difficult times, it will take all of us, all generations working together, to solve our problems. As Hogg so clearly stated in an interview with the *Washington Post*:

> *One question I always ask groups of people when I'm speaking somewhere to people older than me is, "Raise your hand if you think this generation is going to save the country." And they all raise their hand. And I look around, and they all feel good about themselves. Like, yeah, we did a good job raising this generation. And then I say, "You're wrong." It's not going to be this generation that saves America. It has to be all of our generations working together in combination with the fury and energy and vigor of the youth and the wisdom of older generations. The trail has been blazed before, but it's very overgrown. We have to come back and figure out where that path is, and not make that same mistake again so other generations don't make it when they come back down this path* (Ottesen, 2019).

Transformation From Within

This chapter provided a brief overview of how our education system evolved, and it begins to consider how the educational system might further evolve to meet our current needs. I once believed that education transformation had to come from the top down. But now I'm certain that with empowerment and will, this transformational process can and must begin in individual classrooms, schools, and districts with individual, empowered educators, students, and parents leading the way. But before this can happen, we need to build the capacity to transform this archaic and oppressive system from the inside out. Chapters 2 and 3 present the matrix of stressors that are the source of teachers' burnout and the personal strengths that teachers need to elevate their profession to the status that is required for twenty-first-century education.

But before we move on, a caveat: I want to stress that I do not see teachers as the only responsible parties in this transformational process. I do not wish us to shoulder the whole load. Society has been burdening teachers with this for most of our history, and I do not wish to add to it. That said, as a result of economic and social factors that this book will highlight, teachers today are uniquely positioned to claim the power to engage students and parents to transform the system. I say "claim" rather than "reclaim" because we never had this power in the first place. While we have been saddled with the responsibility, we have had little power to determine how we engage our students to promote learning. Now, this must change. The burnout crisis provides an opportunity for us to turn around our educational systems so we can do the job we love: supporting our students' learning and development.

CHAPTER 2

The Stress Matrix

There is no question that teachers experience very high levels of occupational stress. Numerous scientific research reports and policy briefs have made this crystal clear (Greenberg et al., 2016). When we examine the stressors that teachers experience, we see a multidimensional matrix of lines and pressure points that extend from the micro to the macro levels of the education system (teacher, student, student–teacher relationship, classroom, school, district, and society).

Examining Demands and Resources

In this section we examine this matrix of stressors to better understand how the system's pressures impact teachers and how they can be modified from the inside out to both relieve the pressure and transform the system. The key is to recognize these points and empower ourselves to affect changes in this obsolete, decaying system. As teachers, we can address many of these stressors directly and proactively. Other stressors will require minor shifts in the system that we can influence in other ways, with the support of an informed community of parents and other citizens. In Part II, we will learn how applying a systems thinking lens on our educational system can help us recognize critical leverage points.

Teacher

As the teacher, your identity and personal and professional development can be viewed as points of pressure. Teacher education may prepare us with the knowledge and skills to develop engaging lessons and to manage student behavior. However, our personal development is typically completely ignored during our preservice and in-service professional learning. There are so many personal factors that can contribute to teacher stress. The preconceptions about teaching and learning you bring to your professional identity can create tension between your ideal and reality. You may need support to manage this particular kind of occupational stress. You may need assistance learning how to manage your career ladder so you don't end up feeling trapped in a dead-end profession. There are many other self-imposed pressure points that are the primary keys to unlocking our power. The good news is that we have the most control over these pressure points and once we recognize them and we can build skills to overcome them. This book will address these points of pressure and ways to learn from them in later chapters.

Student

The most critical point and the most micro-level stressor in the stress matrix is the student. While the entire system was created and is maintained to have a positive impact on the child, the system assumes that the student has the capacity and inclination to develop and learn within the constraints of the rigid factory model, which imposes standard academic expectations on students and expects teachers to deliver them. To be clear, these standards are supported by very little empirical evidence (Koretz, 2017). After decades of high-stakes testing, there is no compelling evidence that students who score well on standardized tests go on to live more successful lives than those who don't.

The science of learning and human development has evolved way beyond this narrow conceptualization; we now know that there is huge variability in how children develop, how they apply education to problem solving, and how this relates to their success across their lifespan. This variability is actually a fabulously valuable strength that is mostly overlooked and undervalued, but teachers are nevertheless expected to deliver student achievement results tied to rigid grade-level standards. Therefore, unless the student arrives at school already equipped with the capacity to successfully meet this narrow standard, she immediately becomes a stressor for the teacher who is expected to help her meet it. The focus of the teacher's efforts then becomes helping the child meet the standard rather than supporting whole-child development by cultivating her natural strengths, engaging her in learning about things that interest her, and offering targeted help in areas where she needs assistance. Standardized tests are designed to achieve a normal distribution of scores (the bell curve). As a direct result of this goal, from the first day of school, 50% of her students fall below the mean on these standards—a complete set up for failure.

The factory model system (with the market-driven model add-on) also assumes all students have the same psychosocial and cultural characteristics. But in reality, they are at least as diverse as the population at large. Some students do poorly in academics but shine in other areas, such as arts or sports. Some students are more mature than others across the academic, social–emotional, and physical domains. Students who are academically ahead of their peers are at risk of becoming bored. Students who are behind their peers may feel lost and confused. Students who are more socially and emotionally immature may have difficulty managing their own behavior and engaging in appropriate interactions with teachers and peers. For some, the classroom can feel terribly overstimulating, and they can easily feel overwhelmed, frightened, or just out of control. When students are siloed in age groupings, these differences become particularly noticeable because of the assumption that they will be very similar across these domains (academic, social–emotional, and physical).

Finally, each child comes to school with a unique cultural background that adds further diversity to the student body. When a teacher's race or ethnicity are different from her students', she may have difficulty understanding certain culture-specific behaviors. The assumption that all students can and should meet narrow standards of achievement and behavior, and that the teacher can make this happen, provokes unnecessary stress and often leads to unhealthy interpersonal relationships. In Chapter 7 we examine how teacher leadership can transform instruction and assessments to improve outcomes for students.

Teacher–Student Relationship

The interactions between teacher and student constitute a core microsystem in the educational system. How a teacher interacts with an individual student can make all the difference between successful learning and behavior and serious problems. When teachers engage with students who don't fit the standard well, for whatever reason, it can be distressing. We may face a moral dilemma, feeling pressure to try to force the student to fit the standard rather than feeling free to cultivate the unique value the student could contribute to the classroom in their own way. Typically, the student doesn't understand the motives underlying our attempts and begins to feel like a failure, not a valuable contributor to the classroom. For example, Mr. Frank is trying to help Lisa, one of his ninth-grade math students. The state government is threatening to take over management of the school, and he feels pressure to bring up his students' test scores. "Lisa, I know you can do better. Let's try again," he presses. But this added pressure is not working. Lisa doesn't understand why Mr. Frank is hounding her. Already doubting her math abilities, Lisa feels even more like a failure.

When a teacher–student relationship becomes conflictual, it can have extremely negative long-term impacts on the student and can increase the overall stress level of the classroom, making learning more difficult for everyone. As learning is interrupted or impaired, the teacher feels even greater stress and pressure from the system, creating a negative feedback loop that leads to a "burnout cascade" (Jennings & Greenberg, 2009). In this chapter we will explain how teachers can cultivate a prosocial classroom based in our most basic superpower: connection.

The Classroom

The classroom is a highly complex system: a pressure cooker with numerous stress points created, in many cases, by arbitrarily constructed structures and processes. The feelings of confinement and unpredictability are inherent in the typical classroom context. The bells that regularly ring create an ongoing feeling of time urgency. There is never enough time to finish a lesson, and learning gets artificially compartmentalized into specified time periods that have no basis in research on learning. Given that we know some students process information more quickly than others, the expectation that 20 to 30 kids can all learn to master something within a 50-minute time block is inhumane. Stress in the classroom is contagious: once one person begins to feel stressed, others are sure to begin to feel stressed. (Oberle & Schonert-Reichl, 2016). If the teacher feels pressed to finish a lesson within a certain time period, the students begin to feel anxious as well. When students become anxious and distressed, they may feel agitated and act inappropriately, unintentionally interfering with the teacher's agenda. When teachers feel time urgency, they frequently interpret disruptive student behavior as intentional, which further upsets the teacher and further interferes with the lesson, thereby increasing the sense of time urgency and student anxiety: a vicious cycle of stress and disruption. However, this chapter and Chapter 3 offer techniques teachers can use to reduce stress and promote a classroom climate that is more conducive to learning.

School

The average U.S. school is not set up to promote a teacher's sense of community, efficacy, or agency, which are all elements that support teachers' well-being, enjoyment of their jobs, and sense of purpose. Teachers often report that they feel isolated in their classrooms, spending hours of their day with a group, or groups, of students and having few opportunities for adult interaction. When they do have time together, usually it is either for a brief period in the teacher lunchroom or lounge, which is not typically known for its collegiality, or for a boring faculty meeting, which is often scheduled, or extends, outside of work hours. For exhausted and burned-out teachers, these interactions may become opportunities to vent, spreading negativity about the school, parents, and children.

As discussed earlier, the factory model of the school views the teacher as a compliant worker, expected to follow the dictates of the administration. This explains why teachers are rarely, if ever, invited to participate in or contribute to policy decisions that affect them. Often, teachers learn that they will be adopting a new curriculum or procedure without any advance warning whatsoever. When teachers are invited to the table, it is often with an unspoken understanding that the "invitation" is perfunctory and that the school will be making the change whether the teachers like it or not. The good news is that several new trends are growing that transform teachers' roles and professionalism for the better. We will learn about these trends and how to engage with them in Part III.

District

The way schools and districts are organized, with several executive leaders overseeing other administrators and teaching faculty, creates a top-down power dynamic that impedes transformation and favors the status quo. In contrast to organizations that espouse and regulate the standards of a profession, such as law (American Bar Association) or medicine (American Medical Association), educators have relied on teachers' unions, which were originally formed to advocate for workers' (teachers') rights. When the stress on teachers becomes unbearable or one of the pressure points in the matrix ruptures, resulting in an actionable problem, the union steps in to advocate for the teachers. This often creates a dialectic that ends in a strike or a meager victory, hurting students or maintaining the status quo (Gordon, 2019). Furthermore, since the Supreme Court ruled in 2018 that public sector unions cannot force workers to pay dues, the power of unions has diminished, and teachers' unions have become even less influential (Janus v. AFSCME, 2018).

Districts rarely provide teachers with adequate support. The recession of 2008 left states strapped for school funding, so programs and salaries were cut. The economy rebounded, but in many cases, funding was not restored. We have no idea how the financial impact of the COVID-19 pandemic will affect teachers' employment and salaries in the near future. Teachers' pay is not commensurate with professions that require similar training and entail similar responsibilities. The Economic Policy Institute (EPI) reported that professions requiring a college education pay higher salaries. In fact, teachers earn 19% less than comparable professionals. Referred to as the "teaching penalty," this disparity has increased significantly over the past 20 years—from approximately 2% in 1994 to 19% in 2017 (Allegretto & Mishel, 2018). Underpaid teachers often work in under-resourced classrooms that lack critical equipment, such as furniture, books, and computers. Teachers often purchase supplies out of their own pockets because their annual allowance is far from adequate.

However, in recent years teacher labor actions have begun to have some impact on raising salaries and improving in working conditions. Because they recognize how dire the situation has become, there have been an unusual number of parents and students joining the teachers on the picket lines. In Chapter 7 we explore these developments further and discuss other ways teachers can lead their districts in school transformation.

Society

Teachers have suffered the effects of low status throughout American history (Goldstein, 2015). Most recently, we teachers have become the scapegoats for school failure. When an archaic system begins to fail, it's easiest to blame those at the bottom of the hierarchy rather than examine the system itself. In the next section of this chapter, we examine a myth that has undermined teachers' work since the early 1980s.

A Nation at Risk?

The Reagan Era Report *A Nation at Risk: The Imperative for Educational Reform, April, 1983* (U.S. National Commission on Excellence in Education, 1983) reported a decline in SAT scores between 1963 and 1980, which sparked nationwide panic that U.S. schools were failing to meet the challenges of modern educational demands. However, this report was not an objective study of reliable data on our nation's schools; it was politically motivated, authored by educators who believed that the quality of schools was declining and looked for data to support that belief. The alarmist language in the document was designed to bring the nation's attention to American schools. And while this report is still widely cited, an official federal government analysis of standardized test scores (Stedman, 1994) showed the opposite of what was claimed in *A Nation at Risk*.

In 1994, Lawrence Stedman (1994) published a more rigorous longitudinal study of student achievement that explained this decline. This second study, published in the *Sandia Report*, controlled for differences across subgroups of students when they examined SAT scores longitudinally between the late 1970s and 1990 and found steady improvement. Before 1970, only the top students took the SAT and went to college. During the following 20 years, the pool of SAT takers expanded to include a broader range of students. The resulting change in test-taker profiles resulted in a drop in mean scores. However, this change indicated progress toward, not failure of, expanding educational opportunities to larger numbers of students. The 1994 report received very little attention, and the myth propagated by *A Nation at Risk* has continued to shape educational policy. We have been living with the panic *A Nation at Risk* incited for more than three decades.

Throughout this period of panic, teachers have been left out of the conversation. Teachers know from experience that focusing on standardized testing is shortsighted and adds unnecessary stress to our teaching and our students' learning. We also know that these tests are incredibly unreliable because they are so narrowly constructed. The public and policy makers continue to use test scores as indicators of teacher quality despite hard data arguing against this practice.

There is another myth: that teachers can and must raise these test scores (Koretz, 2017). This myth has been perpetrated by the test designers themselves to make money. Standardized tests are created to result in a normal distribution of scores. This means that in any given population, 50% of the students will fall above the mean and 50% will fall below the mean. If this doesn't occur, the test is not considered standardized. Parents, teachers, and the public have been fooled into thinking that on average, our students should all score higher than the mean, results that can easily be manipulated through test design and interpretation by the test developers and politicians (Hursh & Martina, 2016). We teachers have been subject to this arbitrary and unreliable testing regime, created by policy makers driven by failing neoliberal politics, that has been commodifying our educational system in ways that simply don't work. In some states, this testing regime has been applied to create metrics of teacher value, based on the assumption that teachers are the primary driver of tested achievement gains. However, we now know that teacher instruction accounts for only a small percentage of students' tested achievement scores. What actually creates the gap in student achievement is income inequality, which has become dramatically more disparate in the United States over the past several decades (Berliner, 2013).

It may seem like teachers have no control over this testing regime that we and our students are subject to. However, when we understand the limitations of standardized testing, we can relieve ourselves from the burden. I'm not saying we should stop caring about how our students do on these tests, I'm saying it does no good to stress over them. In fact, we now know that the stress generated by testing pressures actually impairs test taking cognitive capacity. So, rather than focusing on test prep and spending time "teaching to the test," we can instead spend time on what we know helps our students flourish.

We can rely on our own eyes, ears, and hearts. With regular formative assessments, we know what our students are learning and how we might address any gaps we see. We can engage our students in their own self-regulated learning process by teaching them how to set their own benchmarks and goals so that they can evaluate their own learning. Focusing on ongoing, formative assessment promotes a sense of certainty—we can readily speak to how each student is progressing, regardless of how they perform on a standardized test. We can share this knowledge with parents and administrators, demonstrating that we know our students well and recognize the diverse strengths they contribute to our classroom community of learners. In Chapter 7 we will consider how teachers can lead the way on transforming assessment.

The Power of Connection

We have examined a complex matrix of stressors that impacts teachers' work and well-being; many of the stressors involve contextual factors that teachers have no direct control over. In the rest of this chapter we'll look at teachers' own psychological resources and how these can be enhanced to manage some of the stressors.

We can build our internal capacity to transform this decaying system from the inside. To build up this capacity, we must recognize our mindsets and dispositions and cultivate those that provide us with a sense of agency, resilience, creativity, and persistence to shed the oppressive stress matrix and hack the educational system.

First let's consider that crucial superpower that has long been overlooked in educational settings: connection. One of our most powerful leverage points is our students' engagement, and the best way to use this leverage is to cultivate our students' feelings of belonging to a community. When students feel recognized as valuable contributors to their classroom community, they thrive.

Mr. Leon started off the school year by making sure all his kindergarteners knew they were valued and felt like they belonged to the classroom community. Having studied the time-tested methods outlined in the Responsive Classroom model, he had all the tools he needed to start the year right (Denton & Kriete, 2000). He spent the first few weeks cultivating a classroom climate with a tone of warmth and safety. He did this by explicitly teaching his students the schedule and the routines of the school day. He also taught them specific expectations for behavior during each of these routines and what these expectations look like, sound like, and feel like.

> "Often we expect our students to know what they're supposed to do, but I have learned that they often don't. We can tell them to do this or that, but it really helps to show them and give them time to practice the routine so they

can embody it," he told me. "Once they have a clear, embodied understanding of routines and expectations, they feel empowered rather than confused. When they see that I'm here to help them learn these routines and expectations, I become their ally and it's much easier to engage them in learning activities, even if they are challenging."

I visited Mr. Leon's classroom after he had completed the orientation process. The connection the students had to him and their classmates was obvious. Mr. Leon started the day by greeting and welcoming each of his students individually at the door. He then led the class in morning meeting, giving students opportunities to lead some of the morning routines, such as the calendar and reviewing the agenda for the day. At the end of morning meeting, he led them through their regular calming and focusing routine he learned from my book *Mindfulness in the PreK–5 Classroom* (Jennings, 2019a).

"To prepare ourselves for learning, we practice calming down and paying attention. Who would like to lead us in our calming practice today?" he said. A flurry of hands went up as the students expressed their desire to lead. He chose Jeremy, who knew just what to do. He said, "Mr. Leon, today I'd like to lead with the Hoberman Sphere," and he walked to a shelf and reached for a multicolored geodesic toy. As he held the sphere out in front of him, he reminded his peers to take three deep breaths with the sphere. As he expanded the sphere, the students took a deep inhalation. As he closed the sphere, they all exhaled together. "Now notice how you are feeling," he said. "Does anyone feel calmer?" They all raised their hands. Next Mr. Leon said, "Jeremy, please choose a classmate to lead us in the focusing practice." Jeremy chose a girl named LaShonda, who gracefully walked to the shelf and picked up a chime. She gave them instructions: "Close your eyes or lower your eyes to the ground and focus your hearing on the sound of the chime. When you don't hear it anymore, look up at me." The students all sat silently as they listened to the bell. As the bell subsided, the students began looking up at her. "Now notice how you are feeling," she said. "Do you feel more focused?" Students smiled and nodded. Mr. Leon thanked the students and was ready to start the day.

Looking around the room, I saw lots of evidence that Mr. Leon was building a strong and supportive learning community. Each student had a place for belongings labeled with their names. There was a bulletin board with photographs of each student, again with name labels. Above the photographs, letters spelled out "Our Learning Community" and Mr. Leon told me that he was collecting photos of students' families to add to this bulletin board so students knew that their families were part of the learning community.

When students like Mr. Leon's feel seen, cared about, and included, they thrive.

The field of social and emotional learning (SEL) promoted by the Collaborative for Academic, Social, and Emotional Learning (https://casel.org/) has for years supported rigorous research showing how teachers can use SEL programs to build community and to promote students' social and emotional skills. Particularly notable: when students gain these skills, they also do better academically (Durlak et al., 2011). The positive enhancements to youth development are durable. A meta-analysis of 82 SEL programs found that students who were engaged in SEL programs did significantly better than students in the control group in social–emotional skills, attitudes, and indicators of well-being (Taylor et al., 2017).

The Prosocial Classroom Model

While SEL programs show great promise, they require that the teacher understands how her own behavior and social and emotional skills impact the teaching of these skills to students. Observational learning is powerful, and if our behavior does not align with the behaviors we are teaching, our students may become confused and the instruction will be ineffective (Jennings & Frank, 2015; Jennings, Minnici, et al., 2019). We can start by examining the teacher's role in the prosocial classroom. What role does the teacher's own psychology and well-being play in creating and maintaining a classroom where everyone feels safe, connected, and engaged in learning?

I became interested in teacher stress and burnout and how it impacts the quality of the classroom climate when I worked as an instructor at a university supervising intern teachers and spent 15 years observing preschool and elementary classrooms. I concurrently taught students classroom management. Time and time again, I witnessed teachers and interns becoming agitated and reactive to relatively minor incidents involving student behavior. I also saw them unintentionally provoke incidents with students because of a misperception of the behavior or the underlying intent. These behaviors were causing palpable tension in the classroom environment. It was my job to mentor these interns, and I tried to explain what I was seeing, but hit a brick wall because the interns had a very different understanding of what had happened and could not hear my feedback without becoming defensive. This conundrum is what motivated me to return to graduate school and study stress. I wanted to understand why teaching is stressful and why it's difficult to see a situation clearly when under stress. I believed that this would unlock the key to helping teachers manage stress and promote effective teaching, and thus prevent burnout.

When I began studying emotions and the stress response, everything became clear. I saw how the typical classroom setup itself provokes stress and strong emotions; the typical setup still includes some of the most oppressive remnants of the factory system described earlier. As we have already seen, when people are confined to a space and put under time pressures, the stress response is automatically triggered. Humans are very sensitive to being physically confined and time constrained, and without the awareness of this and a proactive approach to address it, everyone can feel uneasy. Since this routine has been the norm for decades, no one thought to consider the impact it has on teachers' occupational health and student behavior and learning. The body and the mind interpret confinement as a threat, and the stress response is easily triggered under these conditions (Jennings & Greenberg, 2009). Therefore, it takes extra effort to help everyone feel safe and secure under these conditions.

Next, when stress levels increase, the classroom can become chaotic and unpredictable. When you have 18–30 young people in a room, together with their individual emotional baggage and their immature social and emotional skills, conflicts can erupt and feelings can get hurt easily. The environment offers little if any privacy, so when teachers or students feel threatened by an incident and strong emotions arise, they have to respond to the situation without any opportunities to self-regulate in privacy. This is difficult for everyone, but especially for young children and adolescents who are still developing self-regulation skills.

Consider most adult workplaces. If a conflict arises, there are opportunities for individuals to cool off in private before attempting to resolve the situation. In the classroom, no one has this option. For teachers, this can be particularly challenging because of the implicit messages we receive about the expectations for our behavior. We are not supposed to get angry and raise our voices, so we often suppress emotional expression, causing harm to our health and sending conflicting messages to our students. Added to this stress is the assumption of top-down control inherent in this old factory model. The teacher gets the message that she must control all her students at all times, when we now know that engagement, not control, is the aim of classroom management. Top-down control is an old idea from our autocratic past when social hierarchies dictated power and authority. As policy makers tried to figure out how to scale public education systems, they saw women as more compliant and intentionally grew a predominately female teaching workforce overseen by male supervisors. Teachers were to control the behavior and learning of their students using this same autocratic approach.

Despite the fact that our understanding of human nature and learning has evolved, in many ways we are still stuck in the past. We now know that agency and autonomy are critical to engagement in work and learning, but our school systems, for the most part, do not intentionally cultivate those elements (Ryan & Deci,

2017). While there have been numerous reform movements attempting to overcome this shortcoming by encouraging a more democratic and egalitarian approach, none have been able to transform the entire system. Indeed, each time these reform movements arise, there's usually a backlash, because of the system's built-in expectation to show immediate positive results, which are completely unrealistic and improperly measured. This has resulted in a constant pendulum swing in multiple facets of the system from curriculum (e.g., phonics vs whole language) to classroom setups and scheduling (e.g., multiple ages, open classrooms, and choice and comfort versus standardized seating, age-segregated, and contained classrooms). This has left many of us teachers feeling unmoored because we can't teach the way we want to and every year we are subjected to a shift in approach.

In 2009, *Review of Educational Research*, a premiere education research journal, published an article, written by my friend and colleague Mark Greenberg and I, articulating a theoretical model stressing the importance of teachers' social and emotional skills and well-being for successful student academic and behavioral outcomes (Jennings & Greenberg, 2009). We reviewed all the existing research on teacher stress and burnout, teacher–student relationships, classroom management, social and emotional learning, and classroom climate. We were astounded to learn that throughout this literature, the teachers' own strengths, weakness, characteristics, and psychological well-being were completely ignored. It was like the teacher was a "black box," their inner workings shrouded in complete mystery. The closest literature I could find on teachers' psychological states was a small bit of research on teacher emotional labor, but this was mainly about how teachers "surface act," or suppress emotions, when they feel strong negative emotions, which is likely one of the reason they were feeling stress.

Having spent many years as a teacher myself, I knew there was a lot more to the psychological dimensions of the teacher than anyone was examining. I had firsthand experience navigating the complex demands of managing a classroom and successfully engaging students, so I became determined to better understand the competencies and well-being that teachers really need to successfully manage all these demands. It was very clear to me that teachers need a very high degree of social and emotional competence to do this. The average adult would not be able to step into a teacher's job and be successful. Most of us are not prepared to handle the emotional and cognitive demands of today's classroom; it requires additional learning and development that is not typically available in professional learning for teachers (Schonert-Reichl, 2017). Fortunately, a whole body of research has been built on this model over the past decade, leading to a new understanding of how teachers' psychological, social, and emotional skills impact their teaching. I address these skills in detail in Chapter 3.

Overcoming Moral Distress

Ms. McKenny is facing a familiar conundrum. Her fifth-grade student Jason is not doing his assigned work. She knows that the reading assignment is too advanced for him, but she hasn't been able to convince her principal, Ms. Akiva. Jason and his mother recently moved to a new home, and he joined the school a few weeks ago. His school records are spotty. It's clear that he and his mother are experiencing hardship and that he's been moving from school to school. The annual standardized testing is coming up soon, and Ms. McKenny has been instructed to focus on the test's eighth grade content to ensure her students do well on the test. But she knows it's futile to ask Jason to perform at this level, especially because he's new to school and has not yet had a chance to connect with her and his peers. She knows that he needs opportunities to feel like he is part of the community and that asking him to read something above his level only makes him feel more like he doesn't belong.

Ms. McKenny is experiencing moral distress. Originally used to describe moral conundrums in nursing, moral distress is defined as knowing what is ethical to do in a situation but not being allowed to do it (Jameton, 1984). Today, teachers face moral distress because they are asked to teach and to interact with students in ways they know do not benefit those students. Lack of agency compounds moral distress. Teachers feel that there is nothing they can do to change this situation, no way to teach the way that they know will help their students as whole children, not just as test takers. While many teachers understand that the social and emotional climate of the school and the classroom are critical to kids feeling safe and ready to learn, they often complain that there isn't enough time to build this sense of community.

The first step in building the capacity to transform the system from within involves cultivating the psychological strength to overcome the moral distress and oppressive, implicit messages that the antiquated system continues to impose on us. The factory model inculcated a passive and submissive teaching culture by design to insure standardization and compliance. It pressed the profession into the blue-collar worker status, making union action the only realistic means of professional support (Goldstein, 2015).

While teachers have made great strides over the years in improving salaries, benefits, and working conditions, remnants of this submissive teaching culture remain. One example is the tendency for policy makers to address education reform from the top down, assuming that schools operate under a simple, hierarchical structure and that to change the system you simply need to direct administrators to tell teachers what to do or add a market-based incentive. In this mechanical model, teachers are just a cog in a wheel that needs to be modified in order to improve the system. Look at all the school reform systems over the past two centuries, and you will see this theme arise time and time again.

Meanwhile, we educators have been left powerless and befuddled, knowing that we have the best on-the-ground knowledge of what our students most need but feeling like no one is listening to us. Not only that, teachers continue to be the scapegoats of the education system. Something's wrong with education? It must be the teachers' fault.

For an example of how school systems maintain teacher compliance and submission, watch the video of Louisiana teacher Deyshia Hargrave get arrested at a school board meeting for speaking out in opposition to a raise for the superintendent when the teachers had not had a raise for years (Strauss, 2018). "I have a serious issue with a superintendent or any person in a position of leadership getting any type of raise," she said. "It's absurd that we're even considering giving someone a raise when these teachers are working this hard and not getting a dime" (Kennedy, 2018). The police officer roughly ushered her out of the room and when she questioned him in the hallway, he threw her down on the floor and handcuffed her. "If a teacher has the authority to send a student, who is acting up and she can't control, out of the classroom to the principal's office, under our policy we have the same rules," board president Anthony Fontana told a local reporter to justify the police action (McElfresh, 2018).

Ms. Hargrave was taken to police headquarters but was not charged. Still, the event epitomizes teachers' sense of powerlessness to affect their working conditions. "Professional respect is the number one problem. Every single teacher I've talked to across the country is facing this every day," she said. "I think it's leading to teachers leaving or people not coming into education. Besides the joy we get from working with the kids, everything is still troubled" (McElfresh, 2018). On the bright side, the aftermath of this event led to the dismissal of both the board chair and the superintendent. Asked a year later about the incident, Ms. Hargrave said she does not regret her actions. How can we work together to build the inner strength and resilience to resist and overcome this antiquated systemic oppression?

Avoiding Pitfalls

We can start by defining for ourselves what it means to be a teacher. This is the deep reflective work of building our own teacher identity. To do this, we must first be aware of how this identity is being defined for us by colleagues, school administrators, students, parents, and policymakers. How does society address these questions: *What are good teachers supposed to do? How do we define good and bad teachers?*

What does good teaching look like? When we explore the subtle messages we receive from society, we may be surprised at how our past can influence the way we think about ourselves and our work.

This will likely involve overcoming our own biases about education as well. It can be helpful to refer to the three primary pitfalls identified by Sharon Feiman-Nemser and Margret Buchmann (1983). The first is the *familiarity pitfall*, whereby a teacher holds a biased understanding about what is true and correct. For example, the bias that a successful class is quiet and orderly, because that was the student's own experience, in spite of research suggesting that some noise and some chaos are signs of learning and engaged students. If we do not recognize and challenge these unconscious biases, we can end up mindlessly teaching as we were taught.

The *familiarity pitfall* is often associated with uncomfortable feelings. For example, my own schooling during the 1960s was very traditional. Students sat in desks all in a row, and the teacher was the commander. When I decided to become a teacher, I was exploring alternative models and found the work of Maria Montessori. When I first started working in a Montessori school, I felt an unexpected level of tension. The students were all engaged in their own activities, which to me appeared chaotic compared to my own experiences as a student. I worried that I was not in control. Once I realized that my familiar mental structure of what school and teaching entail was creating a cognitive dissonance with the independent learning model of the Montessori classroom, I was able to let go of the old model and I began to feel more comfortable with a more fluid model of learning. When I got the hang of it, I found that it was actually much easier to manage a classroom when the students learned to be self-directed rather than teacher-directed. I also learned that this model doesn't arise by itself; it requires a series of intentional steps to prepare the students to make good choices and regulate and monitor themselves—an entire curriculum in itself! Later, I found a similar approach to supporting students' self-management in the Responsive Classroom model (Rimm-Kaufman et al., 2014), a well-organized selection of proven practices from a variety of sources presented in a way that is easy for teachers to apply. If I hadn't been able to reconcile this old mental structure of school with the new models I was learning, I would have continued feeling dissonance between my intentional teaching style and the style I grew up with.

The second pitfall is called the *two-worlds pitfall*. This reflects the tendency to separate our understanding of higher education from our understanding of K–12 education. In a way, this reflects the more commonly understood theory–practice divide. Depending on the particular teacher preparation program, the emphasis may be more on theory or more on practice. Often teacher candidates express frustration that they learn too much theory when they just want to know how to "do" teaching. However, everything we do is informed by some sort of theory, and if we can link our understanding of theory to practices in the classroom, our teaching becomes more intentional. We can express the rationale for the multitude of decisions we make over the course of the day. With an understanding of theory, we are also more prepared to apply research-based approaches in our teaching. While an evidence-based program may have been shown effective in one context, our understanding of the underlying theory of the work helps us understand how to apply it in our particular setting with our particular students, which may involve some minor modifications and adaptations. When teachers succumb to this pitfall, they ignore theory and do what comes naturally, which may be based in biases and preconceptions rather than tested theory.

The third is the *cross-purposes pitfall*. This is the mistaken belief that there is a difference between learning to teach and teaching. The fact is, teaching is an ongoing learning process. As teachers, we never stop learning. Learning to teach requires experimenting with new approaches and taking risks that may result in "mistakes." If we believe that we know how to teach and that we are no longer learning to teach *as* we teach, we begin to go through the motions of teaching, that is, acting like a successful teacher. We just try to get through each day, avoiding risks and mistakes. We misconceive of teaching as a performance for others rather than a constantly changing learning experience. This pitfall is especially important to recognize because it can interfere with our ability to learn as we teach.

Refusing Stereotypes

When I graduated with my master's degree in early childhood education in 1980, my friends and family teased me about earning a graduate degree in "babysitting." These views of teaching as a lowly profession are quite common and arise from the old stereotypes of childcare-giving and teaching. There is a erroneous concept of teachers as people who are unable to succeed at something more lucrative and end up becoming a teacher, as George Bernard Shaw so famously said, "He who can, does. He who cannot, teaches" (Shaw, 1903).

Another myth is that teaching is easy. After all, you only have to work 6 hours a day and you get your summers off. Most adults were students during their childhood and adolescence, and from this experience they believe they have a level of expertise. However, it always surprises me that similar biases do not exist with regard to law or medicine. I don't think I have any expertise in these fields, other than as an informed consumer of services, just because I've seen doctors and lawyers over the years.

Whereas the early American schools focused on didactic skills and knowledge acquisition delivered by subservient women teachers, more recent theorists, including Froebel, Piaget, Montessori, and Dewey, viewed teachers as experts in content and pedagogy who create opportunities for students to construct their own learning. Another view of teaching is "noble work focused on democratic social change" (Olsen, 2016, p. 4), a political act that aims to promote progressive social goals, such as honoring diversity and overcoming societal inequities.

Once we recognize how all these views of teaching influence us, we can intentionally shape our own professional development and identity. Without this reflective process, we may feel like we're being battered about like a ship in a storm. Years of attempted school reforms have created confusion in our teaching identities, and we are constantly subjected to mixed messages. In later chapters, I will explain how the growing teacher shortage is producing an opportunity to more intentionally construct our own identities as teachers rather than falling victim to society's biases.

Collective Efficacy

"Never doubt that a small group of thoughtful, committed citizens can change the world: indeed, it's the only thing that ever has."

—Margaret Mead (as cited in Keys, 1982, p. 79)

Today we teachers face a conundrum: we are asked to teach to standards that we know won't prepare our students for the future. We know in our guts that the old idea of transferring a specified body of knowledge to our students is outdated and leads students nowhere. There's just too much information to process these days, so if transferring ever increasing amounts information is the goal, it's impossible to keep up. Meanwhile, the increasing rate of social and technological change makes it hard to predict what students need to learn.

In the early years of mass education, the amount of knowledge that was necessary for future success among the general public—basic math and reading—was limited. Today the knowledge base is growing at such a rate that each day it is more difficult to know what, beyond the basics, our students need to know. It used to be that an expert in a field could keep up with all the research literature in that area. Due to the sheer volume of information today, this is no longer possible. This abundance of information forces expertise to favor either depth, becoming ever narrower, or width, becoming broader but shallower. It also creates the condition that we can no longer work on a project alone. We need others to help us fill in the gaps, whether we work in academia, business, information technology, or health care. The old factory model was the best at the time, but now we are in the twenty-first century, facing a whole host of problems that are looming over our future, from climate security threats to political upheavals. The current COVID-19 pandemic is a perfect example. Successfully tackling a new virus requires us to quickly learn and adapt, stretching our healthcare, medical research, and political systems. To continue to educate as if we must fill the minds of students with knowledge that can be evaluated individually using standards specified by some governmental agency is absurd. Teachers can sense that the task they have been handed is impossible, and their students can sense this too.

The good news is that we have the power of collective efficacy to change the system, beginning with our own classrooms and schools. Stanford psychologist Albert Bandura noticed that the more confident a group of people working together were, the more successful they were at accomplishing their task. Bandura described this phenomenon as *collective efficacy*, which he defined as "a group's shared belief in its conjoint capability to organize and execute the courses of action required to produce given levels of attainment" (Bandura, 1997, p. 477): in other words, future-oriented judgments about capabilities to organize and execute the behaviors necessary to achieve a particular outcome.

Since Bandura's observation, numerous studies of people working in various domains have confirmed the collective efficacy phenomenon. A meta-analysis of collective efficacy and student achievement showed that teachers' beliefs about the efficacy of the school faculty and staff were significantly associated with student achievement (Eells, 2011). Based on these data and his meta-analysis of 1,500 meta-analyses, John Hattie identified collective efficacy as the most influential factor in promoting student achievement, much higher even than students' socioeconomic status, prior achievement, quality of their home environment, and parental support (Hattie, 2016). Even more surprising, he found it to be more predictive of student achievement than student motivation, concentration, persistence, and engagement. Given these findings, it's clear that promoting collective efficacy among a school faculty staff should be a very high priority!

These findings are not the least bit surprising. As mentioned earlier, humans are wired to engage in collective efficacy, to work together to address challenges and solve problems. When we harness the three superpowers, we can accomplish huge tasks. Connection, communication, and cognition have been the keys to our survival and ability to thrive as a species throughout history, so it makes sense to turn to them now. When we accomplish together things that we find valuable or enjoyable, we get about the best feeling possible. Indeed, emotion researcher Barbara Fredrickson defined love, in the universal sense of feeling connected, as two or more people sharing a positive emotion (Fredrickson, 2013). It's the spark that ignites our collective creativity and motivation to accomplish great things.

So how do we cultivate collective efficacy? One proven factor that contributes to the feeling that our school community can achieve excellence is an ongoing examination of evidence. When we see concrete examples of our students thriving, we know what we are doing is working. Students demonstrate that they understand the thesis of a novel by the way they explain the character development and plot. Students show that they understand the concepts of empathy, compassion, and justice through what they write about the history of enslaved African Americans. Their higher order thinking is evident in their answer to a complicated engineering puzzle, in the creative zeal expressed in a carefully articulated drawing. Too often we are so focused on the test scores that we overlook other important indicators of a whole variety of learning types. These demonstrations point to the importance of teachers taking the lead on assessment in our classrooms and schools, which will be discussed further in Chapter 7.

Collective efficacy is validated with more than the kinds of outcomes we teachers focus on, it's also the feeling of connection to one another. I would argue that the first step in building a school with high collective efficacy is building feelings of connection at all levels of the school. Connection requires feelings of safety, affiliation, and collective sharing of positive emotions. First, administration, faculty, and staff need to feel like they're all on the same team. If the adults in the building don't feel connected, it's going to be difficult for the students to feel connected to the school, which impairs teachers' ability to successfully implement effective classroom management strategies (Sebastian et al., 2019). If cliques of adults are in competition or conflict with one another, students tend to unconsciously imitate this behavior.

School leaders can build a sense of community among all adults by expressing appreciation for the work that every member contributes to make the school a success, from the people working in the cafeteria to the principal. They can create opportunities for groups to work together to solve problems, not only within their specific area or job but also across areas. These groups can be formed based on affiliation, task, or administrative need.

For example, one important task that all school personnel deal with is keeping the school well-maintained and clean. When a task force of members representing all groups (not just the custodians) takes responsibility for the quality of the physical environment and supports the custodians, who do the large share of the work, the custodians feel their work is valuable and appreciated. When problems occur that make their jobs difficult, they can draw on the support of the whole community. A task force also can relieve some of the heavy burden on the administration by overseeing the problem-solving process.

At Lyon Middle School, spitballs in the bathrooms was becoming a big problem. Mr. Baker, one of the custodians, brought the problem to the School Environment Council, formed from one representative of each stakeholder group: students, teachers, parents, staff, and the administration. As the council members discussed the problem, the student representative had an excellent idea for a solution. Rather than a typical response that involved monitoring bathrooms and identifying and disciplining culprits, Benji suggested, "How about if we start a campaign to keep our bathrooms clean?" Everyone liked this idea and felt that if it came from the students themselves it would have a stronger impact, so Benji was tasked with forming a student campaign to promote clean bathrooms. He found that he was not alone in his desire to maintain clean bathrooms and soon he had a team of 8 students, who made posters and announcements across the whole school. They came up with catchy contests between the boys and girls to see who had the cleanest bathrooms, and they invited the janitorial staff to be the judges. Soon the spitballs were gone, and the bathrooms were much cleaner. Not only did the spitballs stop, but so did the litter. The paper towels were all neatly placed in the trash bin rather than strewn all over the floor. The whole school became proud of the cleanliness of all the bathrooms. The student committee made a 2-minute video showing off the clean bathrooms and examples of good bathroom etiquette, thanking the whole community for the effort. This video was shown in every advisory period and was posted on the school's website. The acknowledgement, documentation, and broadcast of the achievement is critical to the collective effort's positive feedback loop. When everyone sees that they can work together for a common cause, collective efficacy has taken root.

This may seem like a trivial example of collective efficacy, but it's a critical first step. If the school can rally around a simple goal like clean bathrooms, it's not so difficult to expect a collective initiative to achieve academic goals as well. This feeling of connection and collective accomplishment needs to start with simple steps that everyone in the school can accomplish together. Once the feeling of connectedness and collective accomplishment has been established, the community goals and objectives can become more challenging. Step by step, the community can build strong collective efficacy. When together we feel that we all had a part in this achievement, we feel more connected and even more collective efficacy, creating a positive feedback loop.

As the school year progresses, various communities within the school can take on tasks and initiatives on behalf of school well-being. One science class can decide to figure out how to save energy to reduce the school's spending on utilities. A professional learning community (PLC) of math teachers can work together to improve the math curriculum by creating opportunities for students to apply their math knowledge to real world situations. For example, the Lyon Middle School administration received district funding to resurface the blacktop in the playground. Rather than just hiring contractors to do this, the math teachers engaged the students in calculating how much they could expect to spend on the project. They calculated the square footage of all the separate areas and came up with an estimate based on the average price per square foot, which they found on the Internet. They delivered this estimate to the principal, Mr. Moreno, which saved him the time and energy of doing this himself. As they delivered their calculations to the principal, he beamed with pride and thanked them whole heartedly for their help. He also thanked them during the morning announcements the next day. When the blacktop was resurfaced, students felt pride that they had contributed to this improvement in their playground.

Over time, the school began to see reductions in behaviors that called for disciplinary action. They also saw a steady upward trend in evidence of learning, in both formative and summative evaluations. Once the upward trajectory began, Mr. Moreno made intentional efforts to share this good news with the whole community. Rather than highlight one individual who showed outstanding achievement, he showed off group achievements. He made sure to mention these accomplishments in the regular announcements over the intercom and in written newsletters and on social media. He encouraged parents, faculty, and staff to share these items on social media as well. Every now and then, he submitted a press release to the local news, and a few times the school's achievements were highlighted in the evening TV news and in the local newspaper. All these activities created a positive, reinforcing group sense of efficacy, leading to even greater accomplishments.

This chapter examined the stress matrix that the current school system has imposed on teachers and students. It also showed that many of these are factors under teachers' control and that some can be influenced in a variety of active and proactive ways. Taking charge of our own personal and professional development and intentionally forming our own teacher identity can go a long way toward lifting stressors from our work experience and enhancing the joy of teaching. The next section explains the specific social and emotional skills that research has found to support teacher well-being and professional performance.

CHAPTER 3

Building Inner Resilience

Over the past 40 years, students' home lives have changed dramatically. As income inequity increased and wages remained stagnant, two-income families became a necessity, putting additional pressure on parents as they tried to raise their children and also make ends meet. At the same time, more and more children began to come to school less prepared and with more learning and behavior problems, even as early as preschool (Gilliam & Shahar, 2006). The growing diversity of the student body resulted in more English language learners, and teachers needed to learn to be culturally responsive.

In response to these increasing demands, research has begun to highlight the critical importance of teachers' social and emotional competencies (SEC) in their ability to build and maintain supportive relationships with students, manage the classroom effectively, and teach social and emotional skills to their students (Jennings & Greenberg, 2009; Jennings, 2016). These skills include self-awareness, self-management, social awareness, relationship skills, and effective decision making (https://casel.org/what-is-sel/). Because of the particular demands of the classroom context, along with inadequate preservice training in teacher SEC (Schonert-Reichl et al., 2017), teachers can benefit from professional learning to help them build these skills. My research has demonstrated how supporting teachers' social and emotional development results in improvements not only in teachers' own well-being and functioning but also in the quality of their classroom interactions and student engagement (Brown, et al., 2017; Jennings et al., 2017).

The classroom context and the demands of teaching require exceptionally high levels of SEC. The traditional classroom contains 20 to 30 young people and one adult, confined to a room for a period of time. As mentioned in the previous chapter, confinement is an automatic stressor, acting like an emotional pressure cooker. In a confined room, there are a myriad of social interactions among, between, and across individuals and groups, including the teachers' interactions with individuals and groups of students. In this context, strong emotions such as anger and fear can be easily triggered.

These emotions—anger and fear—signal threat, the fight, flight, or freeze response. When threat is perceived, brain functions shift into survival mode, resulting in hypervigilance or disassociation. While these states of mind can help us survive under serious conditions of threat, they are counterproductive for learning. Just imagine trying to figure out a difficult crossword puzzle while fearing that someone is breaking into your house. Imagine trying to immerse yourself in a good book when you know a hurricane is approaching. It's very difficult because all your faculties are focused on survival.

The threat response is contagious. This makes sense because when one of us is threatened by dangerous conditions, we are likely all threatened, and children are particularly good at sensing adults' emotional states. So, in a sense, our well-being is a bellwether for our students' well-being. When we feel stressed out, for whatever reason, so do they. Indeed, research has demonstrated that when teachers report higher levels of stress, their students exhibit more interpersonal problems and externalizing (acting out) and internalizing (acting in) behaviors (Milkie & Warner, 2011). So, we are not just leaders of our students' learning and interactions, we are their emotional leaders as well. In this role, intentionally managing our stress and emotions can make a huge difference in our students' engagement, motivation, and prosocial behavior.

That our threat-response, designed to help us survive physical threat, can be triggered even when there is no actual physical threat at all is uniquely human. Because we have minds that can interpret and imagine a calamity in the future and remember and ruminate on a trouble of the past, we can get stuck in anxious and depressed states of mind and we can overreact to situations that are not presently threatening our survival. And when we are under stress, we can easily take things personally, assuming that someone is intentionally trying to annoy us or make trouble for us when in fact they are not.

For example, Ms. Asfour was leading a read-through of a script based on *The Diary of Anne Frank* (Goodrich & Hackett, 2017) in her eighth grade English class.

Several students were assigned to play each role, and they were taking turns reading their parts. As they read, she kept looking up at the clock, feeling pressed for time. I could see that she only had about 5 minutes left before the bell would ring.

One of her students, sitting in the back and clearly bored, was getting antsy and fidgeting with his pencil. Suddenly the pencil flew into the air and fell on the head of the girl reading the part of Anne Frank. She was so absorbed in the reading that the flying pencil shocked her. She turned and glared at the boy behind her. This interruption clearly annoyed Ms. Asfour, and she began to lash out at the boy. It was clear to me that it was simply an accident. He didn't mean to hit the girl with the pencil. He was just bored and fooling around, understandable given he was just sitting there, listening to his peers read out loud, and watching the clock, but with a very different state of mind than the teacher. But because she was already feeling time pressure, Ms. Asfour immediately imagined that he had intentionally flipped the pencil to disrupt the lesson and to annoy her and the girl. This, too, is understandable, given that Ms. Asfour felt she just *had* to get through the reading before the bell rang. However, if she had realized that she was feeling this time pressure and that it was likely that she was not going to get through the reading anyway, she could have calmed herself down and shifted the lesson to something more engaging for everyone, instead of feeling stuck doing what she had already planned. Then, when the pencil flew, she could have viewed it as comic relief rather than an intentional, hostile act.

In this case, there was no real threat. The pencil flying was annoying, but it didn't hurt anyone. The time constraints were real, but not really physically threatening. It was obvious that Ms. Asfour was not going to finish the play during the time she had, but she felt she had to try. The time pressure was self-imposed. Often we don't notice the feelings associated with this process while it's happening because our attention is focused outward: on the lesson, the students, and the clock (Jennings, 2015). Also, it is the nature of "negative" emotions like annoyance (teacher-code for *anger*) to reinforce our perception that our interpretation of the situation is right. I'll explain more about that in a bit.

As Robert Sapolsky articulated so well in "Why Zebras Don't Get Ulcers" (Sapolsky, 2004), our stress system is often triggered by things that we can't control (and that are not really life-threatening), like the frustration we feel when we're stuck in a traffic jam, and that threaten our sense of self, like the bitter feeling that arises when we hear a snide comment from a coworker, or like the worry we feel when a friend doesn't text us back right away. All day, things happen that can trigger teachers and students due to the pressure-cooker quality of the classroom.

These are not real-life threats, but our bodies may respond to them by cranking up our stress hormones and neurotransmitters to give us the extra strength and endurance we need to run away fast or fight. In these cases, we don't need the extra strength. We sit in our car fuming while these unused biological substances wreak havoc on our bodies, ultimately leading to chronic disease, such as diabetes, heart disease, and yes, ulcers (Seaward, 2018).

One time, I was faced with a similarly time-pressured situation. I needed to finish a lesson, but Jill kept interrupting me. I felt my heart rate rise as I became annoyed with her. All of a sudden, my patience evaporated, and my words and the tone of my voice became harsh, "Jill, I'm trying to get through this lesson. Will you just listen?" In my state of mind, this felt like a reasonable request, but to her it was an attack. Jill was actually listening, she was listening deeply, but she was confused about something and was trying to sort it out. My sharp comment shut her down. Shame and embarrassment flooded her body, and she no longer cared about the lesson.

When incidents like this happen, students become less trusting. Other students can feel her embarrassment, which can complicate the social interactions and relationships in the classroom. The connection and relational trust that I had built was damaged over a simple, harsh rebuke. So, to function in today's world, we need to find a way to hack this biological function so we don't get so many false alarms that can interfere with our own well-being and our interactions with others.

Over time and with some training in mindfulness and emotion skills, I learned how to deal with these types of situations with much more composure, but it wasn't easy. In my book *Mindfulness for Teachers* (Jennings, 2015), I provide an extensive review of classroom stress and of how engaging in mindful awareness practices and developing emotional skills can help us manage stress and cultivate a supportive classroom learning community. If I could turn back the clock and do things differently, I would have noticed the discomfort in my body from the stress—my shoulders and jaw tightening, heat arising—and this would have signaled to me that I needed to calm myself. Rather than lashing out at Jill, I would have let my students know I was feeling anxious about the time. I might have said, "Jill, I'm so glad you have questions about this lesson. I just realized that I'm feeling some stress about the time. We only have a few minutes before the bell rings, and I was trying hard to finish. I don't think that's going to happen, so I'm going to calm myself down. When I get stressed out, I notice that my shoulders and jaw get really tense. Does that ever happen to you? When I notice this, I can take a few slow deep breaths to calm myself down, so that's what I need to do now." While this may seem like a derailment of my own lesson, it was clear that I wasn't going to make it through my lesson anyway, at least not with my students' full understanding. This is a common dilemma in the current system. There is an arbitrary, artificial time constraint that doesn't give us or our students the time we need for deep teaching and learning. Just getting through the lesson becomes the goal.

In the next section I review each of the CASEL social and emotional competencies (or lack of them) and explain how they are enacted in classroom interactions and sometimes cause stress for both teachers and students.

The five competencies—self-awareness, self-management, social awareness, relationship skills, and responsible decision making—play out in the classroom interactions as an integrated system of SEC. However, to better understand each of them, I will break them down into discrete competencies.

Self-Awareness

Socrates said, "Know thyself" (Plato, ca. 400 B.C.E./1925), and for teachers this is an especially wise maxim. The more we know about ourselves, the better we become at monitoring our thoughts, emotions, and behaviors. Since we now know that teachers' emotional states are critical to our classroom climate, when we can monitor ourselves, we are in a better position to orchestrate the classroom interactions we know will promote learning.

When we're in touch with the values that motivated us to become educators, we are more able to consistently behave in alignment with those values. When we know our overall strengths and weaknesses, we can better work with them; and when we have a clear idea about our cultural, racial, religious, gender, and ethnic background and identity, we can better understand any biases or misunderstandings that arise within us as we interact with others. Having a basic understanding of our personality can also be helpful. Personality can and does change with experience, but it helps to know your underlying tendencies. *Am I typically introverted or extroverted? How conscientious, open to experience, emotionally regulated, and agreeable am I?* To learn more about your personality, I recommend accessing the online inventory at the Synthetic Aperture Personality Assessment project (SAPA Project, 2018), which will give you a report on various dimensions of your personality and cognitive abilities.

As I described in Chapter 2, recognizing the messages people learned about life as they were growing up is important because these messages become biases, "scripts" that may run automatically when they are not paying attention. I call these our *default parameters* because we default to these behaviors when we're not mindful of how we feel and how what we feel is affecting our behavior. For a brief example, let's return again to the issue of time urgency, a common stressor for teachers. In the dominant American culture, time is important. Many of us have learned that being late is disrespectful. As a child, I learned that if I didn't come home on time, I was in big trouble. This was back in the day when young children could safely play unsupervised in the neighborhood, but parents still worried when children came home late. I recall being harshly punished for coming home late, even spanked. I got the message, "Late is very bad."

As an adult, when I'm late I immediately begin to feel anxious. My heart rate rises, and I get a sick feeling in my stomach. If I'm doing something like driving or walking, I begin to rush. In my mind, I imagine the people I'm meeting becoming angry and judging me harshly. All of this is a script that I can hack, but only if I'm conscious. Once I notice that I'm running a script, I can take a breath and calm down. After many years of experience, I know that being a few minutes late is not a big deal. Many times, I've arrived five minutes late to a meeting to find that most of the others have not arrived yet!

This script can play out in my interactions with students, colleagues, and parents. When my colleagues or students are late, the script can flip. Now, I'm annoyed with them for being late. So disrespectful! But I now have years of evidence that my default parameter is culturally conditioned and very context dependent. Yes, if it's a matter of life and death, time is of the essence. In most cases, time is not really a big deal. In fact, traveling in many other countries, I have learned that time is perceived very differently in different cultures, even in U.S. subcultures!

These are all fairly stable self-attributes. Next, let's examine how to monitor inner bodily sensations, feelings, and thoughts. A powerful way to learn these skills is to regularly engage in mindful awareness practices (Jennings, 2015). When I perceive an actual physical threat or a psychological threat, my stress response is triggered, resulting in a physiological and psychological process designed by nature to help me survive. If I feel like someone is interfering with my goals or breaking a norm, anger may rise. Because "anger" is a strong word, and teachers are not supposed to get angry, we usually call it *annoyed* or *frustrated*. Anger is easy to recognize because it triggers the fight response. My blood pressure rises, and I may begin to feel "hot under the collar." My face may actually redden. My shoulders rise and become tense, and I may even find myself clenching my fists and my jaw. My face begins to grimace, and my voice becomes harsh. One marker of anger that is easy to miss when we're feeling anger, but is unmistakable when we are viewing someone who is angry, is the glare. Take a minute to glare. How does it feel? Do you notice the tension around your eyes?

In my years of observing teachers, I have noticed how these anger signals can play out in the classroom. When teachers are conscious of their anger, express it without blame, and model self-regulation, students learn that anger is a normal feeling that we all have. It's not a bad thing, and it can be managed without hurting others or ourselves by bottling it up. It's a signal that things are not going the way we'd like, but to really have an impact, it will be best to calm down and speak clearly about what is happening, what we need to change, and what we want the others to do, specifically.

However, this is not always easy due to the nature of anger. Since anger evolved to help us fight real physical threat, our mind wants to keep us angry until the threat has gone away. It does this by telling us a story about the reason we're angry and how we are right to feel anger about the situation. It exaggerates and personalizes the situation, "He always does this to mess up my lesson!" We make it all about us. Practicing mindfulness can build our capacity to observe this tendency. Once we recognize the script that keeps us angry, we don't need to get so wrapped up in it. Once we let go of anger, we can see that what is really happening is usually not about us at all.

If we are not self-aware when anger arises, we may say and do things we don't intend to and may later regret because it may disrupt the social and emotional climate in our classroom. When I lash out at Jill because of my own feeling of time urgency, I trigger the stress response in her. Like in the example with Jill, the teacher's anger may trigger a student's fear, and they, along with many of their peers, will shut down. Another possible student reaction is anger. A student may feel outraged that they are being unfairly attacked simply because they don't understand. In this case, the teacher unintentionally initiates a power struggle with the student. The student may respond, "I don't understand. You're not explaining it very well." Now I feel personally attacked because this statement reinforces my own script that she's intentionally trying to mess up my lesson. There's only one way power struggles go. They spiral downward until everyone is feeling awful and is blaming one another.

When I was observing classrooms, I became amazed at how often this scenario occurs, damaging the emotional climate of the classroom and derailing learning. When the class has one or more students living in adverse conditions, the power struggle can be even more damaging (for more information about trauma-sensitive approaches in the classroom, see my book, *The Trauma Sensitive Classroom: Building Resilience With Compassionate Teaching.*)

The degree of self-awareness required to function well in the classroom context is quite high. We must not only know our fairly stable attributes but also be able to monitor our scripts and emotional reactivity in the moment, all day long, while confined to a classroom, controlled by an artificially created schedule, and surrounded by young people who are just beginning to learn about themselves and their own emotions.

Along with self-awareness we must cultivate self-compassion: the ability to give ourselves the same kindness and compassion we give others. This is not an easy task for those of us who have inherited this archaic model of the teacher that we sometimes feel we must conform to. We will lose our temper and say things we regret because we are human beings, working under very challenging conditions.

When this happens to you, remember that you can repair the breach in your students' trust by being honest with them. Teachers can model for students how to repair social trust by expressing regret and explaining what happened, how we felt, and what we need. While this can be really difficult at first, because we may have absorbed the message from society that we are supposed to be perfect, you will be amazed at how well students will respond. We can even model self-compassion! "I was feeling so angry I didn't realize I needed to calm down, and I said some things in a way that was harsh. I didn't mean to do that. I was feeling a lot of pressure to get through this lesson, but my relationship with you is much more important than one lesson. Now I'm feeling sorry, and I also need to show myself some care and kindness because I'm human, and we all make mistakes." What a lesson in self-awareness and self-compassion! These lessons are much more vital to preparing our students for the future than the lesson that was interrupted in the first place.

Self-Management

When we think of teaching our students self-management, we often think of emotional and behavioral self-regulation (e.g., impulse control). Indeed, these are two competencies that are critical to success in academic and social learning; these skills help us manage our emotional reactivity and our cognitive functions so we can get along with others and focus on our work. However, self-management is much more than this, and effective self-management requires self-awareness.

Managing stress is a big part of self-management, and when I understand myself enough to know what tends to be a stressor for me, I can proactively manage my stress. I can recognize when I'm tired or emotionally exhausted and engage in self-care activities that will help me build resilience. I can avoid certain situations when I know I'm too stressed to deal with them appropriately, and I can stop and take a breath if I need to deal with those situations right away. This pause for breath allows my nervous system to settle, and my stress response goes down. This reduction in stress helps me think about the situation more clearly, allowing me the ability to reappraise the situation. Is it really so stressful and threatening? Or, am I overreacting because of a script?

When I feel stressed, my motivation declines and I become discouraged. After pausing to calm myself, I also can take a minute to set my intention. This involves three steps:

1. **Recall my values:** *Why am I doing this work?*
2. **Imagine my "best self":** *How do I want to be?*

3. **What is my intention for today?** *Set the intention by focusing on it, by visualizing yourself being this way, or by putting the intention into words. Focus on this intention for a minute or so.*

When I am clear about my values and intentions, I am able to set goals and organize my time and activities to align with my intentions from moment to moment, like the GPS on a phone. This practice can promote self-discipline and self-motivation.

The self-management competency is critical to creating supportive classroom interactions. Because of the stressful nature inherent in the classroom, we need to learn techniques to recognize and manage our stress while we are teaching so our reactivity doesn't creep up on us and surprise us and our students. As the adult in the room, it is our job to make the classroom feel safe and inviting for everyone. If we lose our temper, we disrupt that sense of safety. This is not to say you should try to suppress your feelings. We often confuse suppression with regulation. When we try to suppress an emotion, it tends to leak out in facial expressions and actions, which can be confusing for students. Think about how creepy it is when someone smiles and acts like everything is okay when they are fuming inside. We may also become sarcastic, which can come across as cruel and hostile to students.

If we are overwhelmed by strong emotions, we will find empathizing with those around us very difficult, and it will be easy to forget that our students have very different agendas than we do and that they likely will not understand why we are upset. Most of the time students don't want to upset the teacher, and kids rarely upset adults intentionally because we are so scary to them. However, if a student is feeling confused about how we are feeling and begins to distrust us, she may do things to test us, to see if we're being real or not. Our students don't do this consciously: it's an unconscious protective mechanism. When I'm in the midst of feeling stress, this can seem like an intentional act of defiance or an attack, and my stress can turn into anger, "righteously" directed at the student. But if I do this, it just confirms the student's unconscious sense that I wasn't honestly expressing my emotions and thus I can't be trusted.

Depending upon their experiences with adults, children may prefer the explicit expressions of anger over the sense that the teacher is suppressing emotions and faking that everything is ok. For these kids, suppressed anger is terrifying; perhaps they live with a parent who suppresses anger and then explodes irrationally and unexpectedly (Jennings, 2019b). If we're not careful, we can easily initiate a power struggle with these students because our process inadvertently triggers their feelings of threat, and they become defensive, expressing fear or anger. As soon as a strong negative emotion disrupts the emotional climate of the classroom, academic learning stops, because everyone in the room enters a defensive mode that prioritizes basic survival over learning. Indeed, we now know that when we feel threatened, executive functions of the brain become temporarily impaired and we have difficulty focusing our attention on anything but the threat (Lupien et al., 2007).

Self-management also involves the way we organize our time, our activities, and our surroundings. *Do I put things off to finish them at the last minute, causing myself undue stress? Do I have a self-care routine that supports my physical, emotional, mental, and spiritual health and development? Do I take on more than I have the capacity to accomplish within the time available?* For students, self-management is having all the materials they need to get started on a learning task. It also means being able to manage their learning by taking things one step at a time, keeping focused on the task, and getting help when they need it.

Social Awareness

Social awareness is a crucial skill for teachers. It is the ability to empathize, respect, and take the perspective of others, including those with backgrounds other than our own. Given the history of the factory model and the feminization of the teaching profession, there's a high probability that any given teacher in the United States will be a white, middle-class woman. As a member of the dominant culture, it can take some extra effort for me to recognize and understand cultural differences and the racial, gender, and religious inequities embedded in our systems (Irving, 2014). Social awareness requires open-mindedness and intentional study of structural social injustices and implicit and explicit biases that play out in school, among students, between teachers and students and their families, and between teachers and colleagues.

Indeed, the political climate can exacerbate these embedded systemic biases and cause real harm to students. Tensions in the larger society play out in schools. Stories abound about increases in bullying and racial, ethnic, and religious attacks since the 2016 election. University of Missouri professor Francis Huang and my UVA colleague Dewey Cornell (2019) led a study of Virginia middle school students, examining student reports of bullying between 2016 and 2017 by congressional district. Those districts where Trump won the most votes had significant (17%) increases in bullying compared to those where Clinton won.

"While the ways in which the presidential election could have affected students is likely complex, educators and parents should be aware of the potential impact of public events on student behavior," said Cornell in a statement first published as a press release (Pals & Boylin, 2019) and then republished in the mainstream media. "Parents should be mindful of how their reactions to the presidential election, or the reactions of others, could influence their children. And politicians should be mindful of the potential impact of their campaign rhetoric and behavior on their supporters and indirectly on youth."

Social awareness involves a deep understanding of the social and ethical norms for behavior and differences in these across cultures and other social groups. If we judge the behavior of our students and their families based on our own cultural norms, we may do them a great disservice. If their norms are different than ours, subtle but important differences may cause difficulties in classroom interactions. For example, it is a norm in the dominant U.S. culture that looking someone in the eye when they are talking to you is a sign of respect. In other cultures, including some Hispanic, Asian, Middle Eastern, and Native American cultures, this can mean the opposite—disrespect—especially if the person speaking has authority, like a teacher. I grew up with the dominant norm, and a student not looking me in the eye when I'm speaking to them about something important can feel dismissive. If I have social awareness, I can recognize that the student may have learned a different norm about eye contact and is actually acting with deep respect by not looking at me. If I'm stressed out and don't have the bandwidth to recognize my script about eye contact and respect, I might become annoyed and unintentionally say something that might damage my relationship with the student.

Imagine a teacher asking a student for whom eye contact is considered disrespectful to look them in the eye when they are talking to the student. The student has been taught from a young age that this is disrespectful, especially in relation to an adult with power, so it's very difficult for this student to raise their eyes to the teacher's. The more the teacher forces this behavior on this student, the more frightened and uncomfortable the student becomes. Both are locked in a battle of conflicting norms. In this scenario, the student's trust in school and in the teacher can quickly erode and may never recover.

Social awareness is the recognition of how a social group functions and of how to promote a more supportive and socially cohesive social group. With social awareness, I can consciously impact the social network patterns of my classroom, which can dramatically affect the classroom climate. Another UVA colleague, Scott Gest, has been studying social networks in classrooms. He and his colleagues have shown that teachers can affect social status patterns, such as peer norms and status hierarchies, and social affiliation patterns, such as informal peer groups and friendships (Gest et al., 2014). Indeed, just being more aware of these networks has a positive impact on your classroom. For example, when teachers have a more accurate assessment of the classroom peer networks, peer norms against aggressive behavior are stronger (Neal et al., 2011).

Teachers can also act to reduce status extremes in their classrooms. When we are conscious of the social hierarchies in our classroom, we can intentionally offer attention and responsibilities to students to uplift those who seem socially disengaged or rejected. This may help them become more socially integrated into the peer network. We can also reduce the importance of status by eliminating or reducing competition for special duties, activities, or attention. In their research, Gest and his colleagues found that when teachers take active measures to manage the social hierarchies in their classrooms, their students enjoy learning more and feel a stronger sense of community with their peers and the school as a whole (Gest et al., 2014).

Social awareness involves respect for everyone, including those who are different from us. Indeed, teachers who are socially aware appreciate the diversity of people in the school because they recognize the strength this diversity—of culture, race, religion, gender identity, sexual orientation, language, and physical and learning abilities—brings to the learning community. When teachers and other school personnel recognize that greater diversity equals greater community richness and resilience, each individual is honored, rather than being seen as lacking in some way, for the special difference that they contribute to the diversity of the community.

Relationship Skills

Building and maintaining healthy and rewarding relationships with our diverse students and their parents involves clear communication, good listening, cooperation, and skillful conflict resolution skills. To provide high quality emotional support to others, we must be able to see them for who they are, not who we wish they would be or in terms of how they are "supposed" to be.

As teachers, it's easy to get trapped in the factory mindset looking to achieve the perfect "product" which, in this case, is the outstanding student. However, only a few of our students can fit into this narrow bracket that schools have identified as outstanding. This narrowly defined outstanding student sits still and listens attentively all the time, courteously raises their hand to answer your questions, seems to always understand your lessons, focuses on their work with great enthusiasm and attention, always does their homework, and gets along well with their peers. From this student's perspective, school is a wonderful place—the most wonderful place possible!

However, most kids do not come to school with these characteristics, yet the status quo is to try to mold them into this ideal student. But when we try to do this, we overlook the wonderful strengths, gifts, and interests our students bring to the classroom. We see difference as a problem, rather than a strength. Every student has value, even if they are not completely thrilled with being in school or don't have the academic and social and emotional skills that fit the mold. Indeed, a valuable aspect of human diversity is neurodiversity. In his book *The Power of Neurodiversity: Unleashing the Advantages of Your Differently Wired Brain* (Armstrong, 2011), Dr. Thomas Armstrong explains the evolutionary advantages of pathologized (e.g., ADHD, ASD, etc.) differences in how our brains function.

It's true that we teachers will likely need to modify our instruction and social interactions to meet these students where they are. However, when we open ourselves to the wonderful diversity of all our students, we may find gems. For example, I once had a fourth grade student named Sam who had a really hard time reading. He was several grades behind, and I was working on finding ways to help him catch up. As I got to know him, I realized his general knowledge about the world was prodigious for his age. He knew the names and characteristics of numerous animals, living and extinct. He could describe processes and relate them to other elements, such as evaporation and how it relates to cloud formation. He knew the names of most of the countries of the world and could find them on the globe, but he struggled to read a simple sentence.

With time and patience, I realized that a series of traumatic experiences at school had left him fearful of reading. Earlier in school when he was asked to read out loud, students made fun of him and the teacher failed to help him through the painful situation, leaving him ashamed, embarrassed, and terrified of reading. When the rest of the class was busy working independently, I sat with Sam and tried a new way to reach him. Rather than asking him to read, I decided to focus on writing. He knew the sounds of the letters in the alphabet, so it wasn't difficult to get him started writing about his amazing knowledge base. I said to him, "You know so much about dinosaurs and we're going to study them soon. Could you help me by making a book about dinosaurs to share what you know with the rest of the class?" His eyes lit up and he immediately started drawing pictures of each dinosaur and writing short sentences about each one. I told him not to worry about spelling, just get out a draft, and then we would work together on editing it. After he finished the book and we had edited it together, I invited him to read it to me. He had no difficulty reading the text he had written.

This demonstrated that he actually could read, he just had a block caused by the traumatic incident earlier in his school experience. We continued working on books in this way, and he loved sharing his general knowledge with his peers. Within a few short months, he was able to begin reading books at grade level. Because of his voracious curiosity, he devoured books and his reading quickly improved.

At the same time, Sam's social skills flourished. Other students enjoyed his books and asked him questions about other animals. He became the class expert on dinosaurs and animals in general. He had found a way to make a valuable contribution to the class. By taking a strength-based approach to helping Sam, I had found where he excelled and used this to support him in overcoming his fear of reading. This may seem like hard work, but when we see and connect with our students, teaching becomes so much more enjoyable and our students are more likely to engage in learning. Sometimes it just takes a minor shift in approach to reach a student and help them thrive.

Relationships skills can play a role in school collegiality. Teachers gain more power as the shortage grows, and they can leverage this power in their relationships with principals, other administrators, and other staff to advocate for their students, to advocate for autonomy to teach in their own way, and to create more opportunities for collaboration with other teachers. Teams of teachers working together in professional learning communities can cultivate rich new ways to teach and develop exciting new content. These activities enrich the work of teaching in ways that not only improve our teaching but also reinforce our love of teaching.

As we begin to flex our relational muscles, we learn that minor shifts in attitude and approach can result in significant changes in our schools. Parents, too, can play a supporting role in this transformative process. Recently, there were several successful teacher strikes across the country (van Dam, 2019). What was unusual about these recent, successful strikes was that, in many cities, parents and students joined teachers on the picket lines and this likely made a difference. When parents recognize the critical unmet needs teachers and schools have, they are motivated to help because they see that their children's education is at risk. However, teachers often overlook building bridges with parents by getting to know them and giving them opportunities to contribute. Finding ways to engage parents in meaningful contributions to their child's classroom and school can support the relationships and build community.

Responsible Decision Making

One of the most important social and emotional competencies, which draws on all the others, is responsible decision making. Teachers make tens of thousands of decisions a day in very quick succession. Indeed, this rapid decision making in an unpredictable and multidimensional context can be cognitively and emotionally taxing, resulting in increased stress and reduced performance (Jennings & Greenberg, 2009).

Ms. Fairfax is getting ready for her day: setting up her classroom for an exciting activity that her class will engage in later that day; writing the lesson schedule on the board; preparing supplies for an art project. As she's doing all this, a parent comes in to talk to her. Immediately, she feels time urgency. She thinks, "If I talk to this parent now, I won't get all this set up finished." The distress interferes with her planning and her interaction with the parent. She doesn't want to be rude, so she tries to listen, but she's only half-listening because she wants to get back to her set up. As she "listens," she nods her head robotically and keeps glancing at the clock. She tries to find some words to placate the parent so she can get back to work. The parent finally leaves, after getting the impression that Ms. Fairfax doesn't care about her concerns.

In this scenario, Ms. Fairfax got her classroom set up, but she missed an opportunity to build her relationship with the parent. Because she was so focused on getting her class set up, she missed an opportunity to enlist the parent's help. Here's an alternative scenario. Rewind!

Ms. Fairfax is getting ready for her day. She is setting up her classroom for an exciting activity that her class will engage in later in the day, writing the lesson schedule on the board, and preparing supplies for an art project. As she's doing all this, a parent comes in to talk to her. Immediately she feels time urgency. She thinks, "If I talk to this parent now, I won't get all this set up finished." Recognizing her growing stress level, she takes a deep breath, focuses on her feet and the weight of her body on the floor, and greets the parent with her full attention and friendliness. As she makes an authentic connection with the parent, she says, "I really want to hear about your concerns and I need to finish setting up my class. Could you give me a hand while we talk?" Not realizing that teachers need their mornings for set up, the parent apologizes for interrupting and agrees to help. Ms. Fairfax needs some paper cut for her art project. "Can you help me cut this paper?" As the parent cuts the paper, Ms. Fairfax takes care of other tasks and they talk. It turns out that the parent wanted Ms. Fairfax to know that she and her husband have separated and today is the first night their daughter has stayed with her father at his new home. She came in early to give her a heads up.

This is an example of just one of multitudes of critical decisions that teachers make on the fly all day, identifying and solving problems, analyzing situations, evaluating situations, reflecting, and making decisions that will affect the lives of students and their families. To do this well, we teachers need to think about how our behavior will affect others in the long and short term. We need to take into account the needs of many: our own needs, the needs of our students and their families, and the needs of the community.

One area where responsible decision making is critical is classroom management. The decisions we make about how to respond to our students' behavior can have serious effects on their learning and development. While we may have the expertise and training to be a "warm demander"—the mode science has shown works best when it comes to managing behavior—our stress can get in the way.

Mr. Carroll's fourth grade class was engaged in a lesson on electricity. Students were grouped into teams that were working on creating circuits with a battery, wires, and a flashlight bulb. He noticed a conflict brewing in one group and the students beginning to tussle over the wire. It had been an exhausting day, and Mr. Carroll was tired and feeling stressed out. Jaime, one of the boys, had a history of getting into conflicts with peers. Because Mr. Carroll was stressed and feeling time pressure, he jumped to the conclusion that Jaime was the instigator and immediately took the wire from Jaime. Jaime began to argue with Mr. Carroll, feeling unfairly attacked. This only annoyed Mr. Carroll further, and he told Jaime to go take a time out. What Mr. Carroll didn't know was that Jaime was being bullied because of his Latinx heritage. One of the other boys in his group had grabbed the wire from him when he was connecting it to the battery saying, "Give me that wire. Mexicans can't do science."

In his rush to keep the group on track, he made a quick assumption that Jaime had caused the problem. Since he hadn't gotten to know Jaime well, he didn't know that Jaime was being bullied for his ethnicity and that was why he often was in conflict with peers. Rather than jumping into a conflict situation like this, Mr. Carroll could instead take a moment to observe the interaction. While doing this, he could take stock of his current emotional state, recognizing his feelings of stress. He could take a moment to breathe deeply and focus attention on his feet, which would also give him a moment to observe objectively. He may then notice the expression of contempt on the face of the other boy, and he may hear his comments. He may take reflect on the social inequities Latinx families face in his community, considering that this may play a role in Jaime's experience. In this way, Mr. Carroll can consider all the factors that are playing into the conflict he sees and be able to make an informed decision on how best to respond.

Clearly, in this scenario, Jaime wasn't the instigator. When Mr. Carroll jumped to conclusions about him, he reinforced Jaime's feelings that he is unwanted in this classroom, since both his peers and the teacher pick on him. His growing sense of isolation may lead to further conflict with peers and teachers and eventually lead him to drop out of school. If Mr. Carroll takes the time to assess the situation, he may also notice his own biases about Latinx people and how this bias distorts the way he sees the conflict.

Mr. Carroll holds himself to high standards, and he intends to make decisions that are unbiased and supportive of all his students. However, we are all influenced by the messages we receive from the media and society in general, which result in implicit biases that we may not be aware of and that can surface in stressful situations. Once we understand this normal tendency, how it might play out under stress, and what situations tend to trigger our stress, we are much more able to manage our stress and our reactions, allowing us to engage our social awareness and relationship skills to make a decision that better meets the needs of everyone concerned.

This chapter considered social and emotional competencies and the critical role they play in effective teaching. As we develop these competencies, we will see how they can empower us to better recognize, honor, and express our own needs. This examination of the demands and resources that affect our teaching lives and the ways we can address the stressors we have the most control over—our own perceptions, biases, habits, and skills—concludes Part I of this book. In Part II, we will examine how we can apply systems and design thinking to transforming our school systems from the bottom up.

PART II

PREPARING FOR TRANSFORMATIVE CHANGE

"The thing that really surprised me was that it [Earth] projected an air of fragility. And why, I don't know. I don't know to this day. I had a feeling it's tiny, it's shiny, it's beautiful, it's home, and it's fragile."
　　　　　—Michael Collins, Apollo 11 (Chang, 2019)

At the University of Virginia, I teach a class called Mindfulness in Health and Human Development that I originally intended to prepare students going into helping professions such as teaching, nursing, or medicine. However, the course has become extremely popular and draws undergraduates from across all programs and majors. I am fortunate to have access to a classroom set up well for practicing mindfulness and yoga. The floor space is open and there are shelves stacked with cushions and yoga mats.

We spend two and a half hours a week with our technology turned off, engaging in mindful awareness practices, doing reflective writing or drawing, discussing our experiences and insights about ourselves and our experiences. The first half of the class is designed to help students learn these practices and apply them to supporting their own well-being and development. The second half of the class is designed to help them apply mindfulness and compassion practices to supporting others. On their own, they complete reading and writing assignments through which I get a chance to observe the growth in their self-reflection and understanding of their place in the world. This has been one of the most rewarding teaching experiences in my 40-plus-year career.

Teaching this class has taught me so much about our most valuable human resource: our young adults. They are hungry for purpose; they are hungry for community; and they are super smart and insightful. Fewer of these young adults are choosing to become teachers. Why would they? They will be saddled with huge debt, so earning teacher's salary will not be adequate, especially if they want to live in a large, expensive metro area like New York or San Francisco. This saddens me because many of them *should* become teachers.

For example, Elizabeth enrolled in my course to learn to manage her stress. Bright and energetic, she was graduating with a degree in chemical engineering. She told me she was looking for a job in the pharmaceutical industry, but she didn't seem excited about the prospect. I asked, "Is this what you really want to do?"

"Well, not really. But my parents won't be happy if I don't have a good job that pays well."

"What do you really want to do?" I asked.

"You know, I worked as a volunteer at an afterschool STEM program at a middle school this year and loved working with the kids. I think I would really enjoy teaching." As she told me about how excited the students were to learn about chemistry, her face glowed.

"Sounds like you have some passion there!" I said.

"You reminded me of something. The reason I decided to major in engineering was because of a fantastic teacher I had in high school. She made science thrilling. Maybe I will return to school to become a teacher later," she said.

I certainly hope she does, because we need her!

Teaching this class and getting to know these young adults so well gives me incredible hope for the future. We just need to figure out how to transform education so that it again attracts young people so we don't lose the precious human capital that is at the doorstep of their careers.

So, what can we as a society do? Let's start by looking at the big picture. We see a kind of change that's new for humanity. Not only do we see rapid technological changes, but also social, cultural, economic, biological, climate, and ecological changes. All of these changes converge and impact our lives in ways that interact with one another. Some of this change is exponential, like Moore's law: the development of computing power follows an exponential curve. Some of the change is chaotic and unpredictable, like weather disruptions and social upheavals. Our human brains were not cut out for this, so we try to simplify things to tolerate all this change without becoming distressed. But obviously, this strategy is not working very well.

The COVID-19 pandemic is an example. The verdict is still out at this writing, but it appears that the virus began in bats and mutated to a form that could infect humans. As human beings have encroached on the earth's remaining wilderness, such zoonotic pathogens such as H5N1, SARS, and MERS become more prevalent (Jánová, 2019). Because of the globalization of travel, COVID-19 was able to extend its reach across the entire earth in a matter of weeks. It happened so quickly governments could not stay ahead of the rapidly growing pace of infection and death. At the end of February 2020, there were just a few cases in the United States. But within two short months over 50,000 had died.

The pandemic disrupted our lives in numerous ways, above and beyond stressing the healthcare system. Physical distancing shut down the economy. Millions lost their jobs. We had to rely more on technologies to work and connect with one another. Rising to the challenge to meet students' needs, schools rapidly transitioned to provide remote learning and distribute food. Teachers struggled to provide instruction remotely while also coping with the impact of COVID-19 on their personal lives (Gewerts, 2020). The crisis highlighted existing disparities. While well-resourced students were able to access online learning, many students were completely disconnected from school for the last half of the 2019–2020 school year (Kurtz, 2020). While it's too early to predict what will happen next, the virus has certainly changed our lives in ways we could never have imagined. Unfortunately, the COVID-19 pandemic may be only the first in a string of disasters that our society will need to address.

Even before COVID-19, rapid and unpredictable change had left many of us behind in one way or another. The population of hard-working blue-collar families is being devastated by hopelessness (Kristof & WuDunn, 2020). Globalization, the destruction of union power, and rapid technological change have left them stranded in ghettos of despair that span rural and urban landscapes, riddled with drug abuse, death, and suicide. Highly educated, white-collar professional families are suffering in a different way. They have no other idea of how to prepare their children for the future than to impose great pressure and high expectations. Fearful for their children's future, many are "bulldozing" them into a narrow gorge that they have labeled "success." These parents overcontrol and push their children into the best schools, thinking that this is the only road to a happy future, but that instead leads to increasing levels of drug and alcohol use and mental health problems (Luthar & Kumar, 2018). All of us live with the results of this suffering, and meanwhile, our schools plug along as if doing more of the same is going to improve things. Clearly, it's time to shift the paradigm and shift it quickly. I submit that we teachers are best positioned to lead this change. I hope that the next chapters will show you how we can do this.

CHAPTER 4

Changing the Way We Think About School

I recently was sitting on an airplane and struck up a conversation with a very smart young man, who had recently graduated from high school and was on his way to visit the university where I work. He was taking a gap year to decide what to do next. His parents really wanted him to go to a good 4-year college, but he wasn't so sure.

"All those years of school were mostly a waste of time. I got really good at doing well on tests that didn't prepare me for the world of work at all."

I noted that they probably would help him get into a good university.

"Yeah, but since I'm still not sure what I want to do, I might waste four more years learning more stuff that's not going to help me. And then I might be in debt up to my ears and still working as a barista, like my cousin. That's exactly what I'm doing now, working as a barista, but at least I don't have any debt."

"Sounds like a real dilemma," I said. "But I'm guessing you're not alone." He shared that many of his friends are in the same boat. "It's really hard to figure out what to do next. I don't know what the world will be like in even another five years. What if I get a good job and then it's outsourced to Asia?"

I could really relate to his concerns. Teaching undergraduates, I see a similar conundrum with seniors in my classes. Even though they will leave a top-notch university with a degree, they are still petrified that they either won't find a job or will end up doing something they hate. Many of them have been so parent-pressured that they are gearing up for 2–10 more years of school to study medicine, law, or other advanced degrees, even if they're not really sure that's what they want to do. If they don't make it into their first-choice graduate school, they're devastated.

COVID-19 added to their stress. I was teaching this class when the university was closed and we had to move instruction online. The transition was devastating to my students. All of them were seniors, looking forward to graduation and beginning the next step in their adult lives. Most of them moved home to finish the semester. As I adapted the class to online learning, I made changes to support them during this difficult time. For many of them, the uncertainty was traumatic. The jobs they had accepted were put on hold. A student joining the Peace Corps was told that his program was shut down. Possibilities for graduate school became unclear. Together we built a supportive online community to cope with these challenges and to consider ways that the crisis might inform positive changes in the future.

From Survive to Thrive

As we consider how we might shift the paradigm of schooling, let's return to examining how our ancient ancestors lived and how our bodies and minds adapted to change over tens of thousands of years of evolution. For most of evolutionary history, our ancestors lived as hunter–gatherers. This is a subsistence lifestyle that relies on hunting, scavenging, and foraging plants and other food sources, such as honey. This way of hominin living dates back at least two million years. Groups of early humans relied on one another for survival. Depending on the size of the group and the local resources, this lifestyle required about 500 square miles, so they lived in nomadic bands, from large extended families to larger tribes of up to 100 people. No matter what the size of the group, they coordinated their hunting and gathering to optimize the community food supply. They made weapons, tools, and clothing. They domesticated dogs, they mastered fire, and they invented language. Sometimes these nomadic groups slowly traveled very long distances in search of better food sources. In each new place humans inhabited, they decimated most of the large fauna in the area, resulting in mass extinctions of magnificent large animals: the glyptodonts and dire wolves across North and South America, and the giant goanna of Australia disappeared at the hands of prehistoric humans. Even as recently as about 800 years ago, humans wiped out the huge moa and other large birds in New Zealand.

Over the course of the Neolithic Revolution (12,000 years ago), humans developed agriculture, and some groups settled, growing much larger. Finally, cities rose out of the agricultural landscape. In each new age of development, from the Neolithic to the Industrial Revolution, humans have relied on a limited understanding of cause and effect. We also learned to expect unlimited resources. Having difficulty finding food? Let's just move to the other valley! Our city is suffering economically? Let's raid the city next door! While compassion and connection were still operating at the family and "in-group" level, there have always been vicious conflicts over resources in human history. Our thinking has been, for the most part, very instrumental; making decisions that maximize resources and efficiency by any means necessary.

These thinking strategies are a zero-sum game. You either win or lose. This was necessary for human survival at the time. But now it is clear that this way of thinking is obsolete. Indeed, it's turning out to be a lose–lose strategy; it's killing us and our habitat. Our societies are self-destructing so rapidly it's easy to become depressed. However, if you look at the problems that are now arising as a result of developments of the last century, you can find the keys to transforming our societies into thriving communities rather than just-trying-to-survive communities. Making this transformation will require different ways of thinking and understanding our world. This is where schools and teachers can play an important role.

The Overview Effect

When they see the earth from space, astronauts report a cognitive shift in awareness called the *overview effect*. In 1972, Dr. Harrison H. Schmitt, a crew member on Apollo 17 took a magnificent photograph of the entire earth from space and for the first time, huge numbers of human beings got to see the earth from this view too. Some have argued that this view of earth from above began to transform our understanding of the limits of the earth and the ecosystem (White, 2014). This view, so well captured in Apollo 11 crew member Michael Collins' observation at the start of Part II, has also transformed our ways of thinking by opening up our understanding of large dynamic systems, like the earth, and how important they are to our survival and thriving.

This view is the recognition that we are all interdependent—not just all human beings, but all of life, and indeed, all matter on Earth. This and the advent of particle physics helped us understand that the perception that we are entirely separate entities is an illusion of our minds. The molecules in our body are constantly being transferred from ourselves to our environment and back as part of a system of particles, atoms, molecules, and micro-organisms that operate unseen in the microscopic world. The chair I sit on as I write this is not entirely separate from my body or the pants I am wearing. Subtle shifts of molecules make us truly connected by tiny particles of matter.

From a global perspective of earth, we can recognize that borders are cognitive constructs, and complex global events, such as pandemics and climate disruptions, cross these boundaries. The COVID-19 pandemic demonstrated the futility of counting on borders to protect us from the crisis; public health workers found that the virus had entered the United States early on through travelers from China and Italy. Because the virus is contagious before any symptoms arise and there were no tests available, it was impossible to stop people who were carriers at the borders.

The acid rain crisis in the 1990s made it clear that global efforts are needed to step the negative impacts of environmental degradation and climate change. The sulfur dioxide pollution from coal-fired plants in the northeastern part of the United States was creating acidic rain that was killing aquatic life and forests. While much of it affected the United States itself, enough of it crossed the northern border into Canada to cause an international crisis. However, this problem contained the seed of "the greatest green success story of the past decade" (The Economist, 2002). The Clean Air Act (U.S. Environmental Protection Agency, 1990) included a cap-and-trade approach that required coal-burning companies to cut sulfur emissions in half but allowed them to decide how best to make these cuts. Companies that lowered their emissions more than half could sell these allowances to other companies. This was the beginning of the carbon commodities market, a way to reduce carbon emissions without devastating the economy.

While we can celebrate successes like these, we have a long way to go to shift our thinking to better understand interdependence. Systems thinking can help. Systems thinking involves a shift from win–lose to win–win. In a win–lose scenario, my winning something in the short term might have adverse consequences for others, which may also have a negative impact on me in the long run. When we recognize the interconnectedness of everything, we can see that the only functional way forward is the win–win approach. How do we do this? We change our thinking.

Over the past two centuries, we have solved problems using a mechanistic approach. This is natural, given the limits of our cognitive and technological capabilities during the early modern era. Now, we need to consider much larger complex and dynamic systems. The climate is a very good example. While scientists cannot "prove" that global warming is disrupting the planet, they can point to the increasing probabilities of climate disruptions as the planet warms and can model scenarios based on these probabilities. Unfortunately, like many phenomena, it's impossible to conduct a randomized experiment to determine the exact cause and effect. Indeed, there are multiple causes and effects that interact with one another. Which variables would you examine? Which would you try to hold constant? From this example, you can see that some ways of examining problems have limitations because they attempt to eliminate variability rather than to examine the variability itself.

Thinking in Systems

Systems thinking is beginning to enter education in the form of curriculum. However, why not turn to systems thinking as we transform our school systems? When we look at the school system through a systems lens, we can extend our limited, instrumental way of seeing it to a more transactional view, where everyone and everything is part of a system, and multiple systems interact, forming larger systems.

We can apply systems thinking to all levels of our educational system and think through the problems confronting us in a new way. Starting with the student: We have much more understanding of human development and its potential than ever before. We now know how very plastic our developmental process is, even through adulthood (Glasper & Neigh, 2019). We are incredibly resilient and there's no such thing as a lost cause. Back in the day, if a student didn't do well in school, people thought that they just didn't have what it takes and were innately inferior to others. Now we know that humans are incredibly diverse and have a huge array of strengths and weaknesses. We all have something to contribute if we are given the chance, and this is a "all hands on deck" moment in human history.

We also can't give up on the adults in our system. It's time to stop blaming teachers and start giving them the autonomy they need to help turn this ship around. Teachers are also adult learners and can change quickly when called to the challenge and given autonomy in the classroom. When we teachers address the challenge, there's no stopping us. We can consciously change ourselves in ways that can help us create thriving learning environments (Jennings, 2015; 2019b).

We can apply systems thinking to our classrooms, which are incredibly rich social systems in and of themselves. We can teach our students systems thinking, or better yet, learn along with them by applying it to our classroom system and discovering elements of how our classroom social system is functioning and how to improve it. And guess what? We no longer have to have all the answers (whew! Isn't that a great relief?). Kids learn systems thinking quickly, as we will see in Part III of this book, and when they get engaged, teachers can let them take the helm of their own learning.

We can apply systems thinking to our schools and consider ways to disrupt the old factory model. Many schools are experimenting with mixed age grouping, open classrooms, project-based learning, and flexible scheduling. In Part III, I will share examples of how some schools are applying systems thinking to building school environments that spark deep learning. We can apply systems thinking to our districts and state agencies. Once these ideas take off and succeed, there will be no stopping us. Once school boards see how these changes are transforming our students' lives, they will find ways to provide even greater supports. They might begin to examine school governance and change the imbedded inequities in school funding to ensure all students get equal resources. But now I'm getting ahead of myself. I used to feel discouraged because I had so little hope for change at the top. Now I'm full of hope because I know we can do it. We don't need to wait for the policy makers to give us permission.

Changing Systems

Many have argued that systems thinking is a key competency for twenty-first-century management (Kim, 1999). A system is a group of components that interact to form a unified functioning whole with a specific purpose. The purpose of a system is greater than any of its parts alone—and a system doesn't work well if it's missing any of its parts. Systems maintain stability through feedback loops. A simple example of a system is an HVAC system. The thermostat provides the feedback that signals the system to turn on heating or cooling. Systems thinking involves being able to see processes from three levels of perspective: events, patterns, and systemic structures. This might sound complicated, but kids love learning about systems, and we can learn along with them. Building system-thinking skills with our students will help deepen our own understanding. We can learn terms and tools of systems thinking to communicate to each other our understanding of how systems behave and how we might modify the system to improve the outcomes we're aiming for.

One reason the factory system was efficient is that it created a simple, predictable system. Parts are lined up in an assembly line and workers add one part at a time. Each part is standardized to fit. Each worker has a standardize tool to put the parts together. The end result is a car that meets specific standards. This is a simple context, and at the time it made sense to impose this model on students and teachers to scale education. Classrooms were more homogeneous, content was simpler, and most learning was rote. Sure, some kids fell through the cracks, but this was a necessary trade-off, a function of scaling. At scale, some might argue, there are always products that fall through the cracks, but the number of products that don't outweigh the cost of the loss.

Today our scaling problems and our classrooms are different, and the costs of failure immeasurable. Our classrooms, like our world, are complex, diverse, and often unpredictable. Our students come from multiple backgrounds with diverse home languages and racial and cultural identities and histories. Many are growing up under adversity, poverty, and trauma. Students still need to learn basic skills, but this is the easy part. More importantly, they need to learn how to learn, across their entire life. Right now, our traditional school systems are sucking the life out of learning, for both students and teachers. We know that learning is a very complex and individual process and that we learn better when we have the autonomy to choose what and how to learn (Deci & Ryan, 2002). This is fundamental.

The simple context of the factory model school has evolved into the complex context of the twenty-first-century school. A lot of the stress we experience as educators comes from operating as if we're working in a simple context when we are actually working in an extremely complex system. This new, complex system requires a completely new way of thinking about problems and how to solve them. If we try to solve problems in a complex context using solutions designed for simple contexts, it just won't work. And that's why modern education reforms continue to fail.

The problem is, we humans have been working with simple contexts for most of human history, and we're very good at managing them; it is an automatic human tendency. These tendencies are like our automatic pilot operating system, developed over tens of thousands of years of experience. Today our world is much more complex, and addressing complex problems with simple solutions can actually make things worse. We can no longer rely on this ancient operating system. Complex contexts require a different way of thinking: to slow down and see a situation from multiple perspectives.

Today, so many aspects of our daily lives are unpredictable, and how these aspects will interact with one another is also unpredictable. This causes fear and anxiety. Today it is especially difficult to have a sense of what our children will need to know and to be able to do in the coming decades. With the transformation of work—professions disappearing (such as retail) and the new gig economy growing—our children are likely to be re-inventing themselves and their careers multiple times during their lifetimes (Harari, 2017).

What's particularly difficult today is that our inherent tendencies, what I like to call our "default perimeters," are giving us the wrong signals. You can see this in bulldozing parenting: parents pushing their children to achieve and to aim for a very narrow area of expertise (e.g., Harvard Law, or Yale Medical School). This style of parenting doesn't allow kids to experience failure, which deprives them of the opportunity to learn from failure (Miller & Bromwich, 2019). Perhaps these unfortunate children have a unique gift that does not fit into the parents' chosen path but that will be invaluable in the coming decades. We just don't know. The education system has a knee-jerk tendency to make drastic top-down changes for the sake of improvement that never seem to work out as planned. If they were trying to solve a problem with auto design, that might work, but when dealing with human development in the complexity of the twenty-first century, this approach is incredibly shortsighted.

The old way of thinking is limited because of its adherence to linear cause–effect modeling. It is now evident that a change and the cause of that change are different in systems of different levels of complexity. In simple systems, the linear model works. I follow the recipe, put the oven at the right temperature, and the cookies come out as expected. However, complex systems involve multiple feedback loops that are often difficult to see when viewed through a linear mindset.

The Failure of Linear Thinking

For an example of how applying linear thinking to problems in complex systems can result in unintended and unforeseen outcomes, consider the history of the Class Size Reduction program in California. Achievement in California schools was down, and the idea of reducing class sizes to improve achievement in the early grades was based in scientific evidence. At the time, California had the largest class sizes in the United States (an average of 29 students per class), and results from the Tennessee STAR study clearly demonstrated that students in primary grades do better academically in smaller classes, and the differences were most evident among low-income and minority students (Mosteller, 1995). So, in 1996 California spent $1 billion to reduce class sizes in primary grades, statewide. Simply applying the results of the STAR study in Tennessee to the State of California is an example of linear thinking: kids are not performing well, our class sizes are large, research shows that reducing class size will result in student improvement, let's reduce class size. What's missing in this linear approach is an understanding of the complex and interacting school systems and how making one change might disrupt other learning processes. Two major, unanticipated problems arose when school districts tried to implement this new policy. First, there wasn't a sufficient number of qualified teachers to increase the number of classrooms and decrease class size. Second, schools lacked the facilities to create space for more classrooms. As a result of this policy change, greater numbers of unqualified teachers joined the workforce, especially in areas of greatest need, and the effect was a washout—administrators saw some gains, but they were not able to attribute these gains to the reductions in class size. Also, kids in poorly resourced schools received less support overall. Because of the way education funding works in California and, to be clear, in most of the rest of the United States (e.g., districts with higher property taxes have more financial resources), better resourced schools were more able to take advantage of this initiative without taking funds from other programs. Better resourced schools could afford to pay more teachers and had more facility capacity. They were also more likely to attract qualified teachers from their poorly-resourced neighbors. As you can see from this example, there were multiple causal loops going on in this huge complex system: availability of personnel and space limited change where it was most needed. There were likely many other factors and causal loops that played out in this school reform debacle; I won't go into them here, but you see what I mean.

Rather than rolling out a massive initiative like this all at once, it makes much more sense to start small and pilot test ideas before taking them to scale. This way, all the parts and processes of the system that need to be adjusted can be identified and planned for. Being able to see the entire system, and how its parts interact in causal loops rather than cause–effect dyads, helps us better understand the overall system's functioning and the levers of change inherent in the system. Without a systems view, it's easy to conclude that reducing class size doesn't work. However, when you need to scale a program that requires a massive increase in your teaching workforce without planning ahead, you end up with more unqualified or under-qualified teachers, which causes its own negative impacts on student learning. The primary difficulty with linear thinking is that while it's technically accurate to describe what happened and when it happened, this doesn't help us understand *how* things happened and *why*.

The linear thinking cause–effect model of "lower class sizes equals better student outcomes" becomes "lower class sizes do not equal better student outcomes" when it fails. Those of us who have spent many years in education have seen this cycle repeat itself time and again. Districts experiment with bold, new initiatives without careful planning because of pressure to demonstrate rapid results. The systems view helps us see and understand more of the factors that play a role in the outcome. Meanwhile, a huge body of careful scientific research is helping us understand these systems and what works to promote development and learning. Unfortunately, many policymakers are not well-informed yet are subject to political pressure, leading to attempts at quick fixes. One country that is paying attention to our outstanding education research is Finland. Many of the successful initiatives that have made their school system the envy of the world originated in education research conducted the United States, but not well-scaled here at home (Sahlberg, 2015).

Vicious Cycles

All systemic behavior involves reinforcing and balancing processes. How these two types of processes interact results in most of the dynamic behavior of complex systems. Reinforcing systems result from positive feedback, which in this context means information indicating change in one direction produces more change in that direction. This is an example of how successive changes can add to the previous change and keep the change going in the same direction; a vicious cycle, or downward spiral.

A common teacher–student (and parent–child) interaction that illustrates this type of reinforcing system is the coercive cycle (Patterson, 1982), or power struggle. In a hypothetical example, it is usually assumed that the child starts the cycle by engaging in a behavior that the adult deems disruptive in some way. This upsets the adult, who responds with harsh discipline. The child doesn't understand the adult's actions and feels hurt and angry, so they lash out in vengeance, triggering the adult to engage in even more coercion, and so forth.

While an adult can usually overpower a child, a child can out-tantrum an adult any day, so these types of interactions are extremely exhausting and harmful to relationships. You can see that while this looks like a simple causal loop, there are multiple dimensions that can influence the process and the outcome, including the child's and adult's temperament and personality, the adult's understanding of the child's behavior, and the relationship between the parties (e.g., parent–child versus teacher–child).

Young children themselves can even understand these reinforcing processes. Once I was observing two preschool boys playing in the sand, making a sand fort. Juan was building a tower with a pile of sticks. Sam was digging a hole for the moat, but suddenly he looked up and yelled, "Juan, you can't build it there, someone will fall on it!" Rather than discuss the situation calmly, Sam marched up and kicked the tower, smashing all the sticks to the ground. Juan was furious. "That was my tower and you just ruined it!" He yelled as he got up and smashed the moat with his boot. Soon they were tussling on the ground.

From my many years of working with preschoolers, I knew enough to remain calm. But I quickly walked over to them and stopped the physical fighting. "How do we solve conflicts with our friends?" I asked them both. They knew the answer, and, as they had been instructed to in the past, they went to sit on a bench to discuss the problem using a systems thinking approach. After a few minutes, they came running up to me beaming. "We solved our conflict!" I asked them what they had learned. Sam said, "The tower was getting too close to the slide, and I was worried that someone would smash it, so I smashed it first."

"Then what happened?" I asked.

"Then I got mad because he smashed my tower," said Juan. "So I smashed his moat to get back at him."

"Then what happened?" I asked.

Sam said, "Then I got mad that he smashed my moat and I hit him, and then he hit me back, and then I hit him until you came up and stopped us."

I said, "What did you notice about this situation?"

"It's a loop!" They both yelled in unison.

"Can you say more?" I asked.

"We were just going around in circles, back and forth, until you stopped us."

"What do you think might have happened if I hadn't stopped you?"

They both started to look at me with big eyes. "It would be bad!" said Juan. Sam nodded grimly in agreement.

"What could you do next time so things wouldn't get bad?" I asked.

Sam said, "I could have talked to him about how kids on the slide might smash the tower."

Juan said, "Then I could have moved it to the other side."

When we were back in the classroom, I invited them to draw a picture of the "loop" and they drew a spiral that started out red on the outside and got darker as it closed into the center of the circle.

Virtuous Cycles

In contrast, a virtuous cycle is a balancing process that stabilizes system functioning. These are balancing loops, like the thermostat we visited earlier. The balancing process is always trying to find and maintain equilibrium. While virtuous cycles are ubiquitous, they are often more difficult to see than the reinforcing processes because their function is to keep things as they are, and we are much better at noticing when things change than when they don't change.

Balancing processes include both negative and positive feedback loops that balance the system. There is a gap, or opening in the loop where feedback provides the change mechanism. For example, you want your house to be 70 degrees or cooler; your air conditioning is off in the morning because your house is only 65 degrees after a cool night; as the day passes, the temperature in your house rises. At some point the feedback to the system (in this case the thermometer reaching 70 degrees) triggers positive feedback, and the air conditioning goes on until the temperature is at or below 70 degrees, then it goes off again.

Applying this understanding to our earlier examples, in an adult–child coercive cycle, you can create an opening, or gap, and insert feedback into the system. This might be taking a break from the interaction, engaging in calming and focusing practices, asking another adult to step in, intentional ignoring, etc. What all these approaches have in common is that they disrupt the causal loop.

In the vignette with Sam and Juan, I (the adult) created the gap between the interaction between Juan and Sam. Conflict is not a bad thing, and children can learn from disagreements, but physical violence is never tolerated. In this case, I intervened and gave the boys feedback by directing them to engage in conflict resolution, which allowed them to recover their friendliness towards one another.

When I saw their drawing I asked, "Why is there a dark circle in the middle?"

Sam said, "That's because it would have been really bad."

"But it wasn't bad, was it? Why not?" I asked.

"Because you stopped us," said Juan.

I asked them if they could add this part of the story to their drawing. Sam drew a person holding a stop sign. "Is that me?" I asked. They both nodded.

"After I stopped you what happened?" I said. They thought for a few minutes and Juan said. "We're friends again!" and Sam added, "After we talked about it and I said sorry."

I asked if they could add this to their drawing, and they created a pink circle around the picture and surround it with little hearts.

What I find intriguing about this incident is that the boys actually recognized that the conflict made them feel closer. There's plenty of evidence that human bonds do indeed strengthen after conflict and resolution, which is a really good reason to let our children engage in conflicts, safely. It's important to note that what I did was not meant to control them. I simply created a gap, gently stopped their aggression, and directed them to talk. I made sure they understood that hurting one another was not acceptable, and I invited them to consider what they should do instead. This empowered them to engage in the systems thinking process that helped them resolve their disagreement. They learned and grew closer. See how this is a virtuous cycle?

This is a very simple example of a social interaction system process viewed from a limited frame of time. Some processes are more complex and involve multiple strings of events. Events are things that occur on a day-to-day basis. For example, I become annoyed with Jill's incessant questioning. Patterns are accumulated memories of events. We begin to notice how events in a series play out in similar ways—patterns. When I am under time pressure, I am more likely to become annoyed by Jill's questioning. Systemic structures are how parts of the system are organized. So in this case, I might want to modify the structure by preparing enough time for Jill's questioning so I don't feel pressed for time. Or, I might give Jill some time alone to discuss the lesson.

In these system processes, it's the events that are most salient. Frequently, they feel like they stand alone because they involve a heightened emotional response. Also, our language is very event-oriented. While its usually easy to notice an event, it takes insight to recognize underlying patterns and structures. Events in a system are like the tip of the iceberg. The patterns and structures operate unseen below the surface.

This focus on the events only, rather than the entire system, was adaptive to our survival when we needed to respond to immediate danger and when cause and effect was easier to predict. However, these days, this response can backfire. With our adapting twenty-first-century minds, we can see how to redesign systems, and in this way, we have much greater leverage to affect the future in these times of rapid change.

Finding Balance

The key to unlocking school transformation is systems thinking, but our old factory system is based in a long-outmoded, mechanistic worldview designed to promote linear causal thinking. A student enters the "factory" in kindergarten and each teacher-worker along the assembly line inputs knowledge, year by year, as if the student were on a conveyor belt. The knowledge is compartmentalized by subject area. "We're installing the language arts module this morning." Each learning module is standardized to result in the desired outcome—fact-based knowledge.

The problem is, complex human systems don't work this way anymore, if they ever really did in the past. In fact, few systems, even those in manufacturing, are really this simple anymore. Fortunately, the understanding of complex dynamical systems is growing, and schools are beginning to teach students these ideas. Indeed, new science standards include systems literacy (National Research Council, 2015). However, the goal is not just to learning about systems but to apply systems thinking to learning itself. All across the world, there is a growing field of work to create more dynamic, systemic, and evolutionary systems of learning.

When we practice systems thinking we discover that change is emergent and that outcomes can arise that are more than their constituent parts. Learning itself can be seen as a system. Take a moment to think about how a baby learns mobility. As a young mother, watching my son go through this process was fascinating. First, he learned to flip himself from his back to his tummy. The day he was able to turn over by himself, he was thrilled! It was like a lightbulb went off as he experienced his body flip over. Then he went through the "cobra" stage, where he could push up his chest with his arms, but his legs were still out behind him. Eventually he got his knees bent and his legs under him, but he could only push himself backward, so he ended up scooting into corners and getting stuck. Finally, he figured out how to coordinate his arms and legs to crawl. At this point, he was unstoppable, and we quickly had to babyproof the house!

Which brings me to another system: the house the baby inhabits. If a baby isn't given room to move around and explore, the development of their motor skills may be stymied. On the other hand, if the environment isn't safe for an exploring baby, they can get hurt falling down stairs or sticking fingers into outlets. So, we parents think about the interaction between the baby's emerging mobile body and the home environment. This is a very simple example of how we can apply systems thinking to supporting child development: recognizing the innate drive to learn and creating the environment and opportunities to do so.

The human body is an emergent system, and human mobility is also a system that emerges from the body. Babies don't need a factory to help them learn to walk. We don't have to break down the process for the baby, separating out each step. The baby does this naturally, and eventually the walking-toddler emerges from this dynamic process of experimentation and trial and error, propelled by extraordinary motivation and fierce determination.

To think systemically, we first need to zoom out far enough to see the whole system. Then we need to examine the system from multiple perspectives looking for interdependent leverage points. We need to keep the long-term outcomes in mind and notice where unexpected outcomes materialize. Watch for win–lose thinking and fault-finding, which can stall the process. Tolerating ambiguity, paradox, and chaos will help us look beyond our default perimeters. We can examine flows and accumulations in the system and any time delays that create inertia, or stickiness.

Like Sam and Juan, you can draw maps of systems to see if you can unpack them. When you have a situation that calls for a system analysis, talk it through. What happened? What did you see, hear, and feel? Describe your experience in the fullest detail. Nothing is off limits; it's all part of the system in some way. The responses to these questions can form the key variables in a causal loop, or loops. Don't be afraid to make a mess and start over. There's no "right" answer. There are multiple perspectives. You are hunting for places you can nudge the system to encourage a shift here or there. Often, the process requires a lot of trial and error. Finally, and most importantly, view yourself as part of the system. As my friend and colleague Dr. Alexander Laszlo (2015) says, "Be the system change you wish to see in the world." In other words, know how you impact the systems you create and inhabit. To do this, we really need some deep self-examination, which is discussed in the next chapter.

CHAPTER 5

Mind Traps

So far, I have outlined a basic understanding about how we can apply systems thinking to changing the way we think about school. With this understanding in mind, we need to focus on our own "system" and examine the mental habits that interfere with this perspective. When we examine these mental habits, we see that they are often simple systems, engraved in our psyche. We need to identify our scripts—the grooves or patterns in our socialization process.

Uncovering and Overcoming Scripts

What beliefs do I apply to situations that may limit me? For example, growing up in the 1950s and 1960s, I was taught to be a polite lady. The translation of "polite lady" included: It is not "ladylike" to be assertive. Ladies do not have strong opinions; they are modest, weak, and demure. Although, these qualities do not align with my natural temperament (indeed, as a little kid, I wanted to be a boy), I was socialized to act this way, and for many years, it was very difficult to stand up for myself and to negotiate for what I wanted. The system, for me, worked like this: I want something, I feel bad about wanting something, I don't say anything, I feel bad about not getting what I want. This is a vicious cycle. Each time I run it, I'm reinforcing the script: "I am undeserving of what I want."

Raising a son helped a lot. I found it rather easy to coach him to be assertive, so it wasn't like I didn't know how it's done. Over time and with the help of therapy, I learned to notice the subtle emotional cues that let me know I was restraining my expression of my wants and needs. I got a lot better at asking for what I want and need, although the socialization is still there and sometimes it still feels awkward or uncomfortable.

Society has imposed a social stereotype on the entire profession of teaching. Whether you're older, a baby boomer like me, or part of a younger generation, the history of teaching has left an indelible impression on American society that teachers are semi-skilled workers, most of them compliant and caring (never feisty!) women, who complain too much and have summers off. Heck, anyone with a college degree can be a teacher, right? It is high time to eradicate this oppressive stereotype and empower the teaching profession. Teaching is one of the most complex and demanding professions in the world today, requiring very high levels of cognitive and emotional competence. Indeed, Dr. Lee Shulman (2004), who has studied professional development for over 30 years, concluded:

> Classroom teaching . . . is perhaps the most complex, most challenging, and most demanding, subtle, nuanced, and frightening activity that our species has ever invented. In fact, when I compared the complexity of teaching with that much more highly rewarded profession, "doing medicine," I concluded that the only time medicine even approaches the complexity of an average day of classroom teaching is in an emergency room during a natural disaster. (Shulman, 2004, p. 504)

Besides being a very highly skilled profession, teaching will continue to be valuable well into the twenty-first century. What teachers do is probably one of the most crucial vocations, and it's unlikely that teachers will be replaced by artificial intelligence (Lister, 2018). Once we teachers recognize the value of our work, we can dismantle the old stereotype and build an empowered mindset. We can start by applying self-awareness, noticing the "scripts," the habitual mental processes about our profession and ourselves and also challenging them. We can develop the observer in ourselves so our thoughts are more intentional and less automatic.

Mindful awareness practices can help a lot, and if you'd like to pursue this approach further, I suggest you read my book *Mindfulness for Teachers* (Jennings, 2015). It can help you recognize that uncomfortable feelings are often a clue that there's a script interfering with your perceptions. As I mentioned earlier, time urgency, or stress associated with time constraints, is one of my emotional tendencies, based on an early script. As a child I learned that being late is very bad and disrespectful. When I'm feeling rushed or pressed for time in any way, I can notice the tension rise in my body. Since I learned to notice this, it has become a very familiar feeling that arises quite often. Before I was able to recognize this script and manage my reactivity, the emotions could really get in my way, and depending on the situation, it would play out as either panic and guilt or blame and judgment.

Here's a typical scenario: I notice that I'm late to an appointment, and the first thing that happens is this little panic that says, "Oh, no! You're going to be late! People are going to be mad at you! You better hurry up!" This is my script. I feel my shoulders tensing up and my jaw clenching. If I'm driving, I start speeding up. I have learned to recognize this script, so now I can take a few breaths and calm my sympathetic nervous system. Consciously, I know that if I'm a few minutes late, it's no big deal. But the little girl in my head still haunts me.

When a colleague is late for a meeting, especially if it's habitual, sometimes I catch myself thinking, "Late again! This is such a waste of my time. If I knew he was going to be late I could have finished what I was working on. I don't think he respects the demands on my time." This is my mother script. It reflects the reactions I received as a child when I was late. But now that I'm aware of it, more often I can recognize it and let it go.

This particular script is common among teachers because the old factory system imposes rigid time frames around everything we do. Here's the script: "We are supposed to be on time, our students are supposed to be on time, and we are all supposed to finish everything we start by the time the bell rings." If I were the principal of a school, the first thing I would do is swap out the bells for something more soothing, like chimes or music. In schools, transitions are hard enough without having to be managed by these horrid bells. In many schools they are so harsh the sound is almost traumatizing. With all our new technology there must be a better way.

The way we work today does not fit into this lock-step, bell-regulated system. Deep learning and reflection take time, and when you interrupt learning processes, lots of good progress can be derailed. From my years of experience as a teacher and from working with teachers as a facilitator of professional learning, I know how hard it is to fit everything we have to do into our schedule. It really is impossible, but we keep trying to do it. When anything upsets this tight schedule, it can trigger this time urgency. Many teachers tell me that just the number of daily intercom announcements that interrupt is infuriating. It's no wonder we feel on edge so much of the time.

I believe that it's high time to rethink school schedules and transitions. However, through my years of research, I've discovered that we don't need to feel so oppressed by our schedules. In fact, teachers can take charge of their own social and emotional development and acquire the skills they need to manage the stress of the classroom environment, including this time urgency. My colleagues and I developed a mindfulness- and compassion-based professional development program called Cultivating Awareness and Resilience in Education (CARE) and have tested its efficacy in several federally funded, randomized, controlled trials with elementary school teachers. CARE combines mindful awareness and compassion practices with emotion skills training applied specifically to the emotional challenges we face as teachers in the classroom. In our largest study to date, involving 224 teachers in 36 elementary schools in the Bronx and Upper Manhattan of New York City, we found that the teachers randomly assigned to CARE were significantly more mindful and better emotionally regulated, compared to the teachers in the control group. They were also significantly less stressed by time urgency and had reduced psychological distress (Jennings et al., 2017). Emotion regulation and psychological distress continued to improve into the next school year without further intervention (Jennings, Doyle, et al., 2019).

Many teachers who have participated in CARE have told me that in the process of applying mindfulness to the sense of time urgency, they realized that when they're feeling stressed-out by time, it actually interferes with what they are trying to accomplish. "I'm so busy worrying about all I have to do that I'm not getting things done. It's like my mind is taking me into a black hole of doom," said one teacher. "When I calm down and stop ruminating about it all, I get so much more accomplished." This is a great example of how, by understanding our own internal systems, we can interrupt vicious cycles so they don't derail what we're trying to accomplish.

While it's taken me over 40 years of mindful awareness practice (along with years of therapy) to be able to notice and overcome scripts, my students learn this more quickly. I think as our generations evolve, they outgrow us, as they must, to address this complex world we've created. I've actually been astounded by how quickly the young adults in my classes learn that they have scripts and that they are not the thoughts that play out in these scripts.

Mind Traps

Now that you have a better understanding of how our scripts can run us and how to uncover and overcome them, let's look at some ways our minds get us stuck as we try to address this world of complex systems that we face every day. This complexity affects schools at multiple levels. Just like the growing complexity of the school, family life is also much more complex today. Until the 1980s, most families had a mother at home who took care of children and domestic chores. In 2016, 64.7% of American families with school-age children had two working parents (U.S. Bureau of Labor Statistics, 2017). It's commonly recognized that these families are living complex lives. They are constantly juggling duties, commitments, and demands. On top of that, the higher divorce rate means more children are living in dual households, adding an extra layer of complexity. Today, families are much more diverse in terms of mixed race/ethnicity, gender identity, etc. Finally, growing income inequality has resulted in greater numbers of children living in poverty and exposed to adversity and trauma. So, often the interaction between the complex family system and the complex school system yields undesirable consequences.

Management consultant Dr. Jennifer Berger has skillfully applied adult developmental theory to understanding complexity in her book *Unlocking Leadership Mindtraps: How to Thrive in Complexity* (Berger, 2019). "Part cognitive bias, part neurological quirk, part adaptive response to a simple world that doesn't exist anymore, they are mindtraps," she explains (Berger, 2019, p. 8). As I noted earlier, our default parameter is to approach most problems and situations as if we're dealing with a simple system. In this section of Chapter 5, I apply Berger's explanations of these mind traps to common situations in educational settings to see how we can recognize mind traps and escape from them.

According to Berger (2019), recognizing when you are in a mind trap is a superpower that allows you to see new opportunities and create novel innovative solutions in the midst of complexity. These traps are simple mental habits that were very adaptive during early periods of human history. Years of research in the fields of biology, psychology, behavioral economics, neuroscience, sociology, and human development have uncovered these natural human tendencies. As we have learned more about our human nature, we have begun to experiment with how to consciously and intentionally change ourselves to be more adaptive to this complex world we've created. In this way, we're learning to make friends with complexity rather than letting it overwhelm us.

Berger has discovered that when we are trying to lead in complex and rapidly changing contexts, the places we get stuck are often the ones in which our reflexes are exactly wrong. "Such times seem to clump together in particular ways and create a perverse and inescapable trap: our human instincts, shaped for (and craving) a simple world, fundamentally mislead us in a complex, unpredictable world" (Berger, 2019, p. 7). A critical characteristic of these traps is that they fool us into thinking that we're doing the right thing and that it's not working because we're not trying hard enough, so we try harder. While it's easy to fall into these traps and get stuck, there are proven ways to sidestep them, and that's what I'll address next. Berger

(2019) identifies five primary mind traps: simple stories, rightness, agreement, control, and ego.

During my years supervising and observing student teachers' classrooms, I observed student teachers and their mentors falling into these traps. Since I was still teaching myself, I became more aware of my own tendencies to do the same. I recognized that when we feel stressed, we are much more likely to fall into these traps, because we're operating at the level of the default parameter. In the next five sections, we'll address each of the primary mind traps and how they apply to common conundrums in educational settings.

Simple Stories

Who doesn't love a good story? Humans are wired for storytelling. In his book *Sapiens: A Brief History of Humankind*, historian Dr. Yuval Noah Harari explains how during the Cognitive Revolution (starting around 70,000 BC) humans were able to communicate information about the world around them (Harari, 2014). This allowed them to coordinate survival strategies by communicating where there was danger and where they might find food resources. Humans were also able to communicate more complex and detailed information about the social group, leading to changes in group structure, dynamics, and organization, allowing for larger social groups to form and function.

But Harari attributes the key to our rapid cultural and technological change to our ability to transmit information about nonexistent "things"—constructions of the imagination, such as myths, beliefs, and ideas. This ability allowed large numbers of unrelated strangers to form a larger identity and to cooperate and collaborate on shared goals, which led to rapid changes in social behavior. In some ways, you could say that these abstractions began to form a life of their own, as whole systems of behavior and thinking rose out of them, such as religions, governments, etc. For example, as a citizen of the United States and having grown up in this culture, I identify with the flag as a symbol of my country: I have feelings about a piece of cloth that I don't have about other pieces of cloth. I can also identify with certain myths about the Unites States that have grown out of our history to present aspects of our identity.

Many of these are simple stories about something that happened in our past. Take Thanksgiving, for example. The simple story we have been telling children in our schools all these years is simply not true. It distorts important complexities in the story that reveal aspects of our history we would rather not talk about, including horrors like mass murder (Salam, 2017). The story also distorts the historical import of the colonists, their goals, and their tragic impact on the lives of native people, including the gift of germs that resulted in epidemics that wiped out most of the population of native peoples in Massachusetts before the Plymouth Colony was even settled (Marr & Cathey, 2010). The Thanksgiving myth is only one of many we use to instantiate our shared identity as Americans. Simple stories can blind us to the real story because they are so much easier to remember and transmit to others. For this reason, they hold the power to perpetuate social and political oppression. This is how racism, sexism, and other forms of oppression are systematized so that they are hard for us to see, especially if we belong to the group that is doing the oppressing.

When we humans were beginning to form social alliances in larger communities and needed to cooperate on a larger scale this story-telling skill was helpful. Stories also gave us a sense of meaning or purpose greater than our short human lives. The stories we tell each other and ourselves have a simple plot: beginning, middle, and end. They have simplistic characters, heroes and villains and simple cause and effect processes. If a story doesn't contain these familiar elements, it can cause confusion and anxiety. Simple stories are created by picking and choosing what we remember and putting these things together in a rational cause and effect story. We may embellish the story as we go along if it makes the story sound better. Our minds can't tell the difference between what really happened and how we embellished it. The embellished story ends up feeling like a memory; the simpler the better.

When we look for the reasons something is happening as a way to solve a problem, it's easy to plot out a timeline and look for a cause–effect narrative. In this way, we can confuse association with causation. The fact that two things co-occur doesn't mean they have any causal relationship what-so-ever. But, our minds, used to making simple stories, often overlook this fact. We also project these simple stories into the future by filling in gaps with our imagination to make predictions based on the simplistic narrative. The California Class Size Reduction initiative discussed earlier is a great example of the shortsightedness caused by simple stories. The bulldozer parenting strategy is based in a simple story that if children go to the best schools and do well, they will get into the best colleges and from there will have wonderful successful lives, which completely invalidates the child's passions, interests, gifts, and proclivities.

In our story making, we create simplistic characters: archetypes and stereotypes. First impressions tend to become lasting. Once we have formed a stereotype, we use data to confirm it. This is what's called a confirmation bias: we see only what we want to see (Nickerson, 1998). When I was supervising student teachers and observing classrooms, after the session was over and I was meeting with the student teachers, they often remarked about how chaotic the class was. They were apologetic and embarrassed. Often this was a big surprise to me because my impression was entirely different. I thought the students were all very engaged in learning. Now I realize that they were stuck in the simple-story mind trap, projecting their own story about what a class full of students is supposed to look like: quietly working alone rather than energetically engaged with one another.

This happened so often that I conducted an experiment with my students. I told them about my experience and suggested that they take a moment to calm down whenever they start feeling stress because they think the class is becoming chaotic. I taught them to focus on their breathing and feel the weight of their body on the floor or on the chair. I even suggested that they close their eyes for a minute or so, resulting in many raised eyebrows! The next time our seminar met, I asked them to share any insights from the practice. All of them had tried it and were astonished at how simply calming down changed the whole class. I had to tell them that I didn't think that the class had changed, but that *they* had changed. They changed the way they were perceiving the class. My students and I talked about how often teachers tell each other a simple story about their chaotic classrooms that does not convey the fullness of the complexity of a room full of active learners but is based in an old simple story from our factory model past.

Another example is how we can tend to make up stories about our students. Fifth grade teacher Ms. Moreno was warned about an incoming student named Luke. "He's going to drive you nuts," her colleagues would say, as if they were doing her a favor by preparing her with this information. Clearly the school community had already created a shared simple story about this student. When the school year began, Ms. Moreno made a concerted effort not to review his file. She didn't want to reinforce this story, and she wanted to get to know Luke without more preconceptions. On the first day of fifth grade, she could see that Luke had difficulty focusing his attention and when distracted, he tended to bother his peers. Rather than single him out to talk to him, she decided to do interviews with each of her students to get to know all of them better. She announced this to the whole class, and she scheduled a meeting with each student one at a time during recess. She took this time to learn about their lives and the things that were important to them.

When it was Luke's turn, he sat down looking unhappy. He wore a frown and had his arms crossed against his chest defensively. The first thing she said was that she wanted to get to know everyone better.

"You don't want to know me," he grumbled. Surprised, she asked him why he would say that. "Teachers don't like me, that's all. I'm used to it."

Sadly, he had heard the simple story about himself and believed it.

"What do you think it would look like if a teacher did like you?" asked Ms. Moreno. She was inviting him to make up a new story that had more possibilities, and it caught him off guard.

"I dunno, maybe I wouldn't be in trouble all the time?" In his story, he was in trouble because the teachers didn't like him. In the teacher version of the story, he was causing trouble in class to intentionally disrupt the class and annoy the teachers. For Ms. Moreno, this was a revelation.

"How about if we start this year with a fresh slate," she suggested. "That means we'll both take some time to get to know one another and then we'll see how it goes. What do you say?"

At first his mouth hung open. It was like no teacher had ever spoken to him with the respect we afford to one another as adults. Then his face lit up.

"That sounds great!"

"Ok, then. Let's spend our time now learning about each other."

She learned that Luke was the youngest of 6 and could tell that he rarely got the attention he needed at home. His family had a dog named Molly, whom he loved dearly. It seemed that Molly felt the same about Luke, because Luke told her that Molly slept in his bed with him. Ms. Moreno learned that Luke liked baseball and he was good at catching balls. Beaming, he told her about a fly ball he had caught the previous season.

Over the course of the year, Luke and Ms. Moreno created a new story that was much more nuanced, reflecting the complexity of their relationship. He still had trouble staying on task but was less likely to bother the other students because Ms. Moreno was able to recognize the behaviors that preceded his distraction and realized that he had missed out on developing some important skills. When he hit a patch of work that required these skills, he went off the rails. Together they worked with the school specialists to get him back on track by teaching him to monitor his learning so he could get help when he needed it. Years later, he sent her a message on Facebook telling her that he had become a teacher himself. "You really saw me for who I was, and I really opened up in your class." These kinds of messages from students make all the challenges worthwhile. Now he can help other students unlearn negative and counterproductive stories about themselves too.

Dr. Berger (2019) offers several tips for identifying simple stories. A key question is to ask yourself, "How is this person a hero?" While Ms. Moreno didn't do exactly that with Luke, she did give herself an opportunity to explore different perspectives of him beyond the simple story stereotype of "troublemaker." When you can imagine that the character someone is playing is actually heroic, you might be able to see through the simple story and understand their perspective. While Luke wasn't a traditional type of hero, I think he was doing amazingly well given the gaps in his learning and the story that grew up around him. Quite heroic, I would say.

A key habit to develop is to carry three stories about any given situation. As you find yourself making up a story about the future based on the simple story, make up two more stories. This will help you avoid getting trapped in simple story thinking. Overall, Berger suggests practicing mind flexibility. Try to recognize when your mind is settling on a rigid view.

Rightness

Humans have a tendency to mistake the feeling of certainty as the result of a logical thought process (Schultz, 2010). However, the brain processes the feeling of certainty like an emotion rather than as a conscious thought process (Burton, 2008). Things just *feel* right to us. Also, when we learn we're wrong, we feel terrible, so we construct this feeling of rightness to avoid it. When we feel certain, we can give lots of explanations and justifications for this certainty that make sense because they are constructed after the fact. Indeed, it is our natural human tendency to believe that we are right most of the time (Kahneman, 2011). You can see why this is adaptive. It's a way to simplify a complex process that may be difficult to understand. But that's exactly what we don't want to do when we are working in complex systems.

Rightness is a particularly tough mind trap for teachers because we're *supposed* to be right! We also need to make quick decisions on the fly, so we don't have lots of time to reflect and it's easy to take the short cut and believe what we feel is right. However, there is usually a big gap between what we think is right and what is really right. When we know we're right, we close ourselves off from alternative possibilities that might support some creative new solution.

Our feelings of certainty can impact the way we interact with others. When we're teaching in an active learning environment, we don't often see a whole scenario unfold like you can when you are simply an observer. During my classroom observations, I saw this trap play out frequently. Once I saw two girls, Gina and Amaka, arguing over their art materials. The teacher came over to help them and I heard Gina accuse Amaka, "She took the red marker I was using!" Amaka whined, "That's not true! I had it first and she's trying to take it from me!" Rather than let the girls work out their differences on their own, the teacher immediately decided that it was Amaka's fault and made her give the marker to Gina. Amaka glowered. "Don't give me that look young lady," said the teacher in response.

Later when I was talking with the teacher, I mentioned the incident. "Oh, she's always taking things from other students. She just can't keep her hands to herself," the teacher said. When I asked her if she had seen what happened, she admitted that she hadn't, but she said she was sure it had been Amaka. I hadn't seen what happened either, so I'm not sure who was right, but because she had a history, Amaka became the automatic suspect. Over the years I have learned that when students like Amaka get a reputation, teachers use it to justify their response without really considering whether they are right or not. Other students learn that they can manipulate these scapegoats because the teacher will assume the scapegoat is in the wrong.

How do we overcome the rightness trap? Begin by asking yourself, "What do I believe and how could I be wrong?" Collect questions about the situation. Distinguish between beliefs and truth. Sometimes beliefs feel like truths because of our need for certainty. Another tip is to listen to learn rather than listening to be right, to negate, or to fix the situation. Accept that you might be in error and recognize that to err is to learn.

Agreement

Another human tendency is agreement. This is a powerful force that can band us together or polarize us. Agreement with our tribe, community, or family was critical to human survival. Disagreements could lead to exile and death. However, during times of complexity and uncertainty, too much agreement and too much polarization are not healthy. An important lesson that we humans need to learn is to harness our conflict rather than suppress it. We need to learn how to engage in questioning and disagreement safely so that we can try out multiple perspectives and alternatives.

The factory system imposed a "go along, get along" culture. Teachers were expected to be "nice" people who neither engage in conflict nor express strong opinions. So, while we grumble a lot, we're not used to questioning and modifying the system, because we didn't think we could. We teach our students to question and think critically, but the system hasn't been giving us permission to do this to the system itself. Don't get me wrong, I think educators are some of the nicest professionals, as a whole. But I also know that, from years of oppression, we can sometimes act like martyrs and be passive aggressive, sarcastic, and bitter. So, we have some work to do to create a safe space to question ourselves and one another about everything we are doing in this system.

When I started my doctoral program in human development, I was in for a big shock. Honestly, I had no idea what I was getting myself into. I was virtually starting from scratch in a new field that I knew very little about, although I thought I had some expertise in child development. Sure, I knew about learning theories, but I hadn't thoroughly studied child, adolescent, and adult development. I wasn't used to the tough rigorous questioning that goes on in academia and I took it personally. I told myself a simple story that the professors didn't like me. Over time I learned that the questioning process itself was what we were learning, that the questions directed at me were not personal but were intended to prompt me to think more deeply. I learned that scholars challenge their thinking and question one another. That's how we test our understanding and grow scientific knowledge.

After years of writing and reviewing journal articles reporting scientific findings, it now comes naturally. When I receive feedback about my work, I consider it carefully and learn from it. It usually expands my understanding because I get a different perspective to consider. Shifting my ways of thinking and communicating has sharpened my work considerably. When I think I know something, the first thing I do is to question how and why I think I know it. When I find myself agreeing with others, I ask myself if I have any questions about the situation before I just, automatically, nod my head in agreement. I believe that if we could all have these tough conversations without taking our perspectives and disagreements personally, we would be able to solve many of the difficult social problems in our world today. If we will let go of trying to agree and explore together, we may find out that both perspectives are limited in some ways and come to some understanding that extends beyond both of them. Obviously, to do this we need to build safety into our systems. Social distress is incredibly painful for us humans; it is often experienced in similar ways as physical pain (Ferris et al., 2019). We also need to understand the nature of our minds so that rather than presenting our understandings as "truth" for us to agree on, we can hold them out in front of us and critically examine them together, recognizing that an even better idea may grow out of both views.

The agreement trap leads to the belief that disagreements can be solved by compromise. However, this tends to oversimplify the problem even further, cutting and pasting together the parts of each party's view to form a chimera. This doesn't work in complex contexts where the more options, the better, and where a more wonderful solution may arise from an emergent process than from a process of congealing an aggregate of parts of ideas. Though trying to find compromise wastes time and energy that could result in a more thoughtful approach, this method feels fair to us, and we humans love fairness. The feeling of fairness generates a powerful reward system in the brain (Tabibnia & Lieberman, 2007). However, while it may feel fair at first, the compromise may lose its glow over time. The solution will likely not work well, and the original disagreement may still linger, leading to blame and possibly to polarization.

So how can we sidestep this trap or pull ourselves out of it when we fall in? Dr. Berger (2019) suggests redefining conflict and agreement by asking ourselves how the conflict might help deepen a relationship or relationships. A key habit to cultivate is to view disagreement as an opportunity to expand beyond each of the party's points of view. Recognize that the more possibilities and ideas the better, so rather than working to settle on one, spend time laying out many on the table to examine together. Try some of them out in small ways with pilot experiments. Practice learning together from trial and error with the recognition that in complex contexts there is never just one right answer.

Control

Control is another big trap for teachers because the old factory model has imbedded the belief that we are supposed to be in control of our students though this is actually impossible. Teaching classroom management to teacher candidates, I found that this is one of the most difficult truths my students had to accept. It's impossible to control another person without coercion, and the old punitive methods do not work in our highly complex classroom. Indeed, coercive tactics often backfire, causing power struggles and more disruption (Horner & McIntosh, 2016).

Ms. Chen is teaching eighth grade science. She is a firm believer in active learning and she has planned a lesson on evaporation and condensation that will involve groups of students engaging in an experiment. The groups have been arranged, the materials have been passed out, and the students are busily engaged in setting up the experiment, which involves heating water in a beaker on a Bunsen burner. While she's helping one group, she hears some bickering in the background and begins to feel stress rising in her neck and shoulders.

Looking up, she sees Angela and Marco struggling over the lab worksheet. Angela has a history of being bossy and losing her temper. She's yelling at Marco to give her the worksheet. Ms. Chen's stress level goes from a 5 to a 10, she jumps up and loudly yells, "Stop it!" Rushing over to the students, she grabs the worksheet away and says, "I warned you. If you can't work together peacefully, you can work on the alternative textbook assignment." She had prepared a back-up assignment for students to do on their own if the social interactions got difficult. Five moping students went back to their desks and took out their textbooks to begin the assignment.

Ms. Chen may now feel like she's gained control over the situation, but at what cost? While the rest of the class sullenly goes back to work on the experiment, five students no longer have the opportunity to participate. Also, imagine all the complex social dynamics that will result from this scenario. The trust Ms. Chen had cultivated up to that point may be eroded. Students may say to themselves, "She wants us to be active learners, but we have to do everything exactly right. If we disagree or do something wrong, she might get mad." Kids with internalizing issues, such as anxiety, may shut down, afraid to make a mistake or do anything that might be interpreted as disagreeable. Externalizing students may grow a big chip on their shoulders. They may feel the need to test her sincerity by occasionally doing something subtly defiant or noncompliant. The students in Angela's group are stewing;

they feel Angela was being bossy and that it's unfair to punish all of them. Angela's popularity in eighth grade has just gone down a big notch. And, notice how the learning opportunities just fell through the cracks. Does evaporation seem at all interesting anymore? Obviously, there are infinite scenarios we could imagine here, but this is the nature of complexity. Take a moment and think about how Ms. Chen responded and what alternatives she could have pursued. There's no "right" answer, but you may get a sense that there are multiple outcomes that could have occurred, including Angela learning conflict resolution skills, which would improve, rather than sully, her reputation.

Complexity, by nature, is not controllable because there are just too many interacting variables. Furthermore, in complex contexts it's difficult to pinpoint cause and effect relationships. This makes measuring outcomes very difficult, so we tend to focus on simple targets that are measurable instead of the larger, more complex goals. So, in Ms. Chen's mind, the desired outcome is the students peacefully conducting an experiment, not students learning how to resolve conflict, cooperate, and think together. It makes sense then that school systems have focused on test scores, which are simple, measurable targets, but these do nothing to further the goals of cultivating twenty-first-century learners.

From an evolutionary perspective, it makes sense that we like control, or at least the illusion of it. It gives us peace of mind and a sense of self-efficacy. We actually believe that we *can* control all the important outcomes. When we realize we can't control big things, we settle for control of little things, or proxies of the big things that are measurable. Unfortunately blame often arises when we hold this simplistic understanding of control. If we believe we have control and things don't work out, then it's somebody's fault.

Teachers are also subjects of control strategies. One teacher in a workshop told me about her experience with pacing guides. "The principal monitored all of us, and if I wasn't in the right place in the pacing guide when he visited my classroom, it got written up and saved in my personnel file. This drove me crazy because it was so difficult to conduct my class this way. I was anxious all the time," she said. Pacing guides were instituted to ensure that teachers cover the content on standardized tests—another way to measure a simple outcome that measures another simple outcome—but this may actually be impairing good teaching and student acquisition of twenty-first-century skills. Research has shown that the use of pacing guides narrows the curriculum to tested subjects; instruction becomes primarily teacher-centered and focuses on disjointed, test-related sections of knowledge (Au, 2007). This control tactic puts intense pressure on teachers. Many teachers feel that the guides move too quickly and that they some learners behind (Bower & Parsons, 2016).

In complex contexts, it makes more sense to stop focusing on controlling simple, measurable outcomes and instead cultivate the conditions for active, engaged, self-directed learning. To successfully apply systems thinking to a situation we need to understand emergent properties. This is the understanding that positive, adaptive change can emerge when the conditions are created that allow the possibility for something to happen that we might not have been able to predict, and that is actually better than we could have imagined. Dr. Berger (2019) suggests that we focus on the direction of change rather than specific targets. When we focus on direction of change, we notice opportunities to nudge parts of the system to shift things to go where we are headed. Berger suggests that you ask yourself what is something you can enable (or can enable you) and that you experiment around the edges of the system to see what your nudges do. If we can step back and observe the patterns that are emerging, we can nudge the ones we don't like to move them in the intended direction.

Applying this concept of nudging to the above scenario, Ms. Chen could have noticed the stress she was feeling when she heard the conflict. Recognizing the stress response system, she could have given her own nervous system a nudge. She could have taken a deep breath and excused herself from the group she was helping. Approaching Angela's group, she could have zoomed out to see the situation from multiple perspectives. There was no urgency, just a minor disagreement between two students. Observing the interaction between Angela and Marco, she could have recognized that Angela's behavior might be rooted in her need for control. Let's see what might have happened next.

As Ms. Chen stood up and looked over to the table where Angela and Marco were arguing, the students noticed and suddenly became quieter. She walked slowly over to them.

"What's going on?" she asked.

Angela answered, "I wanted to be the recorder for this experiment, but Marco grabbed the worksheet first. He has horrible handwriting. You'll never be able to read it."

Ms. Chen asked, "How are you feeling about this Marco?"

"I don't care if she writes on the stupid worksheet," he said, "I just don't like her bossing me around. She could have just asked me, but she tried to grab it out of my hands!"

Ms. Chen asked Angela, "What do you think about what Marco just said?"

"Well, I didn't mean to be bossy. I just wanted us to get started."

Ms. Chen continued, "So, can you think of a different way to handle situations like this in the future?"

"Well, I guess I can ask him, or make a suggestion," Angela replied.

"How do you feel about this idea Marco?" Ms. Chen asked.

"Yeah, that would be a lot better. She's right. My handwriting sucks," he said.

Ms. Chen left the group to get back to work.

In this scenario, Ms. Chen created a gap in what was becoming a vicious cycle, she provided feedback, and the conflict was resolved. Both students saved face, and the rest of the class remained happily engaged in the experiment. She observed the interaction that was part of the social system and gently nudged them to resolve the conflict and get back on track.

Ego

These mind traps are based in the perception that we have a solid, permanent self, sometimes referred to as our ego, that needs to be attended to and defended. Applying cognitive science, neuroscience, and philosophy, our understanding of self has evolved, and it is clear that our impression of a self is better described as a "self-system." This self-system is both flexible and context dependent. This self-system presents the perception that I am my self: my body, my thoughts, my emotions are mine. This self-system gives us the capacity for reflexive thinking: we recognize ourselves as an entity that has perceptions, thoughts, and feelings about ourselves and that makes deliberate efforts to regulate our behavior (Leary & Tangney, 2012). While other animals have rudimentary self-systems, humans are unique in their ability to reflect back on themselves. As Descartes (1637–1641/1998) pronounced, "I think, therefore I am" (p. 18). We humans know that we think, feel, and behave, and we can reflect on our thoughts, feelings, and behavior.

Our ability to self-reflect gave us important advantages during our evolution. Being able to imagine ourselves in the past and future allows us to consider options and plan for the future based on past behaviors. However, this self-reflective capacity is a double-edged sword. The recollections we have of the past are often biased, and this mental time travel can distract us from what's happening in the present moment, interfering with our functioning. Thoughts about ourselves in the past and future are often accompanied by uncomfortable feelings, such as regret, shame, and worry. This can leave us in a mental quagmire of rumination, depression, and anxiety, even when things in the present moment are actually just fine (Leary & Terry, 2012). Our self-system can be especially troublesome when we're dealing with complexity and rapid change, because accurate predictions become much more difficult. We need to learn to weigh multiple options and deal in probabilities rather than certainties.

Reflexivity gave us the ability to be introspective. We can consider our thoughts, emotions, and motives. This can promote self-understanding and help us predict situations that might trigger an emotional reaction in us. It also helps us monitor our behavior so that it aligns with social norms, values, and standards. However, it can distract us from what's actually happening in the moment, taking us off an ideal course of action. Furthermore, we often don't know why we feel and act as we do nor how we might feel in the future.

We can conceptualize and evaluate ourselves—our characteristics, skills, and actions—which supports decision-making and self-regulation. However, research continues to show that our self-appraisals are often biased (Gilovich & Griffin, 2002). Self-consciousness can undermine behavior; we can second guess ourselves. Sometimes self-evaluation is unnecessary and actually impairs our functioning. For example, things we usually do automatically, without thinking, can be derailed if we try to use self-evaluation in the process. Most people who know how to ride a bike have no trouble hopping on one and riding away. However, if you ask them to consider their every move, they may find it difficult and maybe even impossible. Self-evaluation often leads us to define ourselves by our own evaluation. People tend to generalize their behaviors to evaluations of themselves. This aligns with Dweck's (2006) theory of mindsets. Rather than focusing on the behavior and reflecting on what we could have done better (growth mindset), we tend to generalize the behavior into a self-evaluation (fixed mindset). Doing poorly on a test becomes "I can't take tests" rather than "next time I should study harder and I'll improve." When we self-evaluate like this, we often limit ourselves. We may also become defensive because we identify so strongly with our behavior, and others' responses to it, that we take situations personally.

Our ability to consider how others perceive and evaluate us supports effective social interactions and appropriate behaviors, but it can also lead to: overconcern with what others think about us, lack of spontaneity, inhibition of behavior under pressure, and letting our concern with our social image interfere with more import-ant concerns. We may become worried about what someone thinks about us when it doesn't really matter, leading us to become socially anxious.

Another aspect of the self-system is the conscious or nonconscious control of thoughts, feelings, and behavior. To some degree, we can control these, but doing so involves a conscious, controlled process that takes time and occupies our attention and cognition. Our self-system also has a nonconscious, or automatic, system that can process information without much effort, conscious thought, or self-awareness. I like to think of this system as a shortcut system because it evolved to help us make quick decisions under relatively predictable conditions. However, in unpredictable conditions, automatic processing can lead to mindlessness, resulting in behavior that is inappropriate to the situation.

Our self-system creates a model of reality. It's not that we create reality itself, but we create a frame of understanding through which we perceive and make sense of reality. We live in it and through it, but we can't see the modeling process itself, which creates the phenomenology of direct experience. We are basically glued to our self-system, the ongoing continuous complex process. However, this self-system has the ability to contract and expand. When we feel threatened, we tend to narrow our perception of ourselves and the context we find ourselves in. This is an automatic function, designed to prioritize survival. If a predator is after me, I need to focus on keeping myself alive and finding an escape route. Anything else is inconsequential. When we feel connected to others, our perceptions of self and the world around us broaden. We are more able to take others' perspectives and recognize ourselves as part of a larger community. Our self-system often sounds the alarm even when we are not really threatened. To overcome this automatic tendency to narrow our self-system, we can ask ourselves, "What's really at stake for me here?" We can also question the reliability of our perceptions by asking ourselves, "How do I know this is true?"

Our self-system can give us the impression that we've changed a lot in the past but will not change much in the future. We tend to model the "self we have become" rather than the "constantly changing self." In some sense, when we unconsciously try to reinforce a sense of a solid, unchanging self, we are fighting against our constantly changing nature. However, we can in many ways consciously transform our self-system. We can change our view of ourselves to include this potential for constant change. When we face situations in the present moment as they are rather than how we think they should be or imagine them to be, we can learn from our experience and change our belief systems, our ideas of who we are or should be, and how we interact with others. To shift our self-system in this way, we can ask ourselves, "Who do I want to be next?" Next, we will explore more ways to escape from egoic mindsets and the other mind traps.

The Escape Hatch

Researchers are beginning to focus on the benefits of quieting the self-system by cultivating hypo-egoic mindsets, such as equanimity, humility, open-mindedness, flow, and mindfulness, that involve minimal engagement with the self-system (Leary & Terry, 2012). We all have access to these mindsets, and we can also cultivate them so they are a more consistent part of our daily experience. When we are experiencing a hypo-egoic state, our self-thoughts are primarily focused on the present and our introspection is limited to what is required to accomplish the task at hand. Some activities require thought but not thoughts about the self-system per se. For example, when Ms. Park is conducting the high school band, she may be carefully observing and listening to her students and monitoring her own movements and eye contact, but she is not engaging in any discursive, evaluative thoughts about herself. Ms. Park is focusing on concrete self-perceptions (e.g., noticing where her arms are and how they are moving). Her self-evaluations are limited to the musical piece she is directing in the moment: "Should I slow down a bit to help them learn this piece?" While she does think about her students, her thoughts are primarily focused on how they are understanding her direction. She's not worried whether they like her or not.

Focusing on the present moment, rather than thinking about the past and future, is one element that can be cultivated with mindful awareness practices. During practices such as a basic breath awareness practice, we focus our attention on the sensation of the air going in and out of our bodies. We notice the feeling of the air going through our nostrils and down our windpipe. We feel our diaphragm expand and contract with each breath. When our mind wanders off into the past or future, the practice is to notice this and gently and kindly return our attention to the breath. With practice, the mind settles and we become more comfortable with being present in silence. The state of mindfulness is not just something that we can experience while meditating. We can also bring mindful awareness into everything we do, including conducting the high school band.

In hypo-egoic states, we notice a shift from self-judgment to discernment. While I'm practicing mindfulness, I may notice myself becoming judgmental, "I can't do this!" or "This is boring." The practice is to notice these judgmental thoughts, just like any other thought, and gently, with kindness and compassion, return attention to the sensation of the breath. The purpose is to develop an attitude of curiosity and acceptance rather than to make ourselves do something. This does not mean that we become indiscriminate, but we can discern without beating ourselves up. I can notice when I'm off track, when I'm doing something that does not align with my intentions. But rather than being self-critical, I can simply notice and recover. If I've said or done something that may have injured another, I can repair it. Then I can let go and move on. Again, this relates to Dweck's (2006) concept of mindsets. Rather than holding a fixed mindset about myself, I recognize that what happened is just one incident, and I recognize that I can do better next time.

When we are in a hypo-egoic state we are aware of ourselves but only as much as is necessary to successfully engage in the behavior. For example, an athlete is aware of where his body is in space, but he's not thinking critically about it. Another example is during mindful awareness practice, when we notice our thoughts, but we don't identify with them or engage in them. We feel less individuated. We have less focus on ourselves as an individual and more connection to the external world, including our relationships with others. We have low ego involvement, which is the degree to which we want something to happen our way. When we are attached to things happening the way we want them to, we have a greater investment in a specific outcome, and we lose perspective of the larger context and implications of the situation. When we are ego-involved, we can become emotionally reactive when things don't go our way. In contrast, when we are in a hypo-egoic state, we may prefer certain outcomes, but we recognize that things might not work out like we'd like, and we don't take it as a personal affront if they don't. Overall, when we are in a hypo-egoic state, we have greater mental clarity, less inner chatter. Our minds are less cluttered with extraneous thoughts, so we can better focus on the task at hand. We can experience negative emotions without the judgement and self-talk that can heighten emotional reactivity. We experience humility, which is not a low opinion of oneself but a realistic self-assessment: we don't believe that our good qualities entitle us to special treatment.

Researchers believe that people are more likely to slip into a hypo-egoic state when they feel safe. There's also evidence that the hypo-egoic state is more likely when we are feeling positive emotions, especially when engaging with others and sharing good feelings (Fredrickson, 2013). Besides engaging in mindful awareness practices, we can promote hypo-egoic states by observing ourselves and noticing when our self-system begins to contract. When this happens, we can intentionally expand it. We can intentionally connect to our body and ground ourselves in our purpose. We can connect with one another and remember what's most important about our humanity, recognizing human dignity as the inherent value in ourselves as human beings. In a complex world, the number and quality of our connections can make a big difference. When together we connect with a deeper purpose, we find that even small shifts can result in big changes. In this way, in a more complex and faster changing world, we can have greater influence to modify the systems that we live and work in.

CHAPTER 6

Design Thinking

Chapter 5 conveyed tips for cultivating systems thinking. In this chapter, I introduce design thinking so you can add it to your repertoire of school transformation tools. First, let's examine the different levels of complexity in systems and a rule of thumb rubric for applying appropriate approaches.

Addressing Complexity

Without first understanding the context of any given situation, it's difficult to apply design thinking.

The Cynefin framework is used to support decision-making (Snowden & Boone, 2007). The Cynefin framework, named after the Welsh word for *habitat*, was created by Dave Snowden when he worked at IBM Global Services (Snowden, 1999). It has been updated and revised several times in collaboration with his colleagues at Cognitive Edge (https://cognitive-edge.com/blog/cynefin-st-davids-day-2020-1-of -n/). The framework identifies four domains, or levels, of complexity and provides guidance for addressing problems or making decisions within each of these levels. The dark center represents the domain of *confusion*, when we don't know which domain we are in.

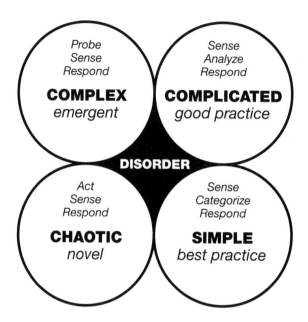

FIGURE 6.1   Simplified Cynefin Framework created by author with permission from Dave Snowden

As you can see in Figure 6.1, the four domains can be mapped out in a rubric where each of the quadrants represents one domain. The *clear domain* represents the "known knowns." There is clearly an existing best practice for the situation, and the situation is stable. The cause–effect relationship is obvious and the constraints are fixed. The best way to respond in this domain is to "sense-categorize-respond." This means we can clarify or sense the facts of the situation, categorize it, and then respond by applying best practice.

The *complicated domain* holds the "known unknowns." The cause–effect relationships are not obvious, and expertise is required to discover them. In this domain, there are a range of right answers, and the framework suggests "sense-analyze-respond" under these conditions. Again, we begin by sensing the facts, but then we analyze the situation, and finally we apply an appropriate practice to the situation. In this domain, a decision requires refined judgment and expertise.

The "unknown unknowns" are prominent in the *complex domain.* There are no right answers, and various cause and effect relationships can only be recognized retrospectively. This requires a lot of brainstorming, experimentation, and trial and error so that the best response can emerge. This process calls for "probe-sense-respond." We probe to gather information, we sense what will work and then we respond by testing various hypotheses.

When the cause and effect relationships are completely unclear, we are in the *chaotic domain*. Events can be extremely confusing, and taking action is the only way to respond. In this domain we can "act-sense-respond." As mentioned in the Chapter 5, we can turn a vicious cycle into a virtuous cycle by creating a gap in the cycle. Therefore, in the chaotic domain we act to establish order and then sense how best to create stability. In this way, we can transform a chaotic event into a less complex event that is more manageable. From this point, we can identify some emerging patterns to prevent the chaos from reemerging and recognize new opportunities for responding.

The black area at the center of the framework represents confusion when it's unclear which domain applies. It is difficult to recognize this domain because of the nature of the confusion. It's a point of cognitive dissonance where one needs to pause and deeply reflect to find one's way out of confusion to see the nature of the problem.

Healthcare professionals responding to the COVID-19 epidemic is a great example of working in the chaotic domain. Since the virus is novel, doctors had no tested protocols to draw upon. They had to quickly assess what each patient needed and attend to the most severe cases immediately. As patients were stabilized, doctors began trying different approaches to support patient recovery. Over time, they learned what worked and what didn't work.

According to the Cynefin framework, as knowledge and expertise are acquired, events can shift from chaotic to simple. However, this shift can result in the development of biases; complacency grows from relying on simple solutions when the event is not as simple as we think. Mind traps can play a role in this process. I might fall back on a simple story to explain something that I think is familiar but that is actually novel, but I don't recognize it. I may then think I'm right and get stuck using the approach for a simple system on a system that is actually much more complex. This can result in a rapid failure in which the situation quickly slips into chaos. Again, the COVID-19 pandemic provides an example. At first many believed that the virus was like a typical flu, and that it would likely resolve quickly. This led to a serious underestimation of the threat and a series of missteps in the response.

Now let's apply the Cynefin framework to classroom management. In my book *The Trauma-Sensitive Classroom* (Jennings, 2019b), I present action steps for problem-solving behavior issues (pp. 102–103). These align well with each of the domains. During each of these stages, teachers are encouraged to engage in self-reflection: recognizing what emotions are involved, considering whether they are taking the behavior personally, considering biases and scripts that might play a role in the situation, and taking a few breaths to calm down before proceeding with any actions.

Stage 1 is routine maintenance, which aligns with the clear domain in which there are "known knowns" and best practices to guide our actions. In the clear domain we "sense-categorize-respond." I recall one year when a teacher I was supervising told me she was having behavioral challenges with a young child named Aisha. Ms. Andreyev complained, "She is just not listening! She's always bothering the other children and doesn't respond to my instructions."

Sensing the situation, we tried the Stage 1 routines based on our categorization of her behavior. These included reminding, reinforcing, redirecting, and logical consequences, which together are a positive behavioral response that is respectful (versus punitive), reasonable (proportionate to the misbehavior), and helpful, in that it promotes learning. Logical consequences can be simplified by these three possibilities: you break it, you fix it; loss of privileges; or a positive time out (Jennings, 2019b, p. 94). These approaches work in a simple context. Most children respond to them quickly. However, Ms. Andreyev and I tried them all to no avail; it was clear that we had a more complicated situation on our hands, so we considered Stage 2.

Stage 2 aligns with the *complicated domain* and involves engaging in "sense-analyze-respond" problem solving. We took some time to speak to Aisha's mother and learned that Aisha was having similar problems at home. I also spent a few hours observing Aisha and interacting with her in class. As I applied my expertise to my observation, I began to sense that she wasn't hearing me. It was difficult to detect because she was actually managing fairly well with body language, but her verbal language was delayed, and that was a red flag. Analyzing the situation, I concluded that she had a hearing problem that was interfering with her responsiveness to adult direction and interactions with her peers. As soon as I had this insight, I called the mother and asked what she thought about my assessment. "Wow, I think you are right. I'm so sorry I missed this," she said. All of a sudden, a complex situation became quite simple and she took Aisha to the pediatrician for a hearing test right away. I was correct, her ears were completely blocked and she needed tubes. Once the tubes were implanted, Aisha could hear fine and her behavior improved dramatically.

If the problem had not been resolved at this point, we would have moved to Stage 3, which aligns with the *complex domain*. This stage is designed to address chronically inappropriate behavior and requires the "probe-sense-respond" approach. We would have engaged other school personnel in probing the issues, such as inviting the parents to meet with us and asking the school psychologist to conduct an evaluation. This may have led to a referral for special education services to meet the complex needs of the student. The special education teacher and the school psychologist would then work with the teacher and the parents to understand the student's behavior and create plans to address it.

While there is no Stage 4 in the action steps model, we've all been in a situation when our classroom has turned into bedlam. This aligns with the *chaotic domain*.

Under these conditions, we have to do something immediately to stop the chaos before someone gets hurt. Often the go-to response is to yell at the students, but often yelling just adds to the chaos. I find that it works better to do something unexpected to draw their attention and then engage in some simple calming and focusing practices afterwards.

For example, years ago I was teaching anatomy to a group of fifth graders. We were studying bones and muscles, and I always like to come up with hands-on learning activities, so I had the bright idea of asking them to bring in a specimen to examine, a bone or a piece of meat. I had not planned ahead very well and when the class began, they all took out the bones and meat they had brought and started teasing each other with them, holding them and shaking them in each other's faces—there's nothing like total chaos with raw meat. You can imagine my mortification. I immediately recognized that this was a really bad idea. It wasn't sanitary, and the kids were not being respectful to their specimens or their peers.

I had to think quickly to come up with a way to halt this failed experiment, so I grabbed a plastic bag out of the classroom garbage can and began singing the "Dem Bones" song very loudly, "Toe bone connected to the foot bone. Foot bone connected to the heel bone." Once I had their attention, I told them that I had made a big mistake and that what they were doing could be dangerous. I held out the bag, and they put the meat in the bag and I threw it away. What a mess. After the meat and bones were discarded and everyone had carefully washed their hands with soap and water, we spent some time taking deep breaths to calm down.

In retrospect, I see so many more problems with this assignment. It was a real waste to throw away the meat. Some students likely did not have the resources to bring in what I had asked. Some might have come from vegetarian families. So, I certainly discourage you from trying this in your classroom. But it was a great example of a classroom in chaos and of a quick and easy way to establish order.

What Is Design Thinking?

Now that we can analyze the type of system we are dealing with, we can see how to cultivate design thinking so we can apply it to studying the needs of our students, classrooms, and school. Design thinking is a mindset based in the belief that we can make a difference by applying an intentional process to generate novel solutions that result in positive outcomes. It can give you the confidence you need to address challenges in complex systems.

The design thinking movement emerged from engineering science to spark innovation in private industry to solve "wicked problems" (Rittel & Webber, 1973).

Wicked problems are difficult to solve because they do not have one obvious solution. They arise from the interaction of multiple perspectives, values, and possibilities. They require that a variety of tools from different disciplines be applied simultaneously. In other words, these are problems that arise in complex systems. Applied to human systems, design thinking democratizes the design process because it allows every person to think and act like a designer, a person who uses the design process to improve a situation or solve a problem.

Design thinking has made its way into education as a complement to project-based, collaborative learning and the maker movement. While it's critical to support our students' design thinking, we can also apply it to designing the classroom and school to address our current and future needs. Designers manifest their intention in the form of a specific outcome based in a thinking process. As educators, we are constantly designing our schools, curriculum, classrooms, schedules, lesson plans, and classroom activities. However, we are often functioning as designers unconsciously. By understanding and applying design principles, we can bring more intentionality to our work, thereby achieving greater impact.

In Chapter 5, we learned about how our mindsets can trap us in unproductive ways of being and how to recognize and overcome such traps to be able to see situations from a wider perspective, one that recognizes the complex interacting systems involved in any process. To add design thinking to our repertoire, we extend this flexible and growth mindset to designing solutions to challenges in our system, whether it be the classroom or the whole school.

Design thinking is focused on human needs and requires collaboration to bring multiple perspectives to the table. Design thinking is experimental, and failing is highly valued because that's how you test new ideas quickly. Design thinking does not have a clean and simple goal. It's an ongoing creative process that opens up vast possibilities through learning by doing. Finally, it's an optimistic approach because it assumes that there is no challenge too difficult to address.

Design thinking can be used to address any challenge, from how we arrange our classroom to designing learning experiences so the content is more closely aligned to our students' interests and needs. You can use it to rethink some of the processes occurring in your school such as scheduling, school discipline policies, and age-grouping.

Begin by being "user" centered. In this case, the "user" is the student. Recognize the talent, skill, and intelligence in the organization, regardless of status. This means recognizing that each and every student has something important to offer the design process. You will need to step out of your comfort zone to experiment and to test novel solutions. Thus, we need to create safety for ourselves and our students, so we value questions of all kinds and failures—the quicker we fail, the better because learning what doesn't work is important.

A critical part of the design process is brainstorming possibilities and becoming comfortable with the chaos and confusion that can arise during deep learning. In this chapter we will explore the functions of the designer that you can apply to your classroom and your school teams can apply to the whole school. With these functions in mind, you will have the tools to intentionally design the change you wish to see in your school.

There are various models of the design thinking process, but they all share the same fundamental elements: empathizing with and understanding the needs of the user(s), engaging in divergent thinking cycles to draw upon diverse sources of inspiration, learning through rapid prototyping and testing, and then scaling and monitoring to ensure needs are being met at scale. This process is nonlinear, messy, and can be time consuming. It may feel uncomfortable at first, because we're so used to rigid, top-down processes. However, you will find design thinking incredibly empowering, and with the increasing complexity of our systems, the only effective way is to consider as many possibilities as we can and to allow novel solutions to emerge from the input of the community.

Design thinking involves a series of recursive processes, comprising an oscillation between divergent and convergent thinking modes, that are all supported by deep reflection. In education, we often consider reflection as critiquing something that we have done. In this context, it's deeper, in that we do more; we also consider how we feel, notice what we are thinking, and allow our wonderings and intuitions to arise in the process. The first step is to examine our identities by questioning ourselves: our values, emotions, biases, and assumptions. Make a list of everything you know about the situation you are addressing in the designing process. This includes the people and the environment and how these interact with the larger system (e.g., classroom, school, district). Then, begin to examine whether there are biased assumptions in this list. Ask yourself, "How do I know this?" Identify areas where you need more information, be it about the people, the environment, or the process. This leads us to wondering about the situation, and we begin to formulate questions. Throughout the process, remember that you are a designer making intentional decisions for a positive outcome. Embrace your beginner's mind by being open to experimentation and possibilities rather than quickly assuming you have the right answer. To learn, we need to get out of our comfort zone to take risks and make mistakes. Try new things, break the routine, collaborate with others within and outside of the school, and have fun! Remember that challenges are design opportunities. You can be the system change you wish to see in the world.

Empathize

When folks in private industry apply design thinking in their work, the focus is squarely centered on the user. Understanding and empathizing with the user is where the design process begins (Kelley & Kelley, 2015). Who are they? What's important to them? What do they need? What's their perspective?

As I described in Chapter 5, one great way to develop empathy for your students is the Student Interview (Jennings, 2015, p. 135). This is simply spending a few private minutes with each student, getting to know them better as well-rounded whole people, not just as students. I have introduced this exercise to many teachers as part of the Cultivating Awareness and Resilience in Education (CARE) program, a mindfulness- and compassion-based professional development program for teachers that helps them manage the stress of the classroom and build emotionally supportive learning environments (Jennings, 2016; Jennings et al., 2017). To introduce this exercise to you, I would invite you to interview one student you wonder about or find particularly troublesome in some way. Tell this student that you'd like to spend a few minutes getting to know them better and schedule a time during a break to speak with them. Ask the student a variety of ordinary questions that may be relevant to students of their age. For example, you might ask, "Do you have any pets?" "How many people are in your family? Will you tell me about them?" "What's your favorite food?" As the student is speaking, listen mindfully with your full attention while tuning into them, building a connection. Don't worry about what you're going to say next. How is the student feeling right now? How are you feeling right now? Allow the feelings to guide your questions. If you find something that really excites the student, probe further to learn why and how they might be encouraged to bring this aspect of their life into the classroom. You'll be surprised what insights can arise and how this simple interaction can transform your relationship with the student.

One example of a dramatic transformation was a story Ms. Rogers told us at a follow-up workshop when participants were asked to share their experiences. Ms. Rogers told us about Missy, a kindergartener who had not yet said one word in school. It was November, so she was beginning to have some serious concerns about the girl. Missy had attended pre-K at the same school and the pre-K teachers had told Ms. Rogers that Missy hadn't said one word the entire year. Applying what she learned in the CARE program, Ms. Rogers realized that the school was starting to create a script about Missy, that something was wrong with her. She could feel the stereotype forming and wanted to nip it in the bud. But to do so, she needed to understand Missy better so she could empathize with her. She told Missy that she was taking a class and that one of her assignments was to interview one of her students, and she asked Missy if she could interview her. Missy nodded her head, beaming, and they made a plan to meet during recess that day. During recess, Ms. Rogers invited Missy to come sit with her, away from the other students on a bench under a shady tree. Ms. Rogers had a note pad on her lap and was holding a pen.

"Thank you for letting me interview you, Missy. My first question is: *Do you have any pets at home?*"

Missy smiled and began telling her about their dog, Peanut. "He has brown hair, and he's about this big," she said, holding her hand up to her knee, which was at the level of the bench.

Ms. Rogers was astounded and relieved to learn that Missy could talk and was actually quite articulate. She asked her more questions about Peanut and learned that he knew how to fetch a ball. As Missy answered each question, Ms. Rogers wrote down every answer on the notepad. We encourage teachers to do this because it lets the student see that we are taking what they are saying very seriously and that we really care about what they have to say. Ms. Rogers shifted to questions about Missy's favorite toys, movies, books, colors, food, and ice cream. She learned that Missy had one older brother and three cousins, who live nearby.

At the workshop, Ms. Rogers ended the story by telling us that since that day, Missy has spoken during class just like the rest of her students.

"It makes me realize how much our students really need to be seen and heard and how sad it is that she didn't feel ready to speak at all during her pre-K year."

One teacher participant conducted the student interview with one of her students, and the other students expressed their desire to have a chat with her too, so she spoke with each of them individually over the course of several weeks. She later reported that she observed a transformation in her classroom culture, the interactions between her and the students, and among the students. The students were much more positive and engaged.

Recently several blog posts written by teachers who shadowed students in the schools where they worked, to understand what being a student there is like, have gone viral. For instance, Ms. Redd and Ms. Wiggins spent a whole day doing the same thing the students they followed did. Both teachers found sitting passively all day exhausting. They both complained that by the end of the day, they felt lethargic and mentally drained. Ashley Redd (2020) shadowed a fourth grader for a day at her school. She "went home with a migraine, a backache, and a hangover of fear and humiliation." The experience was so alarming that she is considering leaving the profession. The teachers she witnessed were so stressed that they had little patience with normal student behaviors, such as socializing in the cafeteria. Ms. Redd left feeling that the primary aim of the students was to avoid getting into trouble. Alexis Wiggins (Strauss, 2014) shadowed two students at the high school where she worked as a learning coach. The first day, she shadowed a 10th grader, and the next day she followed a 12th grader. She noticed how often teachers' impatience made her feel afraid of asking a question.

There are many other ways to learn about and empathize with your students. You can simply observe them in action with "beginner's mind," a mind that is open to new possibilities. You can do informal focus groups with your students to learn about their perspectives and interests. You can encourage them to dream big and imagine what they might do and learn in school.

As you're getting to know your students, avoid pigeonholing. As we learned in Chapter 5, it's easy to create simple stories about others that are simply wrong. There are numerous stereotypes that we hold about students: the teacher's pet, the troublemaker, the class clown, the smart kid, etc. Avoid falling into this mind trap by intentionally looking for the wide diversity of all kinds within and among your students, with an eye for gems of difference that can make a valuable contribution to your classroom, such as the student who loves to draw and is really talented; the student who is an avid sports fan and can name all the players in every team along with their stats; the student who thinks differently, for whatever reason. They are all part of this rich tapestry of human gifts we can engage, nurture, and draw upon.

Understanding the Challenge

After building empathy with the user, the next step in the design thinking process is to identify the design challenge and consider how best to approach it. This is a good time to use the Cynefin framework to determine the challenge's level of complexity. As you begin to learn this process, you might want to start with challenges that are complicated, but not too complex. As you learn and develop design thinking skills, you'll be able to tackle more complex challenges.

Once you have identified a challenge, remind yourself to frame it as an opportunity by stating it as a series of "how might we" questions. Write down the challenge in simple language. Next decide on goals for the design challenge. You might want to create a timeline of action steps. *What are the deliverables and when should they be delivered?* Next define the measures of success. *How will we know when we have met the challenge?* These should be concrete, measurable outcomes. You may come up with additional outcomes as you move through the process, but it's good to have a basic idea up front. Be sure to define constraints to keep you on track. I've found that, during the design process, it's easy to get lured into going down a rabbit hole, following some interesting idea that is completely irrelevant.

Breckenridge Elementary school faced a challenge with scheduling. Several of the teachers wanted to experiment with longer work periods because they felt the schedule was forcing them to stop in the middle of deep learning for transitions, and the shrill bell was annoying. They were experimenting with collaborative, project-based learning and found their students had to quit right as they were figuring out how to solve a problem. The principal encouraged teacher experimentation and leadership, and she invited these teachers to come up with a new schedule design.

A team of six teachers gathered to apply design thinking to the challenge. First, the team spent time talking to each teacher to learn about what they needed from the schedule. They observed some of the classes in which teachers felt they didn't have enough uninterrupted time. This helped the team empathize with the teachers so that they could tailor the design to meet the teachers' needs. In this case the question was "How might we arrange the school schedule so there are longer periods of sustained engagement in learning?" They hoped to design a schedule that accommodated these longer work periods without disrupting the schedule of special periods (e.g., art, library, and PE), lunch, and recess. Since school was already in session for the year, they realized that this change would need to wait until the following school year, which gave them plenty of time to work on the design challenge. They defined success as "Every student has at least one 90-minute time period for sustained learning engagement per day, and every student has two special classes per week." The team wrote a brief that outlined the problem and proposed goals, a timeline, and desired outcomes. They presented the brief in a slide show at the next faculty meeting, where they received considerable feedback from the other teachers. Most thought it was a good idea, but many were skeptical that it would be possible to make such a change.

Needs and Insights

To apply the empathy process to recognizing the needs of and gleaning insights from your user, you can create an Empathy Map (Gray, 2017). This tool can be applied to understanding the needs of an individual, a group, or your entire class or school staff. In Figure 6.2 you will see a diagram of the Empathy Map Canvas from Dave Gray's blog "XPlane." Starting at the top, the first two questions center on the goal of the process: *Who are we empathizing with and what do they need to do?* The answers to these questions should be framed in terms of observable behaviors. Next, work clockwise around the map completing the Seeing, Saying, Doing, and Hearing sections. These sections are opportunities to reflect on observable phenomena that can provide insight into what it feels like to be the user. Next you focus on what is going on inside their heads with the question: *What do they think and feel?* Examine

Empathy Map Worksheet

Designed for: [   ]   Designed by: [   ]   Date: [   ]   Version: [   ]

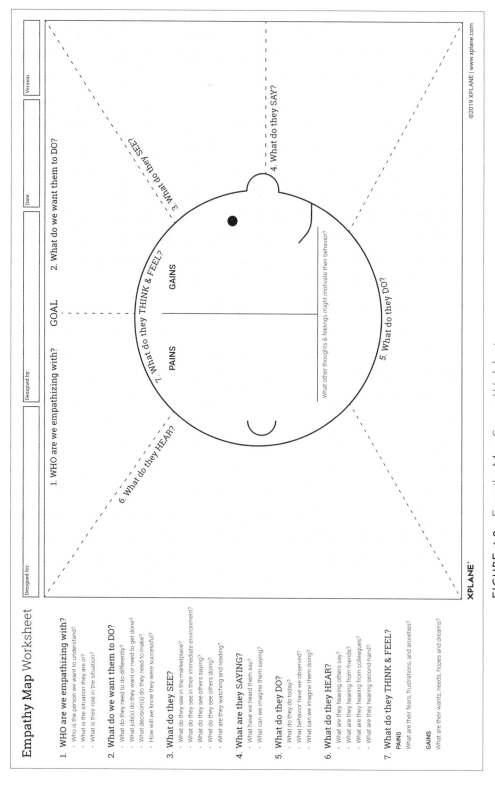

1. **WHO are we empathizing with?**
   - Who is the person we want to understand?
   - What is the situation they are in?
   - What is their role in the situation?

2. **What do we want them to DO?**
   - What do they need to do differently?
   - What job(s) do they want or need to get done?
   - What decision(s) do they need to make?
   - How will we know they were successful?

3. **What do they SEE?**
   - What do they see in the marketplace?
   - What do they see in their immediate environment?
   - What do they see others saying?
   - What do they see others doing?
   - What are they watching and reading?

4. **What are they SAYING?**
   - What have we heard them say?
   - What can we imagine them saying?

5. **What do they DO?**
   - What do they do today?
   - What behavior have we observed?
   - What can we imagine them doing?

6. **What do they HEAR?**
   - What are they hearing others say?
   - What are they hearing from friends?
   - What are they hearing from colleagues?
   - What are they hearing second-hand?

7. **What do they THINK & FEEL?**

   PAINS
   What are their fears, frustrations, and anxieties?

   GAINS
   What are their wants, needs, hopes and dreams?

XPLANE®   ©2019 XPLANE | www.xplane.com

FIGURE 6.2 Empathy Map Canvas Worksheet
Source: Created by XPLANE

their pains and gains, what they fear or are frustrated about, and what they want, hope, and need.

As you observe the user engaged in their own problem-solving, you can begin to recognize places where their learning can use a nudge. If you discover a "wicked problem," you can brainstorm to find as many creative solutions as possible. All solutions are considered. Nothing is too crazy to mention. It helps to limit comments such as "Yes, but" and replace them with "Yes, and. . ."

Often, we can manage this process on our own, but it helps to engage with a team. This can occur in IEP/504 meetings that include several members of the school staff, the parents, and sometimes the student. School leaders can apply design thinking to these meetings to find novel solutions to sometimes intractable problems with student learning and behavior. For example, Larry Dailey (2016) reported on an IEP meeting that was transformed by applying systems thinking to the student's needs. The meeting began with a state-appointed facilitator trying to run the meeting and control the agenda. As tensions arose, the parents became so upset that they withdrew their consent, and the facilitator left the meeting before it was finished. Since everyone else remaining in the room wanted to complete the meeting and the IEP process, they decided to reset and apply design thinking to the meeting format. He noted:

> So, instead of listening to lengthy, preformatted presentations from only a few of the meeting's participants, we agreed that everybody in the room would take turns presenting one thought at a time. Each idea would be posted on a sticky note and placed on a table. Posted ideas would be brief, so that we could build on them later. The parents', teachers', child's, and administrators' contributions would all be treated equally. And we agreed that everybody would present at least three ideas (Dailey, 2016).

After all the ideas were out on the table, the group began considering and prioritizing them and came up with novel solutions that they all felt good about. Even the student left saying that the meeting was fun!

The next step in the design process is to build a prototype. You can do this as a drawing or a model, whichever will get your ideas across. This should be like a rough draft. Remember to maintain flexibility at this stage. It's easy to get attached to our ideas (thinking we're right or that there's a simple story), so be careful not to fall in love with your ideas. Once you have a prototype, test it by experimenting. This can be a real test run, a process, or a thought experiment trial. During this process, be sure to encourage honest feedback and allow for repetition of the prototype testing process. It usually takes several iterations to come up with a great solution.

Throughout this stage, everyone engages in deep reflection so be sure to make time for the reflection process. Sometimes it takes time for insight to arise, so create the space and time for this to occur. Remember to check in with how everyone is feeling. Make sure there's time and safety to work out any uncomfortable feelings.

Brainstorming

Once you have empathized with the user and acquired insight regarding their needs, it's time to brainstorm ideas. This is where the divergent thinking happens, so it's good to set some ground rules to promote exploration. It also helps to have someone act as a facilitator to lead the team through the process and to start with a warm-up activity to get your team in the mood to brainstorm. At this stage, there are no bad ideas, so put on the table any ideas that emerge. Welcome wild and seemingly crazy ideas. Even if an idea is totally unrealistic, it might spark another way of thinking about the challenge that will result in a novel solution. The process involves scaffolding ideas on one another by thinking "and" rather than "but."

Remember to keep your brainstorming session focused on the specific challenge by writing it on a board or chart, because it's easy to get side-tracked during this stage of the design process. Be sure everyone in the team has the tools they need to share ideas, such as pens and Post-it pads. Then ask each person to write the first idea that comes to mind. This gives each team member an opportunity to consider an idea without input from teammates. Facilitate the brainstorming by inviting team members to share their ideas. Ensure that everyone involved has an opportunity to voice an idea. Monitor the time each person takes, and make sure no one is dominating the stage. Use chart paper to illustrate ideas. Sometimes a simple diagram is easier to grasp than a complex explanation of an idea. Aim for lots of ideas; the more, the better.

Going back to the story about our school schedule challenge, the team gathered, and one teacher, Mark, facilitated. Once the team had completed the warm-up steps and gone over the ground rules, they all wrote their first ideas on Post-its. Nadine wrote "eliminate the schedule," which she knew was a totally crazy idea. When they began sharing ideas, everyone chuckled when Nadine shared, but her idea did get them thinking about what the schedule in the school is actually for. As they brainstormed, they began to realize that they had to stretch their thinking to get out of the old factory model framework of regimented time schedules. This freed them to explore many more "crazy" ideas, and they challenged each other to see who could come up with the craziest idea. By this time, they were all laughing and joking about the challenge and the crazy solutions, but soon they had a large batch of sticky notes on the wall.

The next step in the process is to spend a few minutes grouping together similar ideas. Mark began to put all the "crazy" ideas over to the side when Marsha had an insight, "Wait, don't put that one in the crazy pile. I think it should stay with the rest." This idea was to let students create their own schedules. While it was hard to imagine how this idea was feasible, Mark put it back in the group of ideas they were considering. Next Mark invited the team to choose their favorite idea by marking it with a bright pink dot. Then they discussed the favorite ideas, and afterward, Mark asked them to pick three from the six.

Converging and Emerging

The teachers had employed an emergent thinking process to come up with several solutions. Based on the ideas and who originated them, they broke into three pairs to illustrate each of the ideas. As Nadine and her partner began to diagram their idea on a piece of chart paper, they continued to brainstorm how they might bring the concept to life so others would understand it. They had decided to focus on the simplest solution possible, which involved beginning each day with an approximately 20-minute morning meeting followed by a 90-minute work period. Each teacher could decide which content area, or areas, they would use this for. The use of this longer work period could be consistent or vary from day to day, depending on the situation. Special teachers could use the time for planning and for assisting other teachers with learning activities. Special classes would begin right after the 90-minute work period, and each class would have their special periods scheduled at the same time of the day. This gave each teacher a planning period at some point during each day and created a consistent routine for the students. As they thought this through and created the diagram, they questioned assumptions and thought through possible unforeseen consequences. Then they were ready to share their ideas with the team.

Overall, the team found their proposal intriguing. The team gave them constructive feedback and came up with a few possible issues that Nadine and her partner hadn't considered. After each group presented their ideas, the team settled on refining Nadine's idea. They examined the solution in greater depth and mapped out a hypothetical day that included every grade and class. They made a list of possible barriers. For example, they knew that the special teachers might not want all their free time at the beginning of the day. Through the process, they refined the idea to the point where they felt ready to share it with the school community. They even came up with a name for the idea, "Flex Time." Nadine used her smartphone to take photographs of the charts and sticky notes to document the entire process so what they had learned would not be lost.

The team presented their idea at the next faculty meeting. One colleague high-lighted a few issues they had completely forgotten about. For instance, due to lim-ited space, the school had to use the gymnasium for recess on rainy days, which would interfere with one of the daily PE special sections. The team realized that they would have to go back to the drawing board, revisit the other ideas, and brainstorm some new ideas. While this was disappointing, it gave them an idea for creating a better visual of the school schedule so they could juggle all these variables. At their next team meeting, they created a diagram of the entire week and the elements of the schedule, and they used different colors of paper for each class. As they played around with the model, new ideas began to emerge.

As you can see, the design thinking process involves a series of repetitions of divergent thinking and converging on possible solutions. It involves finding ways to map out or illustrate an idea to share it with stakeholders. Feedback from numer-ous stakeholders can help identify problems with the idea so that it can be further refined. In some cases, you might want to pilot test the idea or create a prototype. In this case they couldn't pilot test the idea, but they were able to create a realistic model of all the possible ways to rearrange the schedule. Because they had the whole school year to work on this, they had plenty of time. As the end of the school year approached, they began to settle on a novel idea. They designed a schedule that began with a 30-minute morning meeting followed by four 90-minute blocks. One of the blocks was split in half for lunch and recess. This resulted in longer special classes, but there were fewer each week. It also gave teachers much more flexibility to create their own schedules with long blocks of uninterrupted time. When they presented this idea to the faculty, they found that the special teachers really liked the idea. "We always lose so much time during the transition to and from the gym that we don't have a full period to complete activities as it is," said the PE teacher. The art teacher was also happy to have longer class periods. Except for lunch, recess, and specials, the plan otherwise left scheduling up to individual teachers. If teachers wanted to schedule longer blocks of learning time, that was up to them. They could also vary the amount of time they spent on each subject from day to day. Overall, the teachers appreciated the prospect of having autonomy over their schedules and the principal was happy to eliminate the need for the bell.

This concludes Part II of this book. In the next section, you'll see how we, the teaching workforce, can elevate our profession, transform our teaching and learning environments, and cocreate a new story about the important work we do and how it can contribute to society's progress over this century.

PART III

EMPOWERING TEACHERS

It's easy to assume that changing the educational system involves a monumental leap, dictated from the top down, or to assume that without everyone's buy-in, nothing will happen, even with grassroots support. This can paralyze us with doubt. However, as explained in Part II, we can make meaningful change in large complex systems by nudging around the edges. The teacher leadership movement is demonstrating that we *can* change the system from the classroom up (York-Barr & Duke, 2004; Wenner & Campbell, 2017).

Teachers are uniquely positioned to recognize needs and promote change in schools because we know our students and we understand the complexities of teaching and learning (Mangin & Stoelinga, 2008). Research has demonstrated that teacher leaders contribute to school leadership capacity by cultivating teacher collaboration, modeling and sharing best practices, promoting professional learning, and supporting differentiation and content area needs. Teacher leaders are advocating for changes in policy at all levels of government. The 2016 National Teacher of the Year Jahana Hayes (CT-05) was elected to Congress in 2018. She is the first Black Democratic woman elected to Congress from Connecticut. When asked why she decided to run for office she said, "I think we're in a critically important time. And it's going to require regular people, community people—the people that are most affected by decisions that are being made—for us to stand up and make our voices heard" (Herndon, 2018).

To be clear, I recognize that this is no easy task; school bureaucracies can be bogged down by inertia and red tape. But sometimes the system needs a wake-up call, and we are in the midst of a big one right now: the teacher shortage. Teachers are voting with their feet. In 2016–2017, 69% of districts surveyed reported that a shortage of candidates for open positions was "a big challenge." This was more than double the number reporting the same struggle in the 2013–2014 survey (American Association for Employment in Education, 2017). Due to population growth, the demand for teachers is increasing, and the concomitant decrease in the number of students choosing to enroll in teacher education programs is accelerating the increasing demand for new teachers (see Figure III.1; Sutcher et al., 2019).

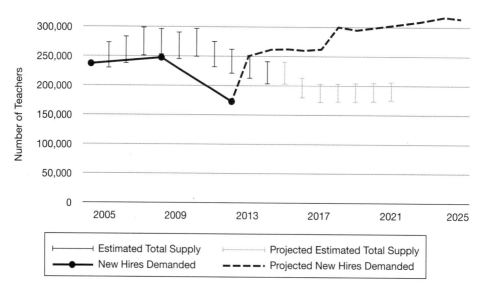

FIGURE III.1   Projected Teacher Supply and Demand

Source: From "Understanding teacher shortages: An analysis of teacher supply and demand in the United States" by L. Sutcher, L. Darling-Hammond & D. Carver-Thomas, 2019, Education Policy Analysis Archives, 27, p. 21. CC-BY-SA.

This demand and the cost of the shortage gives existing teachers, many who already have years of experience, greater value, creating a key opportunity for these teachers to step up and claim a larger role in school leadership and reform. Teachers are already taking on this challenge and building opportunities for themselves and their colleagues to contribute to meaningful changes that can improve our schools and our working conditions. In Part III, I will describe the ways educators are cultivating leadership, collaboration, and empowering students.

CHAPTER 7

Taking the Lead

As researchers and policy makers examine the teacher shortage problem, they find that teacher dissatisfaction is driving teacher attrition. Teachers leave because of dissatisfaction with teaching conditions (e.g., class size and salaries), administration (e.g., lack of support, input on school decisions, or classroom autonomy), and oppressive policies, such as high-stakes testing. Indeed, the most frequently cited cause of dissatisfaction are accountability pressures due to test preparation and sanctions for low performance (Goldring et al., 2014).

The growing teacher shortage has implications for the quality of the teaching workforce due to the reliance on unqualified or under-qualified teachers filling such positions, resulting in negative impacts on student learning (Podolsky & Sutcher, 2016), especially in low-resourced, high turnover schools (Ronfeldt et al., 2013). A principal of a high-turnover school noted other negative impacts of turnover:

Having that many new teachers on the staff at any given time meant that there was less of a knowledge base. It meant that it was harder for families to be connected to the school because, you know, their child might get a new teacher every year. It meant there was less cohesion on the staff. It meant that every year, we had to re-cover ground in professional development that had already been covered and try to catch people up to sort of where the school was heading (Carroll et al., 2000).

The teacher shortage is costly because schools are constantly spending money on recruitment and professional support for new teachers without realizing the value of these investments because they leave (Darling-Hammond, 2003). When a teacher leaves a district, it increases the demand for teachers and also increases the costs of recruiting a new teacher. Researchers estimate that the cost of teacher turnover nationwide is over $8 billion dollars per year (Sutcher et al., 2019). Overall, research is making a strong case to policy makers that they must reduce teacher attrition—and do it quickly.

The COVID-19 crisis has highlighted the value of teachers' work and the deep inequities embedded in our school systems. As schools recover from the COVID-19 crisis, there may be an opportunity to make the shifts necessary to build up and support the teaching workforce.

Teacher Leadership

The Teacher Leader Model Standards define teacher leadership as, "The process by which teachers, individually or collectively, influence their colleagues, principals, and other members of the school community to improve teaching and learning practices with the aim of increased student learning and achievement" (National Education Association, National Board for Professional Teaching Standards, and the Center for Teaching Quality, 2018, p. 11). Teacher leadership can be formal or informal and can be applied at any moment. We can recognize the influence we already have and create new opportunities for leadership within our current school. Or, we can look for opportunities outside of our current school, district, or community because there are so many teaching jobs available.

When teachers are given opportunities to lead, more talented candidates will be attracted to the teaching profession. Until recently, there was not much of a career ladder for teachers, other than to become part of the school administration. The growing teacher leadership movement is creating new leadership positions, thus providing a longer and more attractive career ladder. Research shows that to attract younger people to a career in teaching, the profession needs to offer decision making opportunities, supportive school cultures that cultivate collaboration and innovation, and time to engage in such activities. Younger workers are looking for high-quality feedback, professional learning, fair pay, and the opportunity to be rewarded for outstanding performance with higher pay. At the same time, these opportunities need to be afforded to the existing teaching workforce to prevent attrition.

There's a move towards reenvisioning schools as lifelong learning communities, where everyone is a learner, including all the adults. In this model, the teacher becomes more of a facilitator of learning. The teacher is continuously learning how to facilitate students' learning, from moment to moment, through skillful interactions, action research, and formative assessments. The students become partners in the learning process. Recognized as autonomous, they are afforded more choice of content and learning methodology, which stimulates motivation (Deci & Ryan, 2012). Students learn in collaborative teams, similar to the way adults work in the most highly skilled jobs today. By this method, we are better preparing them for the future.

In lifelong learning communities, teachers are empowered to exercise greater influence over decisions related to instructional practice. Most experienced teachers have content and pedagogical knowledge that the principal may not have. For this to model work, the principals need to feel secure and have the skills to support these new structures and processes, thus demonstrating that the teachers' work is valued. A collaborative bond of reciprocity develops in which each supports the other's work and both share the responsibility for the outcomes. The Council of Chief State School Officers (CCSSO) and State Consortium on Education Leadership policy document, Performance Expectations and Indicators for School Leaders (2008) states:

> Expectations about the performance of education leaders have changed and expanded considerably in the last decade, extending far beyond the traditional definitions of administrative roles. Responsibilities of education leaders now exceed what individual administrators in schools and districts can be expected to carry out alone. State and federal requirements to increase student learning necessitate a shift in leadership, from managing orderly environments in which teachers work autonomously in their classrooms to one in which administrators, teachers, and others share leadership roles and responsibilities for student learning. Research and best practices indicate the value of collaboration on shared vision, goals, and work needed to ensure that every student learns at high levels (p. 1).

Policy makers are beginning to understand that if teachers are to be held accountable for student learning, they must also have more control over the learning process. Policy makers are also recognizing that to encourage teachers to collaborate, there is a need to reevaluate compensation systems that focus on individual teachers alone:

new evaluation systems that recognize and reward collaboration may be required. There is also a need to better define the teacher leader roles and their associated responsibilities, requirements, and compensation.

The Teacher Leader Model Standards consist of seven domains describing the many dimensions of teacher leadership (Teacher Leadership Exploratory Consortium, 2011):

DOMAIN I: Fostering a Collaborative Culture to Support Educator Development and Student Learning

DOMAIN II: Accessing and Using Research to Improve Practice and Student Learning

DOMAIN III: Promoting Professional Learning for Continuous Improvement

DOMAIN IV: Facilitating Improvements in Instruction and Student Learning

DOMAIN V: Promoting the Use of Assessments and Data for School and District Improvement

DOMAIN VI: Improving Outreach and Collaboration with Families and Community

DOMAIN VII: Advocating for Student Learning and the Profession

Teacher leaders can contribute and collaborate in a variety of ways. Typically they support their colleagues' professional learning, formally and informally, including presenting workshops, coaching, modeling, peer advocacy, and cultivating a collaborative school culture. Researchers have identified self-authoring as an important orientation in teacher leadership (Breidenstein et al., 2012). Dr. Robert Kegan (1994) describes self-authoring as follows:

It takes all of these objects or elements of its system, rather than the system itself; it does not identify with them but views them as parts of a new whole. This new whole is an ideology, an internal personal identity, a *self-authorship* that can coordinate, integrate, act upon, or invent values, beliefs, convictions, generalizations, ideals, abstractions, interpersonal loyalties, and intrapersonal states. It is no longer *authored by* them, it *authors them* and thereby achieves a personal authority (p. 185, italics in original).

In a sense, Kegan is referring to the ability to self-reflect and emerge from the mind traps that can hold us under their sway. Also, self-authoring is consistent with hypo-egoic states that are not as subject to the control of the "self-system." Self-authoring is an ongoing process of lifelong learning and self-discovery, not an end point in and of itself.

The formation and facilitation of groups such as project teams, academic departments, professional learning communities (PLCs), and inquiry groups are highly valued leadership activities. The National Education Association, National Board for Professional Teaching Standards, and the Center for Teaching Quality (2018) highlight evidence for the group-process dimension of its overarching competencies. At the highest level of their rubric, the standards state: "Create new groups or using existing groups and facilitate those groups to overcome challenges and engage diverse opinions and experiences to meet objectives, solve problems, and achieve desired outcomes" (p. 17). Communication skills are highlighted in other sections. For example: "Influence other teacher leaders to build their capacity to effectively communicate and powerfully advocate with stakeholders at many levels," and "use communication to navigate and counter multiple, and sometimes, adversarial power structures" (p. 15). Indeed, research has found that teacher group learning outcomes are improved with good facilitation (Little & Curry, 2009).

What are the impacts of teacher leadership? While the empirical literature is scant, there is some promising evidence. Two studies involving very large samples of teachers have found that leadership that is shared or distributed among teachers can lead to enhanced student performance. A study of collective leadership, defined as the democratic distribution of authority among school administrators and teachers, found a significant impact of collective leadership on student achievement on standardized tests (Leithwood & Mascall, 2008). "The influence of collective leadership was most strongly linked to student achievement through teacher motivation" (p. 554); teachers' perceptions of collective leadership were associated with their motivation, which were associated with improved performance on student outcomes. A study of 199 schools in Canada (13,391 students in grades 3 and 6) found a significant positive impact of collective leadership on student math and reading performance (Leithwood et al., 2010).

A recent review of the teacher leadership literature found important signs of progress, but also the need for theory, clear definitions, and rigorous empirical research (Wenner & Campbell, 2017). Teacher leadership contributes to the quality of the school climate and all teachers' feelings of empowerment. Teachers report that professional learning presented by teacher leaders contributes significantly to school change and is more relevant compared to presentations by nonteaching leaders. Teacher leaders report feeling more confident, more professionally satisfied, and more empowered. Authors of one study noted: "There has been a strong sense of purpose and satisfaction for them [teacher leaders] to realize that they are now leading the change, enjoy the autonomy for school improvement and change, and are empowered as leaders" (Chew & Andrews, 2010, p. 72). Teacher leaders report that their professional growth is enhanced by improved leadership skills and instructional skills. For example, one teacher noted: "My teaching has improved and I am constantly looking for new techniques to use with the pupils. . . . I constantly want to better myself and look forward to the next challenge" (Harris & Townsend, 2007, p. 171).

Redefining Teacher Professionalism

To elevate our profession, we need to reconsider our role. What kind of professional is a teacher? What role do power, autonomy, and agency play in professionalism? As discussed in Chapter 1, this question has plagued the teaching profession for most of American history. Dr. Andy Hargreaves (2000) described the evolution of teachers as professionals in terms of four historical periods: the preprofessional, autonomous professional, collegial professional, and postmodern or post-professional. These categories are associated with linear time periods since the early twentieth century and provide insight into how American society has conceptualized teachers' work during the rise of industrialization.

During the preprofessional period, teachers were viewed as simple technicians delivering basic knowledge to their students. The view of teachers as autonomous professionals evolved during the 1960s when teachers began to gain greater agency and control over what and how they taught and their working conditions. While they won more rights, they still worked mostly in isolation with little professional help or feedback. In the 1980s, the view of teachers as a collegial professional arose. The growth of the knowledge base added a level of complexity to the demands of teaching that required greater collaboration with peers who have various areas of expertise.

When Hargreaves wrote his paper at the turn of this century, his impression was that the future would either grow toward a post-modern professionalism, drawing from both the autonomous and collegial professional models, or become post-professional—a de-professionalization of teaching, similar to the preprofessional era, where the teacher is again viewed as a technician.

There is plenty of evidence that recent reform efforts have been de-professionalizing, taking autonomy away from teachers by ordering scripted curricula and the strict use of pacing guides to control content delivery. However, a promising movement of shifting toward post-modern professionalism is gaining traction. In many places, the social organization of the school is beginning to transform away from a bureaucracy managed from the top down by an individual principal to a stakeholder-led community of learners. In this new model, collegiality and professionalism are highly valued, and teachers become the creators and reformers of the school culture. These schools, called professional development schools, are founded in the constructivist understanding of lifelong learning and distributed leadership (Spillane, 2006). All members of the community are engaged in the construction of new knowledge and understandings that reach well beyond the basic skills learning and test-based curriculum that has been tried and has failed miserably. In the professional development school, teachers learn through teaching and redesigning schools in collaboration with one another and with the students and their parents within the context of the community (Darling-Hammond et al., 1995). Teacher-leaders are engaged in decision-making as it relates to the mission, goals, operations, assessments, and scheduling, so they have a hand in creating a better teaching and learning environment. When we teachers are involved in decision-making, we have a greater sense of ownership and commitment to our profession and our community (DeFlaminis et al., 2016).

Referred to as distributed leadership (DL), this approach to leadership includes ". . .those activities that are either understood by, or designed by, organizational members to influence the motivation, knowledge, affect, and practice of organizational members in the service of the organization's core work" (Spillane, 2006, pp. 11–12). In this model, leadership is embodied within all the members of the school community and all leadership activity is distributed across interactions. Indeed, the leadership practice is inherent within the interactions, rather than instantiated at the top of a hierarchical structure. This leadership model is better adapted to our rapidly changing complex school systems because it recognizes and promotes interdependence and interaction across various roles (leaders and followers) and contexts within the school. This model recognizes that these elements are part of a complex, dynamic system; leadership is fluid, and not inherently attached to a specific role or person. In this sense, distributed leadership is a way to lead from a systems and design thinking perspective. Rather than prescribing a new and more desirable form of leadership, it affirms that leadership is already distributed, just unrecognized as such. Researchers who have studied distributed leadership examine how leadership is actually accomplished in school organizations (Diamond & Spillane, 2016).

We often feel like we have little power when we actually may, and not even be aware of it. Our influence depends on the subject matter, existing relationships, history and power dynamics, and the specific situation we find ourselves in. For example, at a faculty meeting, Mr. Ricci is listening to the principal, Ms. Schwartz, explain her plans for revamping the mathematics curriculum. New to the school, Ms. Schwartz wants to try a novel method that she discovered during her graduate training. Mr. Ricci is thinking, "Oh, here we go again, a new principal with new curriculum ideas," and he sits glumly looking down at his smartphone. He may not realize that his response to Ms. Schwartz's presentation is influencing his peers. Following his lead, none of them show any enthusiasm for this idea, and Ms. Schwartz leaves the meeting disappointed in her leadership skills. Mr. Ricci is known for creating fun and interesting math activities, and he often shares them with his colleagues. He has become the leader when it comes to mathematics instruction. Just by sitting glumly during the meeting, he signaled that he wasn't excited about Ms. Schwartz's plans, and the other teachers followed suit. The faculty became restless and disengaged while Ms. Schwartz felt completely deflated. Because she was new to the school, she was unaware of his reputation among his peers. While in this situation he was clearly the leader, this was not explicitly recognized by anyone. Therefore, his leadership was not as effective as it could have been had Ms. Schwartz investigated the history of the school and discovered who led in the mathematics domain before she began to consider reform activity. Can you imagine how different that scenario would have been if she had invited him to discuss ways to improve their mathematics instruction before unilaterally choosing a path forward?

This is an example of how leadership can be shared across various roles under different situations and conditions. The practice of leadership occurs between the leader and the followers. In the scenario above, the faculty followed Mr. Ricci's lead rather than engaging with the principal in a discussion about a new math curriculum. The distributed perspective on leadership views leadership as patterns of interactions rather than discrete linear actions (e.g., recognizing that the school is a complex system, not a simple one). It recognizes that leadership requires followers and therefore recognizes the interdependence of both roles. Followers are not viewed as subordinates, but as equal actors in a discrete interaction. DL is based on the understanding that change is a dynamic process that emerges from these interactions. It recognizes opportunities for leadership as fluid, not fixed in specific roles, existing in a constantly shifting complex context where any member of the community may act as leader, depending on the situation. This perspective can help us reflect on our school organization and enhance our understanding and practice of leadership in the complex system of the school. As explained in Part II, to effectively respond to any situation, it helps to step back and get an understanding of the bigger picture before taking action.

Looking back at the scenario, from the DL perspective Mr. Ricci was not an obstacle to Ms. Schwartz's leadership, but an influential resource that could be more clearly and explicitly empowered to lead in the area of mathematics. To do this we must sidestep the mind traps and be mindful of what is actually occurring rather than what we think is, or should be, occurring. Indeed, when Ms. Schwartz returned to her office, she began to ruminate about her lack of leadership skills. She told herself a simple story that reinforced a fixed mindset about her own value as a leader. She held this script: Teachers are supposed to engage when a principal presents an idea. The teachers were not engaged; therefore, I am a bad leader.

Had Ms. Schwartz been familiar with design thinking, she could have applied it to this situation. Her first step would have been to get to know her teaching staff so she could empathize with their strengths, challenges, and perspectives. This could have formed the basis for diagnosing what the school might need and how to design ways to address such needs. She would have learned that the teachers' respected Mr. Ricci for his creative math ideas, and she could have formally or informally engaged him as a leader to support school improvements. Together they could have used design thinking to examine the math curriculum, and teachers' and students' views on what they needed, and to develop a plan that would make use of his leadership in this area. Furthermore, with a better understanding of each of her staff members and their leadership skills, she would be better positioned to plan effective professional development activities in the future.

Distributed Leadership

As Ms. Schwartz considered how to improve her leadership skills, she came across the DL approach and read *Distributed Leadership*, leading expert Dr. James Spillane's (2006) classic book on applying DL to schools. Determined to bring the DL perspective to her school, she began by spending time getting to know each teacher. She decided that one way to do this would be to take each of them, individually, out to lunch so they could have time away from the school in a more casual setting. She arranged for each teacher to have coverage so they could take a more leisurely lunch. The teachers were delighted by the invitation; they each got private time with her and had an opportunity for a longer lunch off campus.

Over the course of several months, Ms. Schwartz discovered the teachers' current leadership roles and their potential for new roles. She created a map of the school using chart paper with the current arrangement of the classrooms and their associated teachers. After each lunch, she wrote notes about each meeting on the map. Being a very visual person, she found that this map helped her remember and integrate all she was learning. She discovered that Mr. Ricci was beloved by the staff for his creative math ideas that he was very willing to share. She learned that Ms. Rollins had art skills that the other teachers relied on, and that Ms. McGuire was the go-to person for team building activities for both students and teachers. Quickly Ms. Schwartz came to deeply appreciate the richness and diversity of her staff's interests, skills, and expertise.

The next step was to introduce the staff to DL. After her math curriculum flop, she set up a meeting with Mr. Ricci and to engage Ms. McGuire in leading a warm-up activity at the beginning of the next faculty meeting.

"Until I had lunch with everyone, I didn't know what a great reputation you have for creative math ideas," she said. "I should have spoken with you first, before launching any new math initiative."

Mr. Ricci chuckled, "I guess I didn't realize that I had so much influence with the faculty until that meeting. Afterward, I felt bad that I had derailed your initiative with my attitude."

Ms. Schwartz responded, "Well, it *was* uncomfortable, and it prompted me to question my leadership skills, but that was actually a good thing, because it led me to a new approach to school leadership that is distributed, or more fluid. It's not like really changing leadership per se but recognizing that leadership can shift to different people, depending on the situation. Now, I recognize that you are the de facto math leader at this school, and I think it would work better if I invited you to take a more explicit leadership role rather than trying to come up with a new plan myself."

"Well, I love math, and it's fun to generate ideas to help kids learn, so that would be great, as long as I can fit it into my schedule," he said.

"I'm not asking you to do anything different than what you are already doing. I'm simply recognizing your existing influence and making it explicit rather than de facto," she replied.

Mr. Ricci thought about it for a minute and then replied, "I think I see what you mean. I'm already doing all these things, but since you didn't know it, you didn't realize that a teacher might already be a leader when it comes to math."

Smiling, Ms. Schwartz said, "I'd like to share some ideas I have about bringing distributed leadership to our school community to see what you think. Maybe you could help me find a way to extend this approach to leadership to the whole staff."

Ms. Schwartz's enthusiasm was infectious, and Mr. Ricci began to brainstorm some ideas. Together they came up with a plan to introduce the idea to the staff and to invite them to explore ways to identify and distribute leadership more explicitly and more effectively. At the next meeting, Ms. McGuire led the faculty in a warm-up called "Yes, and." This activity can promote design thinking by expanding possibilities and developing the habit of affirming ("Yes, and") rather than negating ("Yes, but"). The faculty formed groups of three, and one person started by making a statement about the school. The person on the right responded, "Yes, and," adding more information. Then the third person responds the same way, until they had gone around the circle three times. By the time they were finished, they were in a lively and playful mood. Next, Ms. Schwartz told the faculty about her experience at the earlier meeting and how she had discovered DL. She invited Mr. Ricci to share his part of the story and his enthusiasm for DL.

"I admit, I was in a sour mood. I didn't want to have another math initiative imposed on me. At the time, I didn't realize I had such influence with you all." He laughed at himself and told them he felt bad for derailing the meeting. "After learning about DL, I can see that we are all leaders in one way or another."

Ms. Schwartz began a brief introduction to DL and took questions from the teachers. By the end of the meeting, most of them were on board with this new approach. However, after years of working in a disempowering system, the teachers were not used to considering that they had much power, so it took work to transition to a more distributed leadership model.

Over time, the school began to make shifts towards teachers emerging as leaders in multiple ways. Ms. Schwartz reflected, "I had to completely change the way I was thinking about leadership, but when the whole community is empowered to lead and people take on the responsibility, it's exciting for all of us. It relieves me of some of the responsibility, and outcomes can emerge that might never even have been considered before."

Viewing the system through the distributed leadership lens gives us the opportunity to reevaluate our current roles and what it means to lead; we can explore new opportunities for growth and influence. By applying this approach, we recognize ways in which we are already leading, such as professional learning communities (PLCs), sports, committees, or extracurricular activities.

Typically DL teams are cross-functional. They include representatives from all the stakeholder groups, and they focus on an aspect of the school that affects everyone in some way, for example, a team that manages the school schedule or a team that focuses on parent engagement. In contrast, PLCs are primarily focused on continuous improvement in student learning, often working on a content area. They consist of collaborators who share mission, vision, values, and goals and work collaboratively to achieve common goals. Both PLCs and DL teams have the potential to promote growth in both leadership and learning. However, while leading a PLC is an extension of the teacher role, participation in a DL team can be transformative because teachers experience learning at a different level. Rather than simply acquiring teaching and leading skills, teachers feel empowered to change their school from within, and they learn how to do it. They begin to build a new identity as a transformational school leader (DeFlaminis et al., 2016).

How Teachers Become Leaders: A Model

Now that we have explored the value of teacher leadership, you may be asking your-self, "How do I become a teacher leader?" Since teaching, learning, and leadership are all very complex processes, it makes sense to apply systems thinking to the question. While I noted earlier that the empirical research and theory on teacher leader-ship is meager, one study examined this question by accessing teachers' own ideas and experiences and presented a theoretical model of the development of teacher leadership based on this input (Poekert et al., 2016).

This model grew from a program evaluation of the Florida Master Teacher Initiative (FMTI), a collaboration between Miami-Dade County Public Schools and the University of Florida, funded by the U.S. Department of Education. This initiative aimed to improve instruction quality and boost student learning in grades preK-3 by supporting teachers to become leaders. The program offered support in a variety of ways, including providing an early childhood specialization certificate that teachers earn as part of a graduate degree program while continuing to work. The program also offered these graduate students leadership opportunities within schools to present new content and teaching practices in inquiry-based PLCs. Finally, the program provided opportunities for teachers to support administrators as they implemented distributive leadership.

The procedure involved conducting focus group interviews with a sample of these teachers and developing a draft theory of teacher leadership. Next, the theory was refined and validated in response to participant feedback. Finally, the theory was validated in an international context, involving teacher leaders in the United Kingdom. The resulting model presents the teacher leader in the center of concentric circles representing contexts, resembling Bronfenbrenner's (1979) model.

I like this model of teacher leadership because it takes a systems perspective on the process of teacher development, recognizing four dimensions of growth, support (mentorship and coaching), and positive impacts and challenges. The four dimensions of growth are personal growth (located in the center of the model), growth as a teacher, growth as a researcher, and growth as a leader. The layers of the environmental context include the classroom, the school, and the community. The outer layers are the local and national education authorities (e.g., departments of education). Simultaneously, teachers must interact and navigate the opportunities and challenges presented by each of these contextual layers.

For example, the annual testing regime, often imposed by the state government, directly impacts the classroom, in the form of teaching strategies; the school, in the

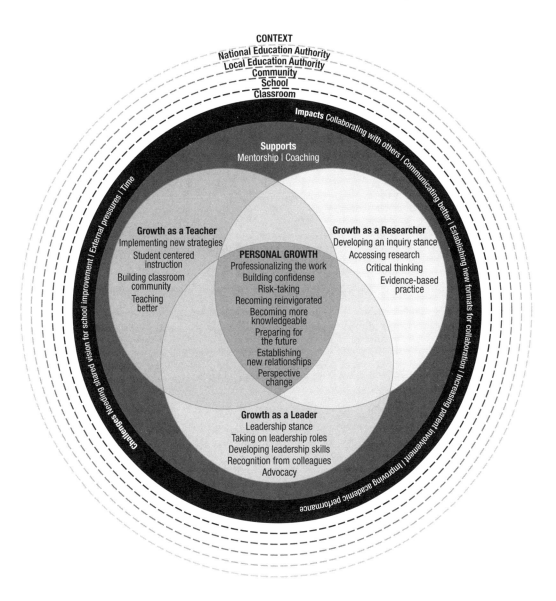

FIGURE 7.1   A model of teacher leadership.

Source: From Poekert, P., Alexandrou, A., & Shannon, D. (2016). How teachers become leaders: An internationally validated theoretical model of teacher leadership development. Research in Post-Compulsory Education, 21, 307–329. https://doi .org/10 .1080/13596748.2016.1226559, reprinted by permission of the publisher (Taylor & Francis, Ltd, http://www.tandfonline.com).

form of potential punitive measures; and the community, in the form of the school's reputation. As teachers build leadership skills, they find they can demonstrate positive impacts while cultivating the resilience to work through challenges. Poekert and colleagues (2016) found that the growth process was not linear, but more itera-tive. Teachers reported that they experienced an interdependent relationship between their own work and the responsiveness of their work environment to implement dis-tributed leadership. Poekert and colleagues (2016) propose that teacher leadership depends on feedback loops between challenges and positive outcomes. The chal-lenges are the barriers to becoming leaders that teachers experience; the challenges may be experienced as negative feedback but may also contribute to the teachers' persistence and fortitude. The positive outcomes teachers experience provide positive feedback in the form of motivation and persistence.

Growth as a Teacher

The model presents four core competencies related to teacher development. The first is growth as a teacher, defined as "use of evidence informed interactional and teach-ing practices to improve child outcomes" (Poekert et al., 2016, p. 317). Teachers found that the model gave them a structure to view and promote their own develop-ment. One American teacher noted,

> I feel almost like a new teacher when I go in with my new strategies . . . I know I've been doing something these past 18 years. But now, I'm going in and I'm building classroom community, and I'm doing all these things now that I don't remember doing before. (Poekert et al., 2016, p. 318)

As teachers developed confidence in their ability to apply new and innovative methods, they discovered that they had more energy and confidence to engage in leadership activities. A teacher from the UK group reported,

> To take on a role as a teacher leader, you need to have confidence to be able to speak to your colleagues on what you're doing and that only comes . . . if you are confident in yourself as a teacher, which comes I think through teaching experience and through upskilling. (Poekert et al., 2016, p. 318)

Growth as a Researcher

The second core competency in this teacher leadership model is defined as "developing a systematic and iterative approach to improving classroom practices" (Poekert et al., 2016, p. 317). One American teacher described this process as follows:

> You look at your own teaching and figure out where to improve, use research and find things people have done. You try to improve your teaching, collect data as you do it so you can see whether you are doing it or not. I did an inquiry on peer teaching—tutoring, pairing students of different abilities low and medium, medium and high, so both get something out of it. Speed and accuracy of math facts went up as a result. (Poekert et al., 2016, p. 319)

Teachers developed improved critical thinking and were more comfortable assessing their own strengths and areas for growth and critiquing their lessons, based in their research aims, which helped them refine their teaching strategies. They found validation in sharing research supporting their work to administrators and peers. Many reported that this process was empowering and motivated them to continue their leadership roles. One American teacher noted:

> I'd like to think that my students had gained something over the years, but now it's like . . . I know the effect that [my teaching] has on them. I can see—and that builds confidence in me. I try to build the same confidence in some of my colleagues. (Poekert et al., 2016, p. 319)

They also found that the inquiry process supported collaboration and collegiality among the staff, and because their confidence was building, they felt safer to self-reflect on their practice.

> When I actually started doing the research and taking on the chartered [certified] teacher, and I started to realize—well I also realized that I knew a lot less than I thought I knew and there was a lot more to even learn, but that was part of that process. And at that point, you do start to grow—you don't just grow in the profession, you start to grow as a person. Your confidence starts to develop, and that's when it all starts to take off. (Poekert et al., 2016, p. 319)

Growth as a Leader

The leadership competency involves the "adoption of a leadership stance to advocate for self and others" (Poekert et al., 2016, p. 317). The word "stance" is intentional here as it refers to your perspective and the way you engage in your world. The leadership stance becomes a way of being with the recognition that everything you do and say will impact your students, colleagues, and the community. Leadership becomes who you are, not just a role you play. An American teacher noted,

> I had the definition [of leader] in my mind . . . you're going to be an administrator or you're going to have a leadership role in the school, and then you're a leader. Otherwise, you're not . . . I wasn't going to do any of those things . . . It's amazing to me how my definition broadened, and I can see ways that I will impact other teachers . . . I need to do this. I have something I can share as a researcher, as a teacher. The confidence, for me[,] came from there. (Poekert et al., 2016, p. 320)

Personal Growth

Finally, personal growth is nested in the center of the model and is defined as "confidence in one's ability to engage in continuous self-improvement" (Poekert et al., 2016, p. 317). This can be seen as part of a virtuous cycle. Each of the other three competencies contribute to teachers' personal growth, and as they grow, the other competencies are also enhanced. One UK teacher noted:

> I would see areas of weakness in the school, and you take it on yourself to develop initiative. You know, at the start, I wouldn't have the confidence that my initiative was going to work, but now I would have that confidence, and it would make me more confident to take on a leadership role and to stay in my leadership role. (Poekert et al., 2016, p. 320)

This growth gave them the persistence and resilience to face challenges and take risks with confidence and courage.

> The more you can sort of dare to change things within you and the way you teach and the way you personally grow in your teaching and teaching approaches, the more you dare to step into the other areas really. (Poekert et al., 2016, p. 321)

As you can see, this study validates the importance of changing the way we think about ourselves, our profession, and our schools. We can step up into the leadership stance and take the initiative to make changes where we see they are needed. We can apply systems and design thinking to investigate our particular system and to address problems with novel solutions.

What Teacher Leaders Say

During my years as a teacher, one of my favorite activities was to observe my class from ground level, sitting on the floor. From there I could get my students' perspective of the classroom, and I could see places to improve that I otherwise would never have noticed. Similarly, we are best positioned to recognize problems in the systems where they touch our students' lives. After all, promoting student learning is the primary aim of these systems. We spend more time with most of America's children than their parents do (Wolk, 2008).

Jennifer Orr, elementary school teacher from Fairfax County, VA, and 2013 ASCD Emerging Leader (Teacher Collaborative and Education First, 2017), notes:

> No one else in education comes to the table with the perspective teachers do. Teachers are doing the daily work of education. Every policy decision, every curriculum adopted, every new regulation, every change in boundaries, impacts that daily work. Teachers have a unique understanding of those impacts.

There are more than 3 million K–12 public school teachers. If you include early childhood educators and teachers working in independent schools, the number is around 4 million, an occupation with one of the largest workforces in the United States. Imagine the collective power teachers have to lead, especially if we teachers join forces with parents and school leaders. When teacher leaders form networks and teams to collaborate on addressing problems, amazing things begin to happen.

> Today's teachers are more than content deliverers. They are dreamers and thinkers who are envisioning students' futures, not just their final semester grade. Veteran teachers possess a breadth of classroom knowledge with insight into changing student cultures and a pedagogical repertoire far more extensive than any teacher prep course could include in a syllabus. (Voiles, 2018, para. 3)

The National Network of State Teachers of the Year (NNSTOY) is building a cadre of teacher leaders. Derek Voiles, one such teacher, is the 2017 Tennessee Teacher of the Year and a member of NNSTOY. In an Education Week blog entitled "Want to Improve Schools? Look to Teacher Leaders," Voiles shared his experience as a teacher leader empowered by the Teacher Leadership Network developed by the Tennessee Department of Education. This expansive program gives districts the resources to network and develop a plan for supporting teacher leadership. Voiles reports,

> Once district plans are in place, Tennessee teachers can grow as leaders in many ways from district level leaders to statewide fellowships centered on various topics including policy and assessment. Teachers leverage their own specialty be it instructional strategies, data analysis, or technology use in the classroom. Many are given an extra period or extended contracts to provide coaching to their peers in these areas. (Voiles, 2018, para. 5)

Voiles is motivated to support his colleagues by his deep commitment to his students:

> I want the best for all my students, which means I want them to experience the best education from the best teachers they can possibly have before, during, and after the time they are with me. The most important thing I can do to strengthen and improve their chances of success is to think beyond the doors of my classroom and be an active participant in the current move toward teacher leadership. (Voiles, 2018, para. 7)

In rural South Dakota, teacher leader Sharla Steever was concerned about the extremely high teacher turnover rate in her school district (Teach to Lead, 2020b). In some schools, all of the teachers would turn over from year to year, making it difficult to cultivate and maintain a supportive school climate and effective teaching. The schools in Steever's district primarily serve the high-need populations of Native American reservation communities. New teachers were not prepared to navigate the complex problems their students were facing, such as community violence, high suicide rates, unemployment, and poverty. Steever wanted to address this problem, so she developed a team that built a mentoring support network for new teachers. They provided in-person and virtual mentoring, seasonal retreats for mentees and mentors to spend time together, and research-based approaches to becoming culturally responsive educators. Sharla noted, "Teacher leadership is about empowering teachers to address the concerns and needs they have . . . in a way that leads to transformation of those issues into solutions." (Teach to Lead, 2020b, para. 4)

Systematic teacher leadership efforts are also developing in Louisiana where the state has adopted a policy to build a sustainable teacher leadership infrastructure. Since 2013 the state has been cultivating thousands of teacher leaders. They created a teacher leader certification process that involves a series of curriculum specific trainings.

Teachers are even addressing the issue of teacher leadership itself. Mississippi consistently ranks at the bottom of educational rankings for student outcomes and teacher quality. Mary Margarett King, Mississippi State Teacher of the Year wanted to develop a state chapter of NNSTOY to develop teacher leaders to advocate for much needed education reforms (Teach to Lead, 2020a). "As teacher leaders, we have a responsibility to empower teachers, to advance the profession, and to impact students," Mary Margarett said. "Teacher leadership is empowering!" (Teach to Lead, 2020a, para. 5).

CHAPTER 8

Teacher Professionalism

Teaching is one of the most valuable and underappreciated professions in the workforce today. To be recognized as professional leaders in educational reform, we must demonstrate our professionalism more explicitly so we may join the ranks of other education professionals, such as central office leaders and education faculty, and contribute to school reform efforts as equal partners. As the understanding and appreciation of the teaching profession deepens and spreads, new systems of employment and compensation are emerging throughout public education. In this chapter, I describe several ways to redefine ourselves as lifelong learners, knowledge workers, and collaborative professionals.

To build a professional identity, we need to understand how theory and research are impacting the field of education. Who knows best how to teach? There is ongoing tension among theory, research, and application sectors in education as they try to answer this question. Theories try to explain how learning occurs, and research tests these hypotheses using empirical methods. The knowledge gained from the application of these theories is just as valuable. Teaching is so situational; in any given moment in the teaching experience, multiple interacting factors are involved. For too long, teachers have been viewed by research and theory as simply deliverers of curriculum, interventions, and other practices. Very little research examined the social and emotional capacities teachers' require to perform this challenging work

(Jennings & Greenberg, 2009). However, recently more research is aimed at studying teaching from the perspective of the teacher and how best to prepare new teachers and support current teachers so they remain in the profession (Korthagen, 2017).

While research can help us understand which practices and interactions are most effective under ideal circumstances, it cannot tell us what practice is best for one specific student at any particular moment. However, when our practice is informed by theory and research, we can refine our understanding of how these can best be applied in our teaching. We recognize the limitations of both theory and research for specific situations that we may encounter and we adapt. For example, a study of a social and emotional learning program that involved a small sample of majority White students from suburban families with high socioeconomic status may show promise for supporting these students; however, the results may not apply to a classroom of students of color living in an urban, low-income area. We may need to make culturally responsive adaptations to meet their needs.

Aligned with this understanding is the concept of funds of knowledge, which refers to the historical accumulation of abilities, knowledge, assets, and culturally significant interactions (Moll, 2019). Public schools have applied a deficiency model to structure instruction for Latinx children that underestimates their families' funds of knowledge. However, when teachers are aware of these funds of knowledge, they have a better understanding of their overall abilities and teachers can draw upon them in their teaching (Rodriguez, 2013). For example, translating from one language to another is a complex and challenging activity requiring excellent language skills in two languages and outstanding interpersonal skills to comprehend the speakers' perspectives and intention. While many of the students coming to school from predominately Spanish speaking homes perform this challenging task for their families on a regular basis, researchers found that teachers were not recognizing and utilizing these rich cognitive capacities (Vélez-Ibáñez & Greenberg, 1992). In this day in age, when diverse funds of knowledge are required to successfully navigate our challenges, recognizing and building upon our students' knowledge assets is critical.

There are also debates over how to define learning. Is learning a cognitive process at the individual level (cognitive theory) or a social process within a context (sociocultural learning theory; Anderson et al., 2000)? While cognitive theory views learning as an internal, cognitive process involving information processing, sociocultural learning theory finds this approach too narrow, proposing that learning is a social activity that occurs within the interactions between individuals and the environment. Applied to learning how to teach, cognitive theory views the teacher as a learner of knowledge that is applied to the classroom. The sociocultural theory views the teacher as a constantly learning individual who creates meaning out of the constantly changing context and interactions in the classroom. This requires us to reflect on ourselves and to view ourselves in society. While the cognitive approach views learning as more of a thing that can be constructed and applied to another situation, the sociocultural position assumes that since learning is context dependent, it must be constructed anew under novel conditions. The two theories are not necessarily mutually exclusive, and they may complement one another.

By engaging in a critical inquiry around the theory, research, and practice of teaching, we elevate our status to that of a highly skilled and creative knowledge worker. From this inquiry process, we develop our own interpretative frame for teaching: a deeply embedded personal and professional perspective. We develop this frame with the understanding of both its necessity and its limitations. The frame can simplify our practice by giving us some rules of thumb, but it can also lead to biases that interfere with our teaching practice. Our teacher identity is both a process and a product: a dynamic system that includes multiple funds of knowledge, our experience applying them, and feedback loops from this experience applied to refining our knowledge base. Becoming aware of the process allows you to take ownership of it to "help you understand the teacher you are becoming" (Olsen, 2016, p. 34). This understanding provides the agency to intentionally direct that process of becoming.

It is also important to learn to become aware of and navigate teacher identity conflicts. For example, when you were a child, what did classrooms look like? If they had identical desks lined up in rows, you may unconsciously feel discomfort in a classroom with more novel seating arrangements. This might give you the impression that the class is chaotic when it's actually going quite well. Another example is the teacher who wears their identity like a suit of armor for protection. This teacher was taught not to smile during the first month of school and has worked hard to create a rigid teacher persona that reflects their understanding of a teacher identity. But this approach does not allow for adaptation to the constantly changing, complex, dynamic systems of the classroom. Furthermore, suppressing emotional expression can be bad for a teacher's health and may lead to burnout (Jennings & Greenberg, 2009).

So how do we take ownership of our teacher identity? We begin with deep reflection on our scripts about teaching and learning that have been automatically and unconsciously built through past experience. Once recognized, these can be intentionally and consciously rebuilt or eliminated altogether. As we become aware of and critically examine the influences that contribute to our teacher identity, we can adjust them to be more aligned with current research, theory, and the goals we have for our students.

Multiple factors can influence our teacher identity development, including school resources, personal experience—such as becoming a parent—our own school experience, and our work with kids in other settings. To examine your teacher identity, you can sketch out the strands of influence that affected your teacher identity development: your family and home environment, your exposure to didactic or constructivist learning environments, your experience interacting with teachers, and your teacher preparation program. What are your views of individualism and success? How do they relate to those of the dominant culture? How might they be similar to or different from those of your students' families? Critique these influences in relationship to the teaching identity you wish to form.

Examine direct and mediating influences. Direct influences occur from some part of history, schooling, or professional preparation that contains specific understanding or perspective on teaching that you have accepted and adopted as part of your identity. For example, Ms. LeRoux continues the practice of writing an agenda on the board each day that she learned from the teacher she interned with as a student. Indirect influences may be more difficult to see, so it's harder to examine them to determine whether you want to include them in your teacher identity. For example, Mr. Watanabe had a difficult relationship with a professor when he was learning about Piaget's constructivist theory. He developed an unconscious bias against this theory because of this difficult relationship.

Support the development of your teacher identity by recognizing the interactions between your personal life and your professional life. Appreciate that learning to be a teacher does not have an end point; it is a lifelong learning process. With this in mind, recognize that you are taking one step at a time toward becoming the master teaching professional you envision. Remember that this process takes time, and be patient with yourself. Recognize your limitations, and maintain a healthy boundary between your personal life and your professional life. Take time to care for yourself. These are vital skills for teachers, and without self-care it's easy to quickly burnout. To support your own development as a teacher, choose conditions that optimize your own growth; choose to work in a school with a comparable philosophy and thoughtful and supportive colleagues.

Teachers as Knowledge Workers

As the Information Age arose, a new professional designation evolved called the *knowledge worker*. These are workers whose main capital is knowledge, and their work requires one to think for a living. Even after acquiring a high degree of expertise, their jobs require ongoing learning. Examples of professions with this designation are programmers, physicians, architects, engineers, scientists, design thinkers, lawyers, journalists, and academics. In this section, we examine what it means to be a knowledge worker and how shifting our identity to align with this line of work can build our professional esteem (Price & Weatherby, 2018). We will also examine the international prevalence of this approach to teacher professionalism, how it impacts teachers' views of their professional esteem, and how teacher professionalism impacts student learning outcomes.

A knowledge worker uses knowledge from formal education or work experience to create new knowledge and then contributes it to the profession (Ramirez & Nembhard, 2004). This knowledge is highly valued, as it supports improvement efforts in education more broadly. While teachers have typically been viewed as merely knowledge disseminators, in reality teachers are constantly discovering and learning new knowledge to share and disseminate. Although teachers rarely receive formal recognition for it, they are some of the most vibrant creators of new knowledge that is often freely shared with colleagues or sold at a very low cost online. Consider the wealth of websites and social media platforms that offer learning activities and ideas for teachers created by teachers. This rich source of creativity has largely gone unstudied. However, recent research shows how teachers are skillfully accessing, adapting, and applying this new knowledge in their classrooms (Hood, 2018). Indeed, the most highly accessed content from Pinterest is educational, and research shows that teachers are savvy and knowledgeable creators and consumers of this content (Schroeder et al., 2019).

Knowledge workers collaborate with fellow workers to learn and to apply new knowledge and skills on the job (Harteis & Billet, 2008). With the advent of professional learning communities (PLCs) and other collaborative professional learning activities, this important aspect of teacher professionalism became widely accepted, although support for such activities varies widely among school districts. Besides PLCs, collaborative knowledge building activities can include instructional rounds, collaborative inquiry and planning, lesson and book study, school networks, action research, data teams, self-evaluation processes, peer review, and learning walks (Hargreaves, 2019).

Years of research have demonstrated that when teachers work in collaboration to build knowledge, these teachers have students who demonstrate higher achievement in reading and mathematics compared to teachers who work under more siloed conditions. The Organisation for Economic Cooperation and Development (OECD, 2016) concluded from its extensive studies of the Teaching and Learning International Survey (TALIS) that a collaborative school culture is one of the strongest factors associated with teachers' self-efficacy and job satisfaction. This is not to say that all PLCs are beneficial to teachers' practice and student learning. We have a lot to learn about how best to organize and lead PLCs for optimal effects (Hargreaves, 2019). However, it is clear that collaborative knowledge work is more important than ever and is key to identifying teacher work as knowledge work.

Teachers who are collaborating can share knowledge and together create new knowledge that they can apply in their classrooms to address specific challenges or enhance learning activities. In our complex and rapidly changing world of work, teachers' learning is continuous because we are constantly encountering new situations and need to respond, often on the spot, with novel ideas.

Knowledge workers require the autonomy and agency to direct their own professional learning, and we are seeing new modes of individualized and differentiated learning and evaluation (Brandon & Derrington, 2019). Such processes are often referred to as transformational learning because they involve a critical examination of the beliefs and assumptions that underly one's practice and the development of alternative perspectives that might broaden one's understanding and refine one's practice (Lysaker & Furuness, 2012). Organizations that employ knowledge workers must remove obstacles for completing transformational learning and provide opportunities for professional learning that aligns with the workers specific needs (Vanthournout et al., 2014). As the sheer volume of knowledge continues to grow, organizations need new ways to manage knowledge by creating professional benchmarks or standards of professional learning, through professional discretion (trust in the knowledge workers' expertise and ability to solve problems), by offering professional growth opportunities, and by providing supportive workplace conditions (Cheng, 2015).

Historically, successful professional work environments develop and maintain a productive knowledge workforce by hiring highly qualified individuals and promoting their learning, providing them autonomy, flattening hierarchical structures, facilitating communication and collaboration across and within groups, providing adequate resources, and building trust between workers and management (Alvesson, 2004). Next we will examine the worldwide prevalence of this view of teachers as knowledge workers.

Knowledge Worker Elements and Their Impacts

How common are factors associated with successful knowledge work in educational work settings worldwide? Examining data from the OECD TALIS (OECD, 2016), the world's first and largest international survey of teachers, Price and Weatherby (2018) looked for evidence of the elements commonly found among successful knowledge professional environments. Below I review their findings regarding each element in the study.

Professional benchmarks. While most teachers in the sample reported having college-level credentials (96%), only 45% perceived that their teacher education adequately prepared them to conduct their work. While 80% of respondents mentioned attending at least one professional development workshop or conference in the past 12 months, most teachers reported that their work appraisal process lacked professional development value. Half of participants noted that the appraisals were conducted for administrative purposes only, with no feedback for improving performance.

Professional discretion. The results showed that many teachers experience opportunities to voice professional opinions and are actively involved in decision-making processes in the workplace (70%). However, their opportunities to collaborate with peers were less common (less than 50%).

Room for promotion. Less than half of the teachers, worldwide, reported that appraisals of their work result in a pay raise, and half reported any opportunity for career advancement.

Workplace conditions. Teachers reported a lack of support from their workplace, especially a lack of professional learning associated with issues of language diversity and special education needs. Despite this shortcoming, most teachers reported satisfaction with their professional workplace climate.

While these findings show promise, they also point to gaps in support for teachers' knowledge worker status. Overall, teachers report that their profession is not valued by society, and this conception is likely related to these gaps. Understanding these gaps can help us advocate for changes that promote our own professionalism and fight against policies that strip professionalism from our work. The greatest gaps were found in the lack of professional benchmarks, professional discretion and autonomy, vertical career movement, and resources—all factors commonly associated with semi-professional work (Ingersoll & Perda, 2008). Indeed, one-third of teachers, globally, do not have the autonomy to determine their own course content and one-fifth have no determination of their assessment policies (OECD, 2014). Finally, teachers, globally, lack basic resources to conduct their work. Twenty-six percent reported that they did not have the basic textbooks they needed, and more than 25% of the teachers in 22 nations, including the United States, lacked adequate Internet access.

While these statics are distressing, there was some very good news in a few countries. For example, in Chile, the 2016 Teacher Professional Development Law improved teachers' working conditions, pay, and professional development opportunities. It also raised the requirements for entry into teacher education programs and established induction programs to support new teachers. It also initiated new performance standards that promote collaboration, innovation, and professional development (Schleicher, 2018).

As we teachers examine these gaps in knowledge professional workplace factors, we can target them in our approach to our own employment. Rather than simply expressing the wish to be viewed as a professional, we can intentionally focus on specific, incremental change in each of these areas. We can focus on developing our own professional benchmarking by earning a higher degree, a specialist credential, or national certification. We can advocate for more individualized professional learning activities that provide more ongoing support than one-off workshops and conferences. We can advocate for greater discretion and autonomy in our selection of learning activities and formative and summative assessment processes. We can support efforts that promote teacher leadership in our communities, which will provide more opportunities for career advancement. Finally, we must lobby for better resources. The TALIS data (OECD, 2014) reveals just how under-resourced our schools are. When more than 25% of U.S. teachers report not having adequate Internet access, it is truly a cause for concern.

You may be asking yourself, "How can I make such huge systematic changes?" As explained in Part II, we can apply systems thinking to examine where we have the leverage to impact change. You may not be able to change the assessment system of the entire district, but you might be able to convince your principal to experiment with new ways of assessment in your classroom, or even the whole school. You may not be able to change your state's benchmarking system for teachers, but you can achieve the highest benchmark for yourself, and in this way, lead the profession in this direction. The more intentional you are in your framing of your teaching identity, the more leverage you will achieve. Remember that there's currently a huge and growing teacher shortage and that this gives teachers an edge to command better working conditions and professional esteem.

The Price and Weatherby study (2018) examined to what extent the factors associated with successful knowledge work in educational settings (i.e., professional benchmarks, professional discretion, room for promotion, and workplace conditions) impact teachers' perceptions of their society's esteem of the teaching profession. Examining evidence of the same elements, they found the following:

Professional benchmarks. Teachers who reported that they received helpful feedback from appraisals of their work that positively impacted their teaching were 1.5 times more likely to perceive that their teaching is valued by their society than teachers who received no feedback. Interestingly teachers who experienced a conference or workshop reported dips in their perceived value of teaching. Perhaps teachers recognize that this type of one-off professional learning activity has limited value in improving teaching and believe that it signals that their professional learning is unimportant. Another surprising result was that the amount of formal training a teacher has does not predict their perceptions of society's value of their teaching. In other words, teachers with more degrees and certificates do not feel that this factor impacts how society esteems teachers.

Professional discretion. The study found that when teachers feel they have professional discretion and involvement in school decisions, they report that their teaching is more valued. Surprisingly, the study's results showed no impact of teacher collaboration on teachers' perceptions of their society's esteem of teaching professionals.

Room for promotion. Researchers found that promotional opportunities and the possibility of a salary raise that is linked to positive evaluations had twice the impact on teachers' perception of professional esteem than participation in school decisions.

Workplace conditions. There was a strong association between the quality of working conditions and teachers' perceptions of society's value of the teaching profession. Teachers who are highly satisfied with their working conditions are more than three times as likely to agree that society values their work compared to those who report less satisfaction.

An important caveat is that the data available did not allow researchers to access teachers' own feelings of value, only their perceptions of their society's value of the teaching profession. However, the results make a strong case that when teachers are treated as knowledge workers, it impacts their sense of how society values their work.

It is interesting to note that initial teacher training is not a significant contributor to teachers' perception of status. It's more important to have collegial opportunities to discuss practices with school leadership, to participate in school decision making, and to have the opportunity to receive feedback that is meaningful and constructive. This highlights the significant value of principal support for a more distributed leadership orientation that has been found in numerous studies (Canrinus et al., 2012; Hulpia et al., 2011; Price, 2012, 2015; Spillane, 2012).

While the TALIS study (OECD, 2014) provided important information about teacher professionalism worldwide, it had several limitations. Some important factors related to teachers' professional identity as knowledge workers were not addressed in this study that have been investigated in other research. Teachers' trust in their school's leadership and their colleagues is foundational to teacher professionalism and organizational commitment (Devos et al., 2014), findings that support other research demonstrating a relationship between the level of professional esteem and attrition. Teachers who feel valued and satisfied with their working conditions are more likely to stay in the profession (Helms-Lorenz et al., 2016). Other research has found a strong relationship between teachers' self-reported sense of professional agency and a variety of positive outcomes (Imants & Van der Wal, 2020).

Collaborative Professionalism

As we build networks of teacher leaders, we can hone our collaboration skills. Since we've spent most of the last two centuries working in isolation, we need to spend time exploring how to build our collaborative professionalism. Isolation is a primary driver of teacher job dissatisfaction and burnout, and policy makers are beginning to advocate for creating more opportunities for teachers to collaborate with colleagues on planning, administration, and evaluation of instruction. Furthermore, there is now strong evidence that professional collaboration in schools can boost student achievement, increase teacher retention, and promote innovation and change (Hargreaves, 2019). The question now is how best to collaborate.

In their recent book, Hargreaves and O'Connor (2018) distinguish between professional collaboration and collaborative professionalism. Professional collaboration describes how workers collaborate within a profession, whereas collaborative professionalism is more rigorous:

> Collaborative professionalism is about how teachers and other educators transform teaching and learning together to work with all students to develop fulfilling lives of meaning, purpose, and success. It is organized in an evidence-informed, but not data-driven, way through rigorous planning, deep and sometimes demanding dialogue, candid but constructive feedback, and continuous collaborative inquiry. The joint work of collaborative professionalism is embedded in the culture and life of the school, where educators actively care for and have solidarity with each other as fellow professionals as they pursue their challenging work together and where they collaborate professionally in ways that are responsive to and inclusive of the cultures of their students, themselves, the community, and the society. (p. 27)

Hargreaves (2000) observed four stages in the development of collaboration in education that have been observed during the transitions from individual work to collaboration: *emergence, doubt, design,* and *transformation.* If you have been working in education for some time, you likely have experienced each of these stages. *Emergence*, which began when research started to show evidence that professional collaboration has positive impacts on student achievement, was the first step away from individualism to collaboration in teaching. During the second stage, *doubt*, some models of collaboration were found lacking because they rely too much on talk rather than action. Examples of too much talk are meetings to talk about how to collaborate without actually engaging in professional collaboration itself. Often referred to as "contrived collegiality," these meetings may result from attempts to promote collaboration through top-down mandates. During the *design* stage, models of collaboration emerged intentionally from specific needs or tasks (e.g., PLCs, data teams, collaborative action research, etc.). The *transformation* stage involved

> . . . deeper forms of collaborative professionalism that are more precise in their structures and methods, more pervasive in their presence, throughout all aspects of teachers' practice rather than taking the shape of add-on meetings, and more rooted in positive and trusting relationships among the people involved. (Hargreaves & O'Connor, 2018, p. 14)

Pointing to the results of numerous case studies, Hargreaves and O'Connor (2018) present 10 tenets of collaborative professionalism:

- Collective Autonomy
- Collective Efficacy
- Collaborative Inquiry
- Collective Responsibility
- Collective Initiative
- Mutual Dialogue
- Joint Work
- Common Meaning and Purpose
- Collaborating with Students
- Big Picture Thinking for All

Collective Autonomy

For collaborative professionalism to thrive, teachers need greater independence from the top-down authority structures and more interdependence with one another. This aligns well with the teacher leadership research discussed in Chapter 7. When teachers collectively take the lead, they can build collaborative teams to address things they see that could be done better.

Collective Efficacy

Chapter 2 presented the power of collective efficacy to improve student achievement (Eells, 2011; Hattie, 2016). Collaborative efficacy is a collective superpower; it only works when we collaborate. According to Hattie (2016), collective efficacy is at the most influential factor that have been shown to influence student achievement. It is more than three times as powerful as socioeconomic status, twice as powerful as prior achievement, and more than three times as powerful as home environment and parental involvement. To top it off, collective efficacy is more than three times more impactful on student achievement than student motivation, concentration, persistence, and engagement. We can see here how critical this factor is to effective collective professionalism. When we teachers have the collective confidence that we can make a positive difference in the lives of our students, we create a virtuous cycle that continuously reinforces positive improvement.

Collaborative Inquiry

When we participate as co-learners inquiring into a problem of practice that we share, we are engaging in collaborative inquiry (Schnellert et al., 2008). The cycle of inquiry involves identifying a focus of inquiry, examining what knowledge and skills we need and building these together, implementing changes in practice based on this inquiry, collecting evidence of learning, and reflecting on the learning to refine the inquiry. We can apply design thinking practices to this inquiry process to deepen it.

Collective Responsibility

Collaborative professionalism depends on our mutual obligation to provide support for one another as we collaborate to support our students. We recognize that all the students in our school and community are "our" students, not just the students in our class or classes this year. It's a reflection of our interdependence; we know that the work we do has impacts for all students in that we are trailblazers in this new frontier.

Collective Initiative

As we begin to take the lead, we find that we need fewer initiatives but more initiative that arises from our shared responsibility. Together we recognize problems and address them because we appreciate that our students need the change and we have the collective efficacy to address it.

Mutual Dialogue

Together we learn to engage in difficult conversations. Aware of potential mind traps, we are open to different perspectives and ideas and feel safe to share them. Rather than succumbing to the mind trap of agreement, we allow ourselves to experience the discomfort of contrasting ideas with the understanding that novel ideas often emerge from putting them all out on the table. Dialogue protocols can help establish ground rules for listening and talking before introducing disagreement.

Joint Work

This is the work that we do together, be it team teaching, collaborative action research, planning, discussing student work, or providing structured feedback to one another. Work often involves a product, such as a new lesson, a curriculum, or a report. Protocols can also help guide our work to keep our work aligned with our mutual goal.

Common Meaning and Purpose

Collaborative professionalism addresses the goals of education and how we can best support our students in flourishing as whole human beings and how we can best value all they have to offer our learning community. It honors the human impulse to find meaning and purpose in life.

Collaborating with Students

As collaborative professionalism deepens, students begin to actively engage in change with the teachers. Student voice is respected and valued.

Big Picture Thinking for All

This recognizes that collective professionalism requires that everyone in the system have access to the big picture. The system has transparency, and everyone who works in the system can see and affect change on the whole system.

These 10 tenets can act as guides for us as we build collaborative networks and teams of teacher leaders in our schools, districts, and communities. When we encounter difficulties with our collaboration, we can review the tenets to see where we need to shore up our processes, helping us stay on track.

Teacher Awarenesses

Teaching is a highly complex activity that involves multiple interacting systems including the teacher, the learner, the context, and the interactions. Our development as expert teachers is based on our awareness of these dimensions. Based on extensive qualitative research, Dr. Vanessa Rodriguez (2014) presented a framework of awareness dimensions that are critical to developing expert teaching knowledge. Called the Five Awarenesses of the Teaching Brain, they are awareness of:

- The learner
- The interaction
- Self as teacher
- The teaching practice
- The context

The awareness of the learner is critical to developing individualized and generalized knowledge about our students. Developing teaching expertise involves being able to understand the learners and what they need, both collectively and individually. For example, when my class of third graders is especially wiggly, I take them on a short brain-break to walk around the school yard picking up trash. This gives them all a break outside and engages them in a community service activity that builds a sense of community. When the principal acknowledges the class during the next morning's announcements, my students beam. In another situation, one student is having a unique difficulty with an assignment. Based on my awareness of this student's needs and abilities, I construct small experiments with alternative teaching practices to see if they help. Awareness of the learner includes awareness of their emotions. When we recognize that a student is upset, we understand that engaging in challenging academic work will likely be difficult, and we give them a chance to recover before we make demands on them.

The awareness of the interaction is a teacher's recognition of the bond that develops between teacher and student that is essential to the teacher's success. With this awareness comes expert knowledge regarding how to connect and how to apply that feeling of connection to motivate learning. As one teacher in Rodriguez's study noted, "When a teacher really knows a kid and can connect to that kid, then, you know, that's going to be the surest path to academic success" (Rodriguez, 2014, p. 142). The interaction requires two active agents engaged in a collaborative learning experience. The teacher recognizes that the interaction has mutual effects. As the student learns, the teacher learns how best to teach.

Teachers in Rodriguez's study noted that they felt what she calls synergy in such rewarding interactions:

> . . . that feeling, you know, of things clicking, things are just clicking, you don't want to stop. You don't want [to stop], and the kids are like, 'I don't wanna go to the gym,' you know, 'I don't wanna go home,' and you're feeling the same thing. And a lot of that is about human connection. (Rodriguez, 2014, p. 146)

As teachers, we all develop a teacher identity, but we may not necessarily integrate the personal and professional contexts we inhabit. The personal context involves internal and external factors: personality, culture, gender, race/ethnicity, and physical appearance. Expert teachers understand that these aspects of themselves affect their view of their students and their students' views of them. This understanding can contribute to successful interactions. The professional context recognizes self as teacher. This involves meta-processing, the ability to take a step back from a situation and recognize the perspectives of the people involved in the interaction. This helps us understand how our students' perspectives affect their learning, and thereby plan learning opportunities that fit this understanding.

Some years ago, I was conducting a study of the CARE program in an Eastern U.S. city that had a city core of predominantly Black families and a ring of suburbs with predominantly white families. While most of the students were Black, most of the teachers were white women from the surrounding rural or suburban areas. During one of our workshops, some teachers mentioned that it was challenging to build relationships with their students because of what their students' parents had told them about teachers. "They tell them to watch out for us, because we might get mad at them. This makes the students shy away from us right from the start," one teacher remarked. The teachers were baffled by this parent behavior and assumed that they were doing it to make things difficult for the teachers. Reflecting on this situation I asked, "Do you think it's possible that these parents had challenging relationships with their teachers when they were kids?" Several of the teachers nodded, aware of the fraught history of racial disparity and injustice in their community. "It seems to me that they are doing what most good parents do, trying to protect their children from something they fear," I remarked. The teachers looked surprised but agreed that this appraisal made sense to them. They realized that to bridge this divide, they would need to make an extra effort to connect with the parents to reassure them that their children were safe in their classrooms.

The more we are aware of our teaching practice, the more we can refine our activities to align with our students' needs and with best practices. This involves monitoring our teaching practice across three domains associated with high quality:

emotional support, instructional support, and classroom organization (Pianta et al., 2008). High quality practice in each of these domains aligns with positive student outcomes. When we are aware of them and how they play out in our own practice, it improves our teaching (Pianta et al., 2017). Emotional support is critical to creating a learning environment that children recognize as safe for taking the risks inherent in learning. This kind of support involves teachers building supportive relationships with individual students, fostering positive peer relationships, and recognizing and responding to students' emotions, needs, ideas, and interests. Instructional support involves providing learning activities that support the development of students' thinking skills by providing activities where students can observe, predict and experiment, brainstorm, plan, and solve problems and by nurturing their natural curiosity and love of learning through drawing on every day experiences to connect new topics with their prior knowledge. Classroom organization involves the way a teacher organizes the classroom's environment and routines to promote student success. Master teachers provide proactive behavior management and well-organized learning routines, and they facilitate learning activities effectively.

Awareness of context involves our awareness of the multiple, overlapping contextual influences that affect our teaching, including the other awarenesses. Context can be viewed from both the micro and macro systemic levels. At the macro level are national and international forces that might influence how we teach. At the micro level are the classroom and school contexts, along with the home contexts of each student. The more aware we are of these various contexts and the roles they play in our teaching, the more expertise we gain.

According to Rodriguez (2014), each of these awarenesses contribute to our theory of the learner. Therefore when we utilize all the awarenesses in our theory, the theory is more comprehensive and accurate. When learning situations fail, we can look to our awarenesses to see what went wrong. For example, Ms. Leary has just presented a lesson on electric motors to a group of eighth graders. In her student-centered classroom, she showed students how to connect a simple electric motor to a battery in preparation for making a simple machine. Aware of her learners, she noticed Jacquina standing in the back of the class, looking down with her arms crossed. She recognizes that due to her own culture (understanding of self as teacher), she might be misinterpreting Jacquina's body language. Rather than immediately assuming that Jacquina was disengaged in the lesson, she decided to wait until the students began to disburse into their learning teams before she engaged with Jacquina. Soon she saw Jacquina deeply engaged in connecting wires to a battery. Ms. Leary realized that Jacquina was probably thinking deeply, not disengaging from the lesson. Had she said something to Jacquina during the lesson, it would likely have been very embarrassing to Jacquina, and it might even have felt like an unfair attack, causing damage to their relationship.

This chapter offers guidance on how to redefine yourself as a collaborative knowledge worker with a high level of expertise. With these tools, we teachers can empower ourselves to take the lead in educational reform efforts. In the next chapter, you will see how empowering your students to direct their own learning can contribute to the reform processes as well. As you will see, when you provide opportunities for students to choose their learning content based on their own interests, you no longer need to expend effort trying to motivate them. Schools can then become places where everyone is actively engaged in transformational learning.

CHAPTER 9

Empowering Students

In education, the primary focus of our work is student learning and development. We want our students to thrive in school and also in their future lives. We know that we have a huge impact on them in so many ways. When we build supportive relationships with our students, it helps them develop resilience and the sense of safety they need to tackle challenges. When we empower our students, we amplify this impact. In this chapter, we examine how to empower our students to become independent lifelong learners. As Alvin Toffler noted, "The illiterate of the twenty-first century will not be those who cannot read and write, but those who cannot learn, unlearn, and relearn" (Toffler, 1970, as cited by Bothwell, 2019).

The first step in empowering our students is to build a supportive and caring community. Typically, it helps to begin the year with this process, but it can be started at any point in time. The key is to cultivate our students' feelings of connectedness with us, with their peers, and with the school. Depending on the age of your students, there are a variety of ways to do this. Social and emotional learning (SEL) programs offer extensive activities and practices for building community.[*]

---

[*] If you are not familiar with SEL, I recommend you access the myriad of resources offered by the Collaborative for Academic, Social, and Emotional Learning (https://casel.org). There you will find many program guides that can point you in the right direction. You can also access a new book series that I

First and foremost, we can build strong and supportive relationships with our students by modeling respectful interactions. Our students are super sensitive to hypocrisy, so we need to make sure we follow our own rules and model the behavior we expect of them. If we expect them to speak respectfully to one another, we need to speak respectfully to them, even when we're feeling frustrated. One teacher who completed the CARE program reported:

"Now, when I'm frustrated, I let them know, but I don't blame them. I don't yell at them anymore. I say, like, 'I need to finish this lesson, but I can't because everyone is talking, so I'm feeling frustrated. No one can hear me. So, my jaw is getting tight, and I can feel my shoulders getting tense, so I need to calm down. Let's all take three breaths together so we can get back on track and I can finish.' And then we're all so much calmer" (Jennings, 2013)

We want our students to feel safe in the classroom so they can focus their attention on learning. When they trust us to keep them safe, from their peers and from our negative emotions, they begin to feel a deep bond with school and can open their hearts and minds to learning. Research has shown that teachers can have a significant impact on their classroom social structures (e.g., hierarchies, friendships, and small peer groups; Gest et al., 2014). To get a sense of your classroom social structures, take a few minutes to step back and observe your class when they are all interacting informally. This could be during recess, lunch, or before school starts. Imagine you are seeing them for the first time. Notice who is playing with whom, who is left out, who is being treated badly. You can affect these dynamics by mitigating status extremes (e.g., not creating competition for status, not showing favoritism), supporting isolated students, managing aggression, and promoting prosocial behavior. Teachers who take more active and proactive steps to manage friendships, aggression, and hierarchies have students who engage in more prosocial behaviors.

Another important step toward creating a safe, supportive classroom is establishing group norms: presenting simple behavioral expectations and consistently reinforcing them. You can engage your students in discussing and creating expectations. One of the books in the SEL Solutions Series, *SEL from the Start,* by my colleague Dr. Sara Rimm-Kaufman (2020), offers a series of activities to begin your school year successfully by introducing your students to norms and SEL skills for

---

edit called *SEL Solutions*. This is a series of brief books—short enough to read over a weekend—that offer evidence-based tips for promoting SEL in your classroom. My books *Mindfulness for Teachers* and *The Trauma-Sensitive Classroom* contain helpful information about building a caring learning community.

the student-centered classroom so they can collaborate with each other successfully. These include active listening, respectful communication, respecting different perspectives, managing frustration and anger, receiving and giving feedback, persevering and resolving conflict.

The key is to be very clear about exactly what you expect and how you want your students to behave. Rules and expectations are norms for general conduct, whereas routines are procedures that students will follow in specific situations. Rules should be simple, general, and stated in the positive. At the beginning of the school year, Ms. Beatty engaged her fifth-grade class in a discussion about classroom rules. She asked them what they hoped to learn this year. Based on their answers, she led them to consider what they need in their classroom to accomplish their goals. A conversation ensued about respecting each other and the materials in the classroom. They came up with four simple rules: treat others with respect, treat the classroom materials with respect, be safe inside, and be safe outside. Once they agreed on these rules, she created a poster with the rules listed in large lettering and displayed it on the wall. These expectations formed the basis for understanding classroom procedures.

Classroom procedures are accepted process patterns or guidelines for social interactions (listening, giving feedback) and accomplishing classroom tasks or specific activities (e.g., walking in the hallway, using lockers, sharpening pencils, attending an assembly, going to the restroom). Procedures form routines that help students meet expectations, do these automatically, manage transitions efficiently, and self-monitor their behavior. Procedures should be succinct, positively stated, and age-appropriate. Keep who, what, when, where, why, and how in mind. Clear procedures, taught and consistently reinforced, are the most critical tool for creating a functional and productive learning environment.

Next, Ms. Beatty introduced procedures. "When I'm giving a lesson, and you want to say something, how can you do that respectfully?" Several of her students raised their hands. "I see you already know this routine," she said smiling. She continued to introduce each basic classroom routine, telling them what she expected and then showing them what it looks like, sounds like, and feels like. The class practiced several of the routines, such as lining up to get ready for lunch, getting a hall pass to use the bathroom, and where and how to store their belongings. With younger students, you may need to simplify this process and engage them in modeling the behaviors you want so the behaviors will become embodied. When students forget the rules or the procedures, you can simply remind them and ask them to show you how to do the procedure correctly. Consistent reinforcement with a firm and warm tone of voice can be a proactive way to prevent behavior problems. When behavior problems do occur, you can follow the actions steps below.

ACTION STEPS FOR PROBLEM-SOLVING BEHAVIOR ISSUES

When faced with inappropriate behavior, engage in the following problem-solving steps.

Teacher Self-Reflections (use throughout all stages)

- What emotion(s) is(are) triggered by the behavior?
- Are you taking the behavior personally?
- Consider possible biases or scripts from your past that may affect your perceptions of the behavior.
- Take a few breaths to calm down or use an "I" message. Model self-regulation to communicate your feelings and teach self-regulation as necessary.

Stage 1: Routine Maintenance

- Check the environment and students' physical needs or issues.
- Consider cultural issues and the student's trauma history, strengths, and challenges.
- Is the expectation developmentally appropriate for this student?
- Check for understanding. Does the student know what the expectation is?
- Does the student need reminding, reinforcing, or redirecting?
- Give a logical consequence with a calm, firm voice (you break it, you fix it; loss of privileges; positive time out).

Stage 2: Problem-Solving

- Interview the student to learn more about him or her.
- Focus on one behavior at a time. Consider which is most important to address first.
- Set up a time to speak to the student's parent to learn more about the student, share concerns, and perhaps develop a strategy involving home involvement (e.g., regular reports, check-ins, consequences at home).
- Plan a problem-solving conference with the student. Be sure to describe the specific behavior and how it interferes with learning. If student agrees to work on the problem, engage in regular check-ins to reinforce improvement.
- If necessary, create a behavior chart that clearly describes what the appropriate behavior is to support learning and reinforce improvement.

Stage 3: Managing Chronically Inappropriate Behavior

- Follow school policies, engaging other school personnel in problem-solving (e.g., school counselor, special education teacher, social worker, administrator).
- Inform and include parents according to school policies.

- Chronically inappropriate behavior may indicate an identifiable issue that merits referral to special education services.

When our students know what is expected of them and they feel connected to their community, they want to make a positive contribution. When they run into difficulty, it's often because they don't have sufficient skills, and it's important to teach them these skills rather than applying punitive action. (Jennings, 2019, pp. 102–103)

Autonomy and Motivation

One of our biggest challenges today is engaging our students in learning. We spend a lot of our time and effort trying to motivate our students. We plan lessons that we hope will be engaging. We search for relevant content. Indeed, students' lack of motivation is a major contributor to teacher burnout and their plans to leave the profession (Skaalvik & Skaalvik, 2016). What if we didn't need to expend all this energy trying to motivate our students? Wouldn't it make teaching much more enjoyable and rewarding?   ·

We can draw upon self-determination theory (SDT; Deci & Ryan, 1985) and associated research to understand how to shift the responsibility for student motivation to our students themselves. Since we recognize that becoming lifelong learners is required to adapt to our rapidly changing world, it makes sense to recognize, support, and cultivate our students' natural motivation to learn now, while they are still young, rather than trying to teach these skills to adults later in life.

Self-determination theory proposes three basic psychological needs: autonomy, competence, and relatedness. We need to be the authors of our own life, we need to master skills, and we need to feel connected to others. The satisfaction of these needs leads to self-determination. I've already discussed feeling connected to others. Next, I will discuss autonomy and competence, which are both associated with intrinsic motivation, the natural, inherent drive to learn and grow, as opposed to extrinsic motivation, which comes from external sources, such as rewards or punishments.

Autonomy involves three primary dimensions: choice of action, internal locus of causality, and psychological freedom. When our students feel free to engage in their choice of meaningful learning activities, they become more motivated to achieve mastery. There is growing evidence that when we provide our students with greater autonomy, they are much more motivated and successful (Jang et al., 2016; Pitzer & Skinner, 2017). They are more intrinsically motivated and engage in deeper learning that they are more likely to retain (Jang et al., 2016). Teachers find that there is less need for behavior management when students are motivated to engage in learning activities they choose (Williams et al., 2016).

Self-determination theory has been applied cross culturally. While research has shown that these needs are the same across cultures, how those needs are satisfied is culturally specific (Church et al., 2012; Ginevra et al., 2015). Therefore, we must consider the cultural values of our students as we apply SDT in our classrooms. For example, in one study involving U.S. high school students, non-White youth were more likely than White youth to report that family responsibilities contributed to their self-determined behavior (Shogren et al., 2014). We must discover what is important to our students rather than assuming that we know.

How can we be more supportive of our students' autonomy? The research shows that three primary actions can make a difference: we can offer choices, make the learning relevant to their interests, and connect the learning to the real world (Cheon & Reeve, 2015). It's not necessary to make drastic changes in the way you're currently teaching. As we have already learned, the classroom is a complex, dynamic system, and it makes sense to try experimenting with a few ideas to see how they work before engaging in a major overhaul. In this way, you can see for yourself how this theory plays out in your classroom, and your students can begin to learn more autonomously.

One simple way to encourage autonomy is to offer choices. For example, fourth grade teacher Mr. Kim offers his students choice of seating. He has arranged a variety of workstations, from standing tables to chairs with bouncy ball bases. Students can even work sitting on the floor with a lapboard. To introduce this new seating arrangement, he introduced an action research project to his students. "I know this is a new way of sitting and working at school. Do you know how we learn about the effects of trying something new?" he asked his students. Darla spoke up, "Can we ask questions about how each one feels?" "Great idea," he said. "Let's do some research. What questions should we ask?"

Mr. Kim continued to engage his students in designing a simple study to learn how each seating possibility was experienced by each student. Over the course of the first few weeks, each student had an opportunity to try each learning station and complete a brief survey. The students decided that the surveys should be anonymous because they wanted honest answers and didn't want to expose anyone to embarrassment. The students were then arranged in teams to work on ways to analyze the results of their study. They learned how to create histograms of the results that showed which workstation was most useful for each purpose. For example, one of the most popular seats was the floor, but only for reading books. For writing, most students preferred sitting or standing at a table.

Next Mr. Kim engaged his students in a social problem-solving activity. "What should we do if we want a seat that is already taken?" he asked. The students brainstormed and came up with some ideas, such as creating waiting lists for seats and using a timer to ensure everyone got a chance to sit where they wanted at some point during the day. This process offered them choices about how to manage the challenges of sharing spaces with their peers.

Third grade teacher Ms. Roose decided to offer a free choice math/ELA extended period during which students could choose to complete their choice of basic math and English language arts activities while she met with one reading group and one math group to present lessons. She provided a wide variety of activities that help students build math and language skills. For example, students could choose to do a math facts game on a tablet. Students logged into the game, so the game kept track of their level of mastery, enabling them to learn at their own pace. Some students chose to do math puzzles or solve problems with manipulatives. Students could choose among several different kinds of leveled reading activities. Some students preferred to work in pairs or small groups on Mad Libs or Concentration with their spelling and vocabulary words. Each of these activities was organized by mastery level, so the students knew which level they needed to do next. They recorded their accomplishments on their daily record sheet so that they and Ms. Roose could keep track of their progress. On a typical day, all Ms. Roose's students were happily engaged in the activity of their choice, freeing her to work with one small group at a time.

Ninth grade English teacher Ms. Bose was beginning a lesson on essay writing. She saw this as an excellent opportunity to provide choice and an opportunity for students to make a difference in their community. She introduced the lesson by inviting them to review the opinion section of the newspaper online. She asked them to pick one opinion essay that reflected their opinion. Next, she invited each of them to share their choice with the class and explain why they chose it. Then she invited them to write their own opinion piece focused on the same topic, including their own experiences in some way. They were also invited to submit their essays to the local newspaper and several of them were published. One student's essay on her perspectives on guns and school violence made it into the syndicated news stream, and it went viral on Twitter.

The Genius Hour/20% Project

Another way to promote autonomy and self-directed learning is the Genius Hour, also called the 20% Project. This idea originated in innovative companies like Google, where workers were allowed to spend 20% of their time working on their own projects. This system successfully launched many new innovations, including Gmail and Google News. In recent years, this approach has been adopted in schools. The school-based approach has five simple guidelines (Juliani, 2017):

1. Choice: Students choose their own project and the form of their final product.
2. Structured Unstructured Time: The 20% time is scheduled, not offered at random times in the day.
3. Peer Accountability: Students receive feedback from peers.
4. Reflection: Students reflect on what they learned and how they learned it.
5. Presentation: Learning is shared in the form of a product.

Inspired by Daniel Pink's (2011) book *Drive* and Carol Dweck's (2006) book *Mindsets*, A. J. Juliani (2017) decided to take a leap of faith and assign a 20% project to his high school English students. After the winter break, he presented the idea to his class:

The 20% Project

1. For the rest of the year, 20% of your time in my class will be spent working on something you want to work on.
2. It has to be some type of learning, and you have to document it (journal, etc.).
3. You'll present your accomplishments to the class twice (and will not be graded on it).
4. That's it. Have fun. Find your passion. Explore it. Enjoy learning what you want. (Juliani, 2017, p. 10).

Accustomed to being told what to do all the time, his students were immediately confused. "What are we supposed to be doing?" they asked. "How are we going to be graded?" He explained that they would not be graded on their presentation, but they would be held accountable. They were expected to document their learning and present it to the class after each quarter. They could do this in various ways, including writing or producing a video. Rather than taking time away from the curriculum, this project allowed the students to achieve beyond the standards. Here's what they were able to accomplish:

My students were able to build computers, learn computer programming, create and produce their own songs, learn how to play an instrument, start learning a new language, design their own clothes, design and create their own game, etc. What they did was a true accomplishment, and I'm sure many of them felt a sense of pride in their work. That initial blog post on 20% time caught fire on Hacker News, and thousands of people were able to start talking about the opportunities we give our students in school. As I began to share and connect online, I found a growing number of teachers who thought just like I did, and were doing something about it as well! (Juliani, 2017, p. 11–12).

Soon Genius Hour/20% Time Project began to spread across Juliani's entire school, and a team of his colleagues created a Genius Hour wiki space, which is now a website (https://geniushour.com/).

Ms. Smith (2017) tried Genius Hour in her fifth grade classroom. She gave her students one hour each week to study anything they wanted. She noted:

They chose subjects I could not have predicted: the architecture of the Czech Republic, blade forging, gender issues in the media. They used a plethora of technology and three-dimensional models. Working alongside my students, my topic was "How to Implement Genius Hour in the Classroom." Our year was successful but also flawed, with room for improvement and refinement. (Smith, 2017, para. 3)

Over time Ms. Smith refined the Genius Hour with a more scaffolded system, which involved four weeks to explore ideas, three weeks to narrow topics, and the rest of the year for learning and making. During the last four weeks of school, they presented their learning to the community. To help keep them on track, Ms. Smith set mini-project deadlines, such as a short video pitch or an interview, for every few weeks. She also found that introducing prompts to encourage reflection on their learning that they would respond to in their reflection journals helped the students. She also used Genius Hour to build supportive relationships among her students. She noted,

"Some students were more adept in some areas. One student, Aiden, was brilliant with big ideas but couldn't complete any work. Aspen, on the other hand, could run a small company. I paired them up and called Aspen a 'consultant.' It wasn't long before Aiden had his project moving along." Students engaged in skill swapping: "Skills like lettering titles, turning a video link into a QR code, and using keyboard shortcuts in typing were swapped throughout the classroom. This workshop environment happened authentically, but this year I will organize it by having a skill-sharing poster where students can log skills they have. (Smith, 2017, para. 10)

During this process, teachers provide ongoing conferencing and encourage self-reflection. At some point, you need to let students work at their own pace. They might get stuck once in a while, but they will learn through the challenges with your help.

Design Thinking and Project-Based Learning

Once you begin to feel comfortable creating opportunities for choice in your classroom, you can extend the choice process by inviting your students to engage in project-based learning activities. As we do this, we are shifting from trying to make a subject interesting to tapping our students' own interests. In this way we help them acquire the knowledge and skills to pursue their passions, fanning the spark of learning. We are also preparing them to engage in project-based teamwork, which typifies the most highly skilled knowledge work today.

In project-based learning, students take the lead; they choose the map, the vehicle, and the destination, and they steer their own learning. They decide on the topic, ask the questions, and choose the tools and what they aim to learn. They work at their own pace. According to Spencer and Juliani (2016, 2017), making is the mindset, design thinking is the process, and launch is the framework. Their "LAUNCH" framework provides a structure for guiding students through this process:

L—Look, listen, and learn. Encourage students to become aware of things that interest them. In discussions, a problem or challenge might arise that ignites their curiosity. For example, students in Mr. Acosta's eighth grade science class expressed concern about global warming, climate change, and the environment. "Understandably, they were worried about their future," he said. "We spent the first week or so discussing what they knew about the topic and what they wanted to learn more about. This discussion got them excited because they began to consider that there might actually be solutions that they could contribute to."

A—Ask questions. Once the students' curiosity is piqued, it's easy to move to the next phase of the launch cycle and ask lots of questions; the more questions the better. Questions can be generated by individual students, or they can be developed by small groups or the entire class. Eventually students come up with one problem that they want to solve. Then they can turn to brainstorming questions that are more directly related to this problem. Part of this process is learning how to generate insightful questions. Mr. Acosta's class wondered why more people were not concerned about the problem and why countries were not doing more to curb the CO_2 emissions that are believed to be the cause of global warming.

U—Understand the process or the problem. This is where students study the problem by first examining the systems and components that make up the problem. The students in Mr. Acosta's class studied the problem and the system of carbon use around the world. They began to see just how dependent most societies are on carbon-based energy. They interviewed their parents and other community members about what they thought about the problem and how people might become more aware of it. They spoke to experts at their local university. They became excited when they learned about carbon footprints and thought these might be key to solving the problem.

N—Navigate ideas. This phase may involve several iterations of brainstorming and consolidating ideas. It can get messy and confusing, but eventually the students will settle on what they want to make. The students in Mr. Acosta's class came up with lots of ideas that were way beyond their capacity to complete in school. However, he let them realize this on their own because their ideas were fascinating and they might have the opportunity to pursue these later, when they're older. On their own, they came up with a project to reduce the school's energy consumption.

C—Create. This is where the students begin to create their project. They may begin by making prototypes or drawings. The students in Mr. Acosta's class created a step-by-step plan to complete this project. The first step in their project was to do an energy audit of the school. On the U.S. Department of Energy website (n.d.), they found do-it-yourself energy audit instructions they could use. They planned to use the audit to generate a report and recommendations for ways to reduce the school's carbon footprint.

H—Highlight and revise. During this stage, students try out their ideas, highlight the data that they will use to evaluate the success of their project, and make appropriate revisions to improve the product. Mr. Acosta's students conducted the energy audit and discovered a lot of cold air coming through leaks in the seals of the doors. They also discovered some old appliances that were using a lot of energy in the school kitchen. They noted that the school was already using low energy lighting. As they began to work on the report, they considered various ways to make the case that the school should invest in new door seals and new appliances. They estimated the cost of the wasted energy and the repair and replacement costs, and they determined that repair would be a cost effective choice. Soon they felt ready to "launch" their project and present it to the school community.

LAUNCH. At this phase, students present their project to an authentic audience— real stakeholders in the issue or problem their project addresses. The aim is to disseminate the project as broadly as possible to experience real-world impact. The day of the launch, Mr. Acosta's students prepared to present their project to the principal, the superintendent, and a representative of the school board. They presented a PowerPoint presentation that reported the steps they took when conducting the energy audit, including photographs of students examining lighting and appliances and looking for leaks. They showed a video of one student testing the doors for leaks. The student demonstrated how to spray water on her hand and place it near the door to feel for air leaking. Another student described how they audited energy use of the old appliances. Both techniques came from tips they found on the Department of Energy website. Then the students presented the cost estimates and showed the adults how much money the school would save if they resealed the doors and replaced the old appliances. They also calculated how much the school's carbon use would decrease if it made these repairs. The superintendent was excited to see how much the students had accomplished on their own and invited them to present their project at the next school board meeting. It was such a thrill for the students to be invited to share their work with the community. Eventually a new budget was passed that included funds for new appliances. The door seals were an easy fix, and the students participated in fixing the seals. Students were so excited about what they had learned that many of them conducted energy audits at home, finding more ways to reduce the community's carbon footprint.

If a huge project like this is too much to take on, try short maker challenges that involve rapid prototyping. Students can complete the LAUNCH cycle quickly and have the opportunity to make something. Often these challenges are STEM related. You can find lots of great ideas on the Teach Engineering: STEM Curriculum for K–12 website (https://www.teachengineering.org/k12engineering/makerchallenges).

As you can see, project-based learning can be incredibly empowering as students engage in real-world problems and come up with actual solutions. These projects often involve multiple content areas. Mr. Acosta's students applied math to calculate energy usage and developed deep knowledge of carbon usage and how to reduce it. They also learned to write up a report and make a convincing presentation to stakeholders. Finally, they learned to assess their own learning. They met all their benchmarks. They successfully completed the audit, the report, and the presentation. They even convinced the school to make the recommended repairs and replacements.

Global Collaboration

Learning how to become a "global citizen" is essential to preparing our students for a world that is becoming more globally connected. Global citizenship refers to the cultivation of a holistic view of the world, recognizing our common humanity, our interdependence, and our shared responsibility to help one another and protect our planet's future. The COVID-19 pandemic and its rapid spread has highlighted this view. As I noted in Chapter 1, our children and youth are hungry for opportunities to address global challenges. As savvy consumers of digital technology, they are ready to break down the walls of their classrooms and connect with peers around the world.

One way to create opportunities for them to engage in collaborative learning with other students around the globe. The Flat Classroom Project (https://en.wikiversity.org/wiki/Flat_Classroom_Project) is just one of many ways to do this. This project idea comes from Thomas Friedman's (2005) book *The World is Flat: A Brief History of the Twenty-First Century*, which addresses globalization and a flattening of global markets offering opportunities for innovation like never before.

In the "flat classroom," students are grouped by topics and collaborate on a wiki, or other platform, with students from all over the world. The creation becomes the final project. Next, students create a multimedia project, based on the wiki project, to share what they learned with other students across the world. One might require that the final presentation include a contribution, such as a short video clip, from a student in another country. The final projects are judged by an international panel, and student teams have the opportunity to win awards.

Another prominent platform is the International Education and Resource Network (https://iearn.org/). They offer a diverse range of projects for K–12 students focused on various school subjects and the United Nations Sustainable Development Goals. The platform builds upon the essential question, "How will this project improve the quality of life on the planet?" They offer 15-week learning circle projects that involve project-based partnerships of schools around the world to address environmental, social, and educational issues that conclude with a media creation and presentation that is shared worldwide. They also offer professional learning courses for interested educators to support the integration of such projects into their existing curriculum.

Flat Connections (https://www.flatconnections.com/) was created by an Australian educator named Julie Lindsay. Similar to iEARN, Flat Connections supports global collaborative projects. For example, in Global Youth Debates, schools form teams to engage in debates with schools across the world asynchronously. Other projects involve teams of students from many schools that collaborate together on projects with the potential for global impact. These projects conclude with collaboratively created products and personal multimedia reflections. They also offer professional learning opportunities and in-person conferences for teachers.

TakingITGlobal for Educators (https://www.tigweb.org/) has designed a platform that engages and connects students in global collaborative learning projects. All their resources are free for teachers, including online professional learning. Their aim is to cultivate globally aware students by focusing on three primary themes: global citizenship, environmental stewardship, and student voice. TIGed offers opportunities such as live webinars with guest speakers, graduate student mentors, and international online conferences. They also offer some exciting projects such as Global Encounters, which is a live video conference that brings students together across the globe to address ways to shape a better future for humankind. Before they engage in the conference, students work with graduate student mentors and peers on related interactive content that prepares them for the big event.

A New Kind of School

Walking into the school building was disorienting at first. The school had the typical double door entryway for security, but there was no obvious school office or place for visitors to check in. One woman was sitting on a sofa with a student. Noticing my confusion, she smiled warmly and said, "Can I help you?" I told her that the principal, Chad Ratliff, had invited me to visit. She pointed to an interior room surrounded by windows and said, "Wonderful! He's over there. Just go on in." Later I learned that the woman who helped me was the school nurse.

Principal Ratliff plays a leading role in school innovation for the county, the state of Virginia, and the nation. Among many other honors, in 2017 the National School Boards Association named him one of the "20 to Watch" educational leaders in the United States. Since 2018, he has served as the principal of two innovative schools under one roof. Soon these schools may be combined into one 6–12 grade school. For now, each school has its own wing: Murry High School on one side and Community Charter Middle School on the other. We had met several years before, when he served as Director of Innovation and Instructional Programs for Albemarle County Public Schools (ACPS) and we were working together on a collaboration between ACPS and the University of Virginia, where I work. ACPS serves more than 14,000 students in preschool through grade 12. Albemarle County is a diverse locality of 726 square miles with a blend of rural, suburban, and urban settings in central Virginia. The urban and suburban area of the county surrounds, but does not include, Charlottesville, a small city of about 48,000 with its own school division. The greater Charlottesville area has a population of about 100,000.

Mr. Ratliff had seen me as I entered the building and came to greet me with a hug. I arrived as the teachers were settling in for their team meetings. Every morning, each school's teachers meet to review the plans for the day. Mr. Ratliff invited me to sit in on the middle school teachers' meeting. As we walked in, he introduced me to the staff of about 12 teachers sitting at a round table. They brought a chair over and invited me to sit with them. This Friday the students were finishing up a project focused on ways to address climate change. Groups of students were presenting their projects to members of the Charlottesville Community Climate Collaborative (C3), a community group aiming to make Charlottesville a carbon neutral city. The teachers discussed the logistics of the presentations and what students can be working on when they are not presenting. Each student needed to complete an ACPS technology survey on their laptops and groups could rehearse their presentations.

The school's two wings are connected by a welcoming central area that feels like a kitchen/living room combination. School starts at 9:30, a policy designed to align with the adolescent circadian rhythm; students stay up and wake up later during puberty (Crowley et al., 2015). As the students begin to arrive, they casually gather in this central area. Some sit on sofas, working at their laptops. Some chat in small groups. As school began, Chad invited me to join him as he presented an orientation to visiting eighth grade students who plan to attend the high school next year.

This is an overview of how things work at these schools. Both are grounded in student-centered, inquiry-based learning, and students are encouraged to independently pursue their own interests through the curriculum. The school has a liberal arts focus and emphasizes creativity, international understanding, cultural identity, and perspective taking. Due to its popularity, students who are residents of the county are admitted by lottery.

In alignment with the original concept of a charter school, Chad envisions the school as a model of innovation. Every design decision that he makes is based on the understanding that it must be feasible and scalable in other contexts. "Everything we try here needs to be transferrable to any other school," he noted. The school is experimenting with a degree of student autonomy not often seen in traditional schools. Murry and Community Charter cultivate self-motivation and self-discipline with the understanding that students will need these skills to succeed in this school model and in the future. The central theme of the school is student choice; students choose how they use their time, how they behave, and what educational goals they wish to accomplish. Students learn from the start that they are responsible for their learning and behavior and will be held to a high standard at these schools.

The school's philosophy is that learning is a continuum and the school aims to prepare students for lifelong learning. Students advance through the Virginia Standards of Learning at their own pace. When they have completed a standard, students are free to advance to the next level. If a student hasn't demonstrated mastery, learning is considered incomplete. Mastery can be demonstrated in a variety of ways, through independent projects, alternative assignment proposals, or completion of Self-Directed Learning (SDL) credits. Assessment is a multifaceted process that considers participation, effort, content mastery, and commitment to learning. For each assignment, students receive an A (90–100%), a B (80–89%) or an NMY (Not Mastered Yet; 79% and below). An NMY is given when a student has not satisfactorily completed all required work by the end of the semester. Students have time to make up the incomplete assignments, and teachers determine the requirements for completion. The high school is a candidate school for the International Baccalaureate (IB) Diploma Programme and is pursuing authorization as an IB World School, schools with a commitment to high-quality, challenging, international education. The full IB Diploma is available to students, or students can take individual IB courses, depending on their educational goals and personal interests. You may be wondering how these students fare on standardized tests. So far, they have exceeded the mean across the county and the state. However, Chad quickly notes that he doesn't want to focus on these scores because they can change from year to year. It's likely too early to be sure what impact the school will have on standardized test scores in the long term.

Students at Community Charter Middle School engage in projects that address authentic problems of personal interest. Academic content is integrated across subject areas, in contrast to traditional middle schools where content is organized into single subject areas. Every day, students spend some time working on reading and math skills related to their project work and some time within flexible learning groups. Though completely individualized, the curriculum is based on the Virginia Standards of Learning. Students engage in projects that run for about two weeks. They begin with a launch event where students are introduced to the content. Groups of students engage in a design thinking process to come up with project ideas. Once they have decided on a project, they collaborate on activities to complete it and then present the final project to an authentic stakeholder whose interests are related to the project topic.

The day I visited, the students were presenting their projects to three members of the Charlottesville Community Climate Collaborative (C3). The first group of students connected a laptop to the large monitor on the wall, and one student introduced their project. This group was concerned about the litter around the school grounds and the surrounding neighborhood. They started their presentation with background information about the problems litter causes to the environment. Next they explained how they studied the local problem by conducting a litter inventory—looking for patterns in the litter, where it tended to gather, and what types of litter were found. Finally, they proposed installing trash containers in these places and suggested that signs be installed to encourage citizens to use the trash containers. The students were poised but clearly excited to be sharing their work with interested adults. The visitors asked a few questions and told them that they liked how the students had done an inventory of the trash around the school to address the problem.

Two more groups presented while I was there. One focused on composting school food garbage and the other introduced the value of eating plant-based foods. As a final project, the latter group had made vegan pancakes from whole ingredients (no packaging) for the whole school the day before. The students reported that they conducted an experiment to see if students' opinions of the pancakes differed depending on whether they knew they were vegan or not. They noted that some students automatically snubbed the pancakes if they knew they were vegan. However, once they tasted the pancakes, these students changed their minds.

I asked middle school Head Teacher Stephanie Passman if I could see the maker spaces. "We have these maker spaces, but we encourage making all over the school, not just in these spaces," she noted. As we entered the middle school space, one teacher was helping a student with a wire between a battery and a bulb that had a short. Ms. Passman asked the student to show me around the space. There were several 3D printers and carvers; an array of woodshop tools, including a drill press; and an area dedicated to supplies for building and projects, including electrical components. Another student gave me a tour of the high school maker space. She showed me an art project she had created with wood and a 3D carver.

As I met with Chad and Stephanie to debrief at the end of my visit, I was struck by how calm and quiet everyone was. From my research, I have found that time urgency is a common stressor for teachers because we're always working against the clock to get through our content. In this school, there are no bells and there's plenty of time for deep learning and quality social interactions among students and between students and teachers. Chad told me about ACPS's commitment to student-centered learning and how he was working with other schools to extend the Murray model. We spent some time talking about teacher stress and teacher leadership, and I asked him if he was employing distributed leadership in the schools. His answer, "No, they are the leaders. They just tell me what I need to do, and I do it."

CONCLUSION

The End and The Beginning

Recently, I had the wonderful opportunity to present the CARE program to a group of teachers and education professionals over four days at the Sorbonne in Paris. This was in late February 2020, right before COVID-19 became a pandemic. Throughout the week I referred to aspects of this book as I addressed the teachers' complaints about the oppressive systems they confront each day. Every CARE program I facilitate, anywhere in the world, I hear the same stories. I see teachers who are passionate about supporting their students' growth, development, and learning, but overwrought by emotional exhaustion and the crushing demands of antiquated systems. As the program progresses, I see these teachers come back to life. As they learn to apply mindful awareness to the stress response and their emotional reactivity, they begin to lighten up and recover.

One of the participants was Luc Shankland, an English professor at Paris 3, Sorbonne Nouvelle University who had arranged for a room in the Sorbonne for the program. At the end of the course, he shared his deep gratitude for our bringing this transformative energy to his university. The Sorbonne is a building in Paris that was the home of one of the first universities in the world, beginning in 1257. Over the centuries, the Sorbonne has transformed again and again to adapt to changes in society and culture. It now houses multiple universities including Sorbonne Nouvelle, the result of a recent transformation.

As I sat in one of the oldest university buildings in the world, it dawned on me that human systems like the Sorbonne have been transforming throughout human history again and again. Now that the rate of change is increasing, we can witness major transformations multiple times within one lifetime, when before it changed slowly and incrementally over many years, or in dramatic ways that only occurred every few centuries. In the twenty-first century, for the first time in human history, we cannot reliably predict what's in store for us and the complex systems we have created. Our schools, and indeed our world, are facing unprecedented challenges. As the old factory model is crumbling, a new vibrant school is emerging that prepares our children and youth for the twenty-first century and beyond. But this requires us to step up to the challenge, show that we know what is needed, and take the lead to affect the system changes we wish to see in our world. The growing teacher shortage gives us a window of opportunity by providing leverage, but we need to know what to do to use it to transform our learning environments into places like Murry and Community Charter.

The COVID-19 pandemic has opened another opportunity for transformation. Attempts to provide learning remotely have revealed the deep inequities in our communities. Millions of children and youths are missing out on school because they do not have the necessary resources to access the schools' supports. Teachers are trying to reach to students whose parents may no longer have jobs and are struggling to put food on the table. They may no longer have phone service and an internet connection, or even a home. I sincerely hope that this tragedy motivates all of us in our society to recognize the need to prioritize investments in our children, families, and schools. Further, this pandemic has illuminated the critical need for systems and design thinking at all levels of society in order to successfully coordinate strategies to meet the current crisis and to prevent future catastrophes.

My deep commitment to the teaching profession and to teachers around the world inspired me to write this book. After years of studying teacher stress and developing interventions to help teachers manage the stress, the larger context of the oppressive school system kept looming in the background. I realized that we can develop our emotion skills and become more mindful, which will not only help us manage the stress of the classroom but will also give us an edge to become transformational change agents. As we change the way we think about schools, and ourselves as professionals, we can empower our students keep the spark of learning alive and pursue their dreams. Over time I am confident that we will look back on the coming decade as the Decade of the Teacher.

References

Allegretto, S., & Mishel, L. (2018). *The teacher penalty has hit a new high.* Washington, DC: Economic Policy Institute.

Alvesson, M. (2004). *Knowledge work and knowledge-intensive firms.* Oxford, England: Oxford University Press.

American Association for Employment in Education (2017). *Educator Supply and Demand Report 2016-17: Executive Summary.* Retrieved from https://www.aaee.org/resources/Documents/AAEE%20Supply%20_%20Demand%20Report%202017%20Ex%20Summary_fnl.pdf

Anderson, J. R., Greeno, J. G., Reder, L. M., & Simon, H. A. (2000). Perspectives on learning, thinking and activity. *Educational Researcher, 29,* 11–13. https://doi.org/10.2307/1176453

Armstrong, T. (2011). *The power of neurodiversity: Unleashing the advantages of your differently wired brain.* New York: Da Capo Lifelong Books.

Au, W. (2007). High-stakes testing and curricular control: A qualitative metasynthesis. *Educational Researcher, 36,* 258–267. https://doi.org/10.3102/0013189X07306523

Bandura, A. (1997). *Self-efficacy: The exercise of control.* New York, NY: W. H. Freeman and Company.

Bennett, M. R., & Reynolds, S. C. (2018, February 2). *What ancient footprints can tell us about what it was like to be a child in prehistoric times.* Retrieved from https://theconversation.com/what-ancient-footprints-can-tell-us-about-what-it-was-like-to-be-a-child-in-prehistoric-times-91584

Berger, J. G. (2019). *Unlocking leadership mindtraps: How to thrive in complexity.* Palo Alto, CA; Stanford University Press.

Berliner, D. C. (2013). Effects of inequality and poverty vs. teachers and schooling on America's youth. *Teachers College Record, 115*(12), 1–26.

Berwick, R. C., & Chomsky, N. (2016). *Why only us: Language and evolution*. Cambridge, MA: MIT Press.

Bothwell, M. (2019, October 17). *How upgrading education will secure the future*. Retrieved from https://www.tofflerassociates.com/vanishing-point/how-upgrading-education-will-secure-the-future

Bower, H.A., Parsons, E.R.C. (2016). Teacher identity and reform: Intersections within school culture. *The Urban Review 48*, 743–765. https://doi.org/10.1007/s11256-016-0376-7

Brandon, J., & Derrington, M. L. (2019). Supporting teacher growth and assuring teaching quality. In M. L. Derrington & J. Brandon (Eds.), *Differentiated teacher evaluation and professional learning*. Cham, Switzerland: Palgrave Macmillan.

Breidenstein, A., Fahey, K., Glickman, C., & Hensley, F. (2012). *Leading for powerful learning: A guide for instructional leaders*. New York, NY: Teachers College Press.

Bronfenbrenner, U. (1979). *The ecology of human development: Experiments by nature and design*. Cambridge, MA: Harvard University Press.

Bruns, H. A. (2017). Southern corn leaf blight: A story worth retelling. *Agronomy Journal, 109*, 1–7. https://doi.org/10.2134/agronj2017.01.0006

Burton, R. A. (2008). *On being certain: Believing you are right even when you're not*. New York, NY: St. Martin's Griffin.

Canrinus, E. T., Helms-Lorenz, M., Beijaard, D., Buitink, J., & Hofman, A. (2012). Self-efficacy, job satisfaction, motivation and commitment: Exploring the relationships between indicators of teachers' professional identity. *European Journal of Psychology of Education, 27*, 115–132. https://doi.org/10.1007/s10212-011-0069-2

Carroll, S., Reichardt, R., & Guarino, C. M. (2000). *The distribution of teachers among California's school districts*. Santa Monica, CA: Rand Corporation.

Carver-Thomas, D., & Darling-Hammond, L. (2017). *Teacher turnover: Why it matters and what we can do about it*. Palo Alto, CA: Learning Policy Institute.

Chang, K. (2019, July 16). For Apollo 11 he wasn't on the moon. But his coffee was warm. *The New York Times*. Retrieved from https://www.nytimes.com/2019/07/16/science/michael-collins-apollo-11.html

Cheng, E. C. K. (2015). Challenges for schools in a knowledge society. In E. C. K. Cheng (Ed.), *Knowledge management for school education* (pp. 1–10). Singapore: Springer.

Cheon, S. H., & Reeve, J. (2015). A classroom-based intervention to help teachers decrease students' amotivation. *Contemporary Educational Psychology, 40*, 99–111. https://doi.org/10.1016/j.cedpsych.2014.06.004

Chew, J. O. A., & Andrews, D. (2010). Enabling teachers to become pedagogical leaders: Case studies of two IDEAS schools in Singapore and Australia. *Educational Research for Policy and Practice, 9*, 59–74. https://doi.org/10.1007/s10671-010-9079-0

Church, A. T., Katigbak, M. S., Locke, K. D., Zhang, H., Shen, J., de Jesus Vargas-Flores, J., . . . Ching, C. M. (2012). Need satisfaction and well-being: testing self-determination theory in eight cultures. *Journal of Cross-Cultural Psychology, 44*, 507–534. https://doi.org/10.1177/0022022112466590

Council of Chief State School Officers & State Consortium on Education Leadership. (2008). *Performance expectations and indicators for education leaders: An ISLLC-Based guide to implementing leader standards and a companion guide to the educational leadership policy standards: ISLLC 2008.* Retrieved from http://npbea.org/wp-content/uploads/2017/05/Peformance_Indicators_2008.pdf

Crowley, S. J., Cain, S. W., Burns, A. C., Acebo, C., Carskadon, M. A. (2015). Increased sensitivity of the circadian system to light in early/mid-puberty. *The Journal of Clinical Endocrinology & Metabolism, 100,* 4067–4073. https://doi.org/10.1210/jc.2015-2775

Dailey, L. (2016, October 28). *Refocusing special needs: Child-centered special education.* Retrieved from http://blogs.edweek.org/edweek/learning_deeply/2016/10/refocusing_special_needs_child-centered_special_education.html

Darling-Hammond, L. (2003). Keeping good teachers: Why it matters, what leaders can do. *Educational Leadership, 60*(8), 6–13.

Darling-Hammond, L., Bullmaster, M. L., & Cobb, V. L. (1995). Rethinking teacher leadership through professional development schools. *The Elementary School, 96,* 87–106. https://doi.org/10.1086/461816

Deci, E. L., & Ryan, R. M. (1985). The general causality orientations scale: Self-determination in personality. *Journal of Research in Personality, 19,* 109–134. https://doi.org/10.1016/0092-6566(85)90023-6

Deci, E. L., & Ryan, R. M. (2002). Overview of self-determination theory: An organismic dialectical perspective. In E. L. Deci & R. M. Ryan (Eds.), *Handbook of self-determination research* (pp. 3–33). Rochester, NY: University of Rochester Press.

Deci, E. L., & Ryan, R. M. (2012). Self-determination theory. In P. A. M. Van Lange, A. W. Kruglanski, & E. T. Higgins (Eds.), *Handbook of theories of social psychology* (pp. 416–436). Thousand Oaks, CA: Sage.

DeFlaminis, J. A., Abdul-Jabbar, M., & Yoak, E. (2016). *Distributed leadership in schools.* New York, NY: Routledge.

Denton, P., & Kriete, R. (2000). *The first six weeks of school.* Wingdale, NY: Brookhillside.

Descartes, R. (1998). *Discourse on method and meditations on first philosophy* (D. A. Crass, Trans.). Indianapolis, IN: Hackett Publishing Company. (Original work published 1637–1641).

Devos, G., Tuytens, M., & Hulpia, H. (2014). Teachers' organizational commitment: Examining the mediating effects of distributed leadership. *American Journal of Education, 120,* 205–231. https://doi.org/10.1086/674370

Diamond, J. B., & Spillane, J. P. (2016). School leadership and management from a distributed perspective: A 2016 retrospective and prospective. *British Educational Leadership, Management & Administration Society, 30,* 147–154. https://doi.org/10.1177/0892020616665938

Durlak, J. A., Weissberg, R. P., Dymnicki, A. B., Taylor, R. D., & Schellinger, K. B. (2011). The impact of enhancing students' social and emotional learning: A meta-analysis of school-based universal interventions. *Child Development, 82,* 405–432. https://doi.org/10.1111/j.1467-8624.2010.01564.x

Dweck, C. S. (2006). *Mindset: The new psychology of success.* New York, NY: Random House.

Economist. (2002, July). The Invisible Green Hand. The Economist. Retrieved from https://www.economist.com/special-report/2002/07/06/the-invisible-green-hand

Eells, R. (2011). *Meta-analysis of the relationship between collective efficacy and student achievement* [Unpublished doctoral dissertation]. Loyola University.

Ellick, A. B., & Ashraf, I. (2009). *Class dismissed in the Swat Valley* [Video]. Available from https://www.nytimes.com/video/world/asia/1194838044017/class-dismissed-in-swat-valley.html?searchResultPosition=1

Feiman-Nemser, S., & Buchmann, M. (1983). *Pitfalls of experience in teacher preparation: Occasional Paper, 65.* East Lansing, MI: The Institute for Research on Teaching.

Ferris, L. J., Jetten, J., Hornsey, M. J., & Bastian, B. (2019). Feeling hurt: Revisiting the relationship between social and physical pain. *Review of General Psychology, 23,* 320–335. https://doi.org/10.1177/1089268019857936

Fredrickson, B. L. (2013). *Love 2.0: Finding happiness and health in moments of connection.* New York, NY: Penguin Group.

Friedman, T. L. (2005). *The world is flat: A brief history of the twenty-first century.* New York, NY: Farrar, Straus & Giroux.

Funk, C., & Hefferon, M. (2019, November 15). *Millennial and Gen Z Republicans stand out from their elders on climate and energy issues.* Pew Research Center FactTank. Retrieved from https://www.pewresearch.org/fact-tank/2019/11/25/younger-republicans-differ-with-older-party-members-on-climate-change-and-energy-issues/

Gest, S. D., Madill, R. A., Zadzora, K. M., Miller, A. M., & Rodkin, P. C. (2014). Teacher management of elementary classroom social dynamics: Associations with changes in student adjustment. *Journal of Emotional and Behavioral Disorders, 22,* 107–118. https://doi.org/10.1177/1063426613512677

Gewerts, C. (2020, April 16). *Exhausted and grieving: Teaching during the coronavirus crisis.* Education Week. Retrieved from https://www.edweek.org/ew/articles/2020/04/16/exhausted-and-grieving-teaching-during-the-coronavirus.html

Gilliam, W. S. & Shahar, G. (2006). Preschool and child care expulsion and suspension: Rates and predictors in one state. *Infants & Young Children, 19,* 228–245. https://doi.org/10.1097/00001163-200607000-00007

Gilovich, T., & Griffin, D. (2002). Heuristics and biases: then and now. In T. Gilovich, D. W. Griffin, & D. W. Kahneman (Eds.), *Heuristics and biases: The psychology of intuitive judgment* (pp. 1–18). Cambridge, England: Cambridge University Press.

Ginevra, M. C., Nota, L., Soresi, S., Shogren, K. A., Wehmeyer, M. L., & Little, T. D. (2015). A cross-cultural comparison of the self-determination construct in Italian and American adolescents. *International Journal of Adolescence and Youth, 20,* 501–517. https://doi.org/10.1080/02673843.2013.808159

Glasper, E. R. & Neigh, G. N. (2019). Editorial: Experience-dependent neuroplasticity across the lifespan: From risk to resilience. *Frontiers in Behavioral Neuroscience, 12,* 335. https://doi.org/10.3389/fnbeh.2018.00335

Goldring, R., Taie, S., & Riddles, M. (2014). *Teacher attrition and mobility: Results from the 2012–13 teacher follow-up survey* (NCES 2014-077). U.S. Department of Education.

Washington, DC: National Center for Education Statistics. Retrieved from https://nces.ed.gov/pubsearch/pubsinfo.asp?pubid=2014077

Goldstein, D. (2015). *The teacher wars: A history of America's most embattled profession.* New York, NY: Anchor Books.

Goodrich, F., & Hackett, A. (2017). *The diary of Anne Frank.* Hawthorne, CA: Snowball Publishing.

Gordon, C. (2019). An analysis of the 2019 Oakland teachers strike. *Monthly Review Online.* https://mronline.org/2019/06/06/an-analysis-of-the-2019-oakland-teachers-strike/

Gray, D. (2017, July 15). *Updated empathy map canvas.* Retrieved from https://medium.com/the-xplane-collection/updated-empathy-map-canvas-46df22df3c8a

Greenberg, M. T., Brown, J. L., & Abenavoli, R. M. (2016). *Teacher stress and health:Effects on teachers, students, and schools.* Retrieved from Pennsylvania State University, Edna Bennett Pierce Prevention Research Center: http://prevention.psu.edu/uploads/files/rwjf430428.pdf

Harari, Y. N. (2017). *Homo Deus: A brief history of tomorrow.* New York, NY: HarperCollins.

Harari, Y. N. (2014). *Sapiens: A brief history of humankind.* New York: HarperCollins.

Hargreaves, A. (2019). Teacher collaboration: 30 years of research on its nature, forms, limitations and effects. *Teachers and Teaching, 25,* 603–621. https://doi.org/10.1080/13540602.2019.1639499

Hargreaves, A. (2000). Four ages of professionalism and professional learning. *Teachers and Teaching, 6,* 151–182. https://doi.org/10.1080/713698714

Hargreaves, A., & O'Connor, M. T. (2018). *Collaborative professionalism: When teaching together means learning for all.* Thousand Oaks, CA: Corwin.

Harris, A., & Townsend, A. (2007). Developing leaders for tomorrow: Releasing system potential. *School Leadership & Management, 27,* 167–177. https://doi.org/10.1080/13632430701237339

Harteis, C., & Billett, S. (2008). The workplace as learning environment. *International Journal of Educational Research, 47,* 209–212. https://doi.org/10.1016/j.ijer.2008.07.002

Hattie, J. (2016, July 11, 2016). Third annual visible learning conference: Mindframes and maximizers), Washington, DC. Retrieved from https://visible-learning.org/2018/03/collective-teacher-efficacy-hattie/

Helms-Lorenz, M., van de Grift, W., & Maulana, R. (2016). Longitudinal effects of induction on teaching skills and attrition rates of beginning teachers. *School Effectiveness and School Improvement, 27,* 178–204. https://doi.org/10.1080/09243453.2015.1035731

Henn, B. M., Cavalli-Sforza, L. L., & Feldman, M. W. (2012). The great human expansion. *Proceedings of the National Academy of Sciences of the United States of America, 109,* 17758–17764. https://doi.org/10.1073/pnas.1212380109

Herndon, A. W. (2018, August 14). This former 'teacher of the year' wants to be Connecticut's first black democrat in congress. *The New York Times.* Retrieved from https://www.nytimes.com/2018/08/14/us/politics/jahana-hayes-teacher-connecticut.html

Hess, F. M. (2010). *The same thing over and over: How school reformers get stuck in yesterday's ideas.* Cambridge, MA: Harvard University Press.

Hogg, D., & Hogg, L. (2019). *#NeverAgain: A new generation draws the line*. New York, NY: Random House.

Hood, N. (2018). Personalising and localising knowledge: How teachers reconstruct resources and knowledge shared online in their teaching practice. *Technology, Pedagogy and Education, 27,* 589–605. https://doi.org/10.1080/1475939X.2018.1535448

Horner, R. R., & McIntosh, K. (2016). Reducing coercion in schools: The impact of schoolwide positive behavioral interventions and supports. T. J. Dishion & J. J. Snyder (Eds.), *The Oxford handbook of coercive relationship dynamics* (pp. 330–340). New York, NY: Oxford University Press.

Huang, F. L., & Cornell, D. G. (2019). School teasing and bullying after the presidential election. *Educational Researcher, 48,* 69–83. https://doi.org/10.3102/0013189X18820291

Hulpia, H., Devos, G., & Van Keer, H. (2011). The relation between school leadership from a distributed perspective and teachers' organizational commitment: Examining the source of the leadership function. *Educational Administration Quarterly, 47,* 728–771. https://doi.org/10.1177/0013161X11402065

Hursh, D., & Martina, C. A. (2016). The end of public schools? Or a new beginning? *The Educational Forum, 80,* 189–207. https://doi.org/10.1080/00131725.2016.1135380

Imants, J., & Van der Wal, M. M. (2020). A model of teacher agency in professional development and school reform. *Journal of Curriculum Studies, 52,* 1–14. https://doi.org/10.1080/00220272.2019.1604809

Ingersoll, R. M. (2012). Beginning teacher induction: What the data tells us. *Phi Delta Kappan, 93*(8), 47–51.

Ingersoll, R.M. and Perda, D. (2008). The status of teaching as a profession. In J. Ballantine & J. Spade (Eds.), *Schools and society: A sociological approach to education* (p. 106–118). Los Angeles, CA: Pine Forge Press/Sage Publications.

Irving, D. (2014). *Waking up White and finding myself in the story of race*. Cambridge, MA: Elephant Room Press.

Jameton, A. (1984). *Nursing practice: The ethical issues*. Englewood Cliffs: Prentice-Hall.

Jang, H., Reeve, J., & Halusic, M. (2016). A new autonomy-supportive way of teaching that increases conceptual learning: Teaching in students' preferred ways. *The Journal of Experimental Education, 84,* 686–701. https://doi.org/10.1080/00220973.2015.1083522

Janus v. AFSCME, No. 16-1466, 585 U.S. (2018)

Jennings, P. A. (2013). Focus group comment. Internal document: unpublished.

Jennings, P. A. (2015). *Mindfulness for teachers: Simple skills for peace and productivity in the classroom*. New York, NY: W. W. Norton.

Jennings, P. A. (2016). CARE for Teachers: A mindfulness-based approach to promoting teachers' well-being and improving performance. In K. Schonert-Reichl & R. Roeser (Eds.), *The handbook of mindfulness in education: Emerging theory, research, and programs* (pp. 133–148). New York, NY: Springer-Verlag.

Jennings, P. A. (2019a). *Mindfulness in the preK-5 classroom: Helping students stress less and learn more*. New York, NY: W. W. Norton.

Jennings, P. A. (2019b). *The trauma-sensitive classroom: Building resilience with compassionate teaching*. New York, NY: W. W. Norton.

Jennings, P. A., & Frank, J. L. (2015). In-service preparation for educators. In J. Durlak, R. Weissberg, & T. Gullota (Eds.), *Handbook of social and emotional learning* (pp. 422–437). New York, NY: Guilford.

Jennings, P. A., & Greenberg, M. (2009). The prosocial classroom: Teacher social and emotional competence in relation to child and classroom outcomes. *Review of Educational Research, 79,* 491–525. https://doi.org/10.3102/0034654308325693

Jennings, P. A., Brown, J. L., Frank, J. L., Doyle, S., Oh, Y., Davis, R., . . .Greenberg, M. T. (2017). Impacts of the CARE for Teachers program on teachers' social and emotional competence and classroom interactions. *Journal of Educational Psychology, 109,* 1010–1028. https://doi.org/10.1037/edu0000187

Jennings, P. A., Doyle, S., Oh, Y., Rasheed, D., Frank, J. L., & Brown, J. L. (2019). Long-term impacts of the CARE program on teachers' self-reported social and emotional competence and well-being. *Journal of School Psychology, 76,* 186–202. https://doi.org/10.1016/j.jsp.2019.07.009

Jennings, P. A., Minnici, A., & Yoder, N. (2019). Creating the working conditions to enhance teacher social and emotional well-being. In D. Osher, M. Mayer, R. Jagers, K. Kendziora, & L. Wood (Eds.), *Keeping students safe and helping them thrive: A collaborative handbook for education, safety, and justice professionals, families, and communities* (pp. 210–239). Westport, CT: Praeger.

Juliani, A. J. (2017, June 17). *The epic guide to student ownership.* Retrieved from http://ajjuliani.com/epic-guide-student-ownership/

Kahneman, D. (2011). *Thinking, fast and slow.* New York, NY: Farrar, Straus and Giroux.

Kegan, R. (1994). *In over our heads: The mental demands of modern life.* Cambridge, MA: Harvard University Press.

Kelley, D., & Kelley, T. (2015). *Creative confidence: Unleashing the creative potential within us all.* New York, NY: William Collins.

Keltner, D. (2012, July 31). *The compassionate species.* Retrieved from https://greatergood.berkeley.edu/article/item/the_compassionate_species

Kennedy, M. (2018, January 10). *Outcry after Louisiana teacher arrested during school board meeting.* Retrieved from https://www.npr.org/sections/thetwo-way/2018/01/10/577010534/outcry-after-louisiana-teacher-arrested-during-school-board-meeting

Keys, D. (1982). *Earth at Omega: Passage to planetization.* Boston, MA: Branden Press.

Kim, D. (1999). *Introduction to systems thinking.* Arcadia, CA: Pegasus Communications.

Koretz, D. (2017). *The testing charade: Pretending to make schools better.* Chicago, IL: The University of Chicago Press.

Korthagen, F. (2017). Inconvenient truths about teacher learning: Towards professional development 3.0. *Teachers and Teaching, 23,* 387–405. https://doi.org/10.1080/13540602.2016.1211523

Kristof, N. D., & WuDunn, S. (2020). *Tightrope: Americans reaching for hope.* New York: Alfred A. Knopf.

Kurtz, H. (2020, April 10). *National survey tracks impact of coronavirus on schools: 10 key findings.* Education Week. Retrieved from https://www.edweek.org/ew/articles/2020/04/10/national-survey-tracks-impact-of-coronavirus-on.html

Laszlo, A. (2015). Living systems, seeing systems, being systems: Learning to be the systems we wish to see in the world. *Spanda Journal, 6*(1), 165–173.

Leary, M. R., & Tangney, J. P. (2012). Handbook of self and identity. New York, NY: Guilford Press.

Leary, M. R., & Terry, M. L. (2012). Hypo-egoic mindsets: Antecedents and implications of quieting the self. In M. R. Leary & J. P. Tangney (Eds.), Handbook of self and identity (pp. 268–289). New York, NY: Guilford Press.

Leithwood, K., & Mascall, B. (2008). Collective leadership effects on student achievement. *Educational Administration Quarterly, 44*, 529–561. https://doi.org/10.1177/0013161X08321221

Leithwood, K., Patten, S., & Jantzi, D. (2010). Testing a conception of how school leadership influences student learning. *Educational Administration Quarterly, 46*, 671–706. https://doi.org/10.1177/0013161X10377347

Lister, J. (2018, January 31). *This is why technology won't replace teachers.* Retrieved from https://hundred.org/en/articles/this-is-why-technology-won-t-replace-teachers

Little, J. W., & Curry, M. (2009). Structuring talk about teaching and learning: The use of evidence in protocol-based conversation. In L. M. Earl., & H. Timperley (Eds.), *Professional learning conversations: Challenges in using evidence for improvement.* Dordrecht, Netherlands: Springer.

Lupien, S. J., Maheu, F., Tu, M., Fiocco, A., & Schramek, T. E. (2007). The effects of stress and stress hormones on human cognition: Implications for the field of brain and cognition. *Brain and Cognition, 65*, 209–237. https://doi.org/10.1016/j.bandc.2007.02.007

Luthar, S. S., & Kumar, N. L. (2018). Youth in high-achieving schools: Challenges to mental health and directions for evidence-based interventions. In A. W. Leschied A., D. H. Saklofske D., & G. L. Flett (Eds.), *Handbook of school-based mental health promotion* (pp. 441–458). New York, NY: Springer.

Lysaker, J., & Furuness, S. (2012). Space for transformation: Relational, dialogic pedagogy. *Journal of Transformative Education, 9*, 183–187. https://doi.org/10.1177/1541344612439939

Mangin, M. M., & Stoelinga, S. R. (2008). Teacher leadership: What it is and why it matters. In M. M. Mangin, & S. R. Stoelinga (Eds.), *Effective teacher leadership: Teacher leadership using research to inform and reform* (pp. 1–9). New York, NY: Teachers College Press.

Marr, J. S., & Cathey, J. T. (2010). New hypothesis for cause of epidemic among Native Americans, New England, 1616–1619. *Emerging Infectious Diseases, 16*, 281–286. https://doi.org/10.3201/eid1602.090276

Matisoo-Smith, E. (2017). The human landscape: population origins, settlement and impact of human arrival in Aotearoa/New Zealand. In J. Shulmeister (Ed.), *Landscape and quaternary environmental change in New Zealand: Atlantis advances in quaternary science* (Vol. 3, pp. 293–311). Paris, France: Atlantis Press.

McElfresh, A. (2018, December 11). A year later, Vermilion Parish teacher doesn't regret speaking up at board meeting. *The Daily Advertiser.* Retrieved from https://www.usatoday.com/story/news/2018/12/11/vermilion-parish-school-board-meeting-teacher-deyshia-hargrave-arrest-protest/2265740002/

Milkie, M. A., & Warner, C. H. (2011). Classroom learning environments and the mental health of first grade children. *Journal of Health and Social Behavior, 52*, 4–22. https://doi.org/10.1177/0022146510394952

Miller, C. C. (2018, September 10). Does teacher diversity matter in student learning? *The New York Times*. Retrieved from https://www.nytimes.com/2018/09/10/upshot/teacher-diversity-effect-students-learning.html

Miller, C. C., & Bromwich, J. E. (2019, March 16). How parents are robbing their children of adulthood. *The New York Times*. Retrieved from https://www.nytimes.com/2019/03/16/style/snowplow-parenting-scandal.htmlMoll, L. C. (2019). Elaborating Funds of Knowledge: Community-Oriented Practices in International Contexts. *Literacy Research: Theory, Method, and Practice, 68*(1), 130–138. https://doi.org/10.1177/2381336919870805

Mosteller, F. (1995). The Tennessee study of class size in the early school grades. *The Future of Children, 5*, 113–127. https://doi.org/10.2307/1602360

National Education Association, National Board for Professional Teaching Standards, & Center for Teaching Quality (2018). *The teacher leadership competencies*. Retrieved from http://www.nea.org/assets/docs/NEA_TLCF_20180824.pdf

National Research Council. (2015). *Guide to implementing the next generation science standards*. Washington, DC: The National Academies Press.

Neal, J. W., Cappella, E., Wagner, C., & Atkins, M. S. (2011). Seeing eye to eye: Predicting teacher–student agreement on classroom social networks. *Social Development, 20*, 376–393. https://doi.org/10.1111/j.1467-9507.2010.00582.x

Nickerson, R. S. (1998). Confirmation bias: A ubiquitous phenomenon in many guises. *Review of General Psychology, 2*, 175–220. https://doi.org/10.1037/1089-2680.2.2.175

Oberle, E., & Schonert-Reichl, K. A. (2016). Stress contagion in the classroom? The link between classroom teacher burnout and morning cortisol in elementary school students. *Social Science & Medicine, 159*, 30–37. http://dx.doi.org/10.1016/j.socscimed.2016.04.031

Olsen, B. (2016). *Teaching for success: Developing your teacher identity in today's classroom*. New York, NY: Routledge.

Organisation for Economic Cooperation and Development. (2014). *TALIS 2013 results: An international perspective on teaching and learning*. Paris, France: OECD Publishing. https://doi.org/10.1787/9789264196261-en

Organisation for Economic Cooperation and Development (2016). *Supporting Teacher Professionalism: Insights from TALIS 2013*. Paris: OECD Publishing. https://doi.org/10.1787/9789264248601-en

Ottesen, K. K. (2019, June 24). Parkland's David Hogg: 'Children having to go through active shooter drills is not what freedom looks like to me.' *The Washington Post*. Retrieved from https://www.washingtonpost.com/lifestyle/magazine/parklands-david-hogg-children-having-to-go-through-active-shooter-drills-is-not-what-freedom-looks-like-to-me/2019/06/24/ee5c8982-8182-11e9-bce7-40b4105f7ca0_story.html

Pals, T. & Boylin, C. (2019, January 9). Study finds link between voter preference for trump and bullying in middle schools. *American Education Research Association Newsroom*.

Retrieved from https://www.aera.net/Newsroom/News-Releases-and-Statements/Study -Finds-Link-between-Voter-Preference-for-Trump-and-Bullying-in-Middle-Schools

Partelow, L. (2019, December 3). *What to make of declining enrollment in teacher preparation programs.* Retrieved from https://www.americanprogress.org/issues/education-k-12/ reports/2019/12/03/477311/make-declining-enrollment-teacher-preparation-programs/

Patterson, G. R. (1982). *Coercive family process.* Eugene, OR: Castalia.

Pianta, R. C., La Paro, K., & Hamre, B. K. (2008). *Classroom Assessment Scoring System (CLASS) manual: K–3.* Baltimore, MD: Brookes.

Pianta, R., Hamre, B., Downer, J., Burchinal, M., Williford, A., LoCasale-Crouch, J., . . . Scott-Little, C. (2017). Early childhood professional development: Coaching and coursework effects on indicators of children's school readiness. *Early Education and Development, 28,* 956–975. https://doi.org/10.1080/10409289.2017.1319783

Pink, D. H. (2011). *Drive: The surprising truth about what motivates us.* New York, NY: Penguin Random House.

Pitzer, J., & Skinner, E. (2017). Predictors of changes in students' motivational resilience over the school year: The roles of teacher support, self-appraisals, and emotional reactivity. *International Journal of Behavioral Development, 41,* 15–29. https://doi.org/10 .1177/0165025416642051

Plato. (1925). *Plato in twelve volumes* (H. N. Fowler, Trans.). Harvard University Press. Retrieved from http://www.perseus.tufts.edu/hopper/text?doc=Perseus%3Atext %3A1999.01.0174%3Atext%3DPhileb.%3Asection%3D48c (Original work published ca. 400 B.C.E.)

Podolsky, A., & Sutcher, L. (2016). *California teacher shortages: A persistent problem.* Retrieved from Learning Policy Institute: https://learningpolicyinstitute.org/sites/default/ files/product-files/California_Teacher_Shortages_Persistent_Problem_BRIEF.pdf

Poekert, P., Alexandrou, A., & Shannon, D. (2016). How teachers become leaders: An internationally validated theoretical model of teacher leadership development. *Research in Post-Compulsory Education, 21,* 307–329. https://doi.org/10.1080/13596748.2016 .1226559, copyright © Further Education Research Association, reprinted by permission of Informa UK Limited, trading as Taylor & Francis Group, www.tandfonline.com on behalf of Further Education Research Association.

Price, H. E. (2012). Principal–teacher interactions: How affective relationships shape principal and teacher attitudes. *Educational Administration Quarterly, 48,* 39–85. https://doi .org/10.1177/0013161X11417126

Price, H. E. (2015). Principals' social interactions with teachers: How principal-teacher social relations correlate with teachers' perceptions of student engagement. *Journal of Educational Administration, 53,* 116–139. https://doi.org/10.1108/JEA-02-2014-0023

Price, H. E., & Weatherby, K. (2018). The global teaching profession: How treating teachers as knowledge workers improves the esteem of the teaching profession. *School Effectiveness and School Improvement, 29,* 113–149. https://doi.org/10.1080/09243453.2017.1394882

Ramirez, Y. W., & Nembhard, D. A. (2004). Measuring knowledge worker productivity: A taxonomy. *Journal of Intellectual Capital, 5,* 602–628. https://doi.org/10 .1108/14691930410567040

Ravitch, D. (2016). *The death and life of the great American school system: How testing and choice are undermining education.* New York, NY: Basic Books.

Redd, A. (2020, January 22). *This teacher spent a day as a 4th grader. Now she's rethinking her career.* Retrieved from https://www.edweek.org/tm/articles/2020/01/21/this-teacher -spent-a-day-as-a.html

Rimm-Kaufman, S. E. (2020). *SEL from the start.* New York; W. W. Norton & Company.

Rimm-Kaufman, S. E., Larsen, R. A. A., Baroody, A. E., Curby, T. W., Ko, M., Thomas, J. B., . . . DeCoster, J. (2014). Efficacy of the Responsive Classroom approach: Results from a 3-year, longitudinal randomized controlled trial. *American Educational Research Journal, 51,* 567–603. https://doi.org/10.3102/0002831214523821

Rittel, H. W. J., & Webber, M. M. (1973). Dilemmas in a general theory of planning. *Policy Sciences, 4*(2), 155–169.

Rodriguez, G. M. (2013). Power and agency in education: Exploring the pedagogical dimensions of funds of knowledge. *Review of Research in Education, 37,* 87–120. https://doi .org/10.3102/0091732X12462686

Rodriguez, V. (2014). *The teaching brain: An evolutionary trait at the heart of education.* New York, NY: The New Press.

Ronfeldt, M., Loeb, S., & Wyckoff, J. (2013). How teacher turnover harms student achievement. *American Educational Research Journal, 50,* 4–36. https://doi.org/10 .3102/0002831212463813

Rourke, A. (2019, September 2). Greta Thunberg responds to Asperger's critics: 'It's a superpower.' *The Guardian.* Retrieved from http://www.theguardian.com

Ryan, R. M. & Deci, E. L. (2017). *Self-determination theory: Basic psychological needs in motivation, development, and wellness.* New York: Guilford Press.

Sahlberg, P. (2015). *Finnish lessons 2.0: What can the world learn from educational change in Finland?* New York, NY: Teachers College Press.

Salam, M. (2017, November 21). Everything you learned about Thanksgiving is wrong. *The New York Times.* Retrieved from https://www.nytimes.com/2017/11/21/us/thanksgiving -myths-fact-check.html

SAPA Project (2018, January 16). Retrieved from https://sapa-project.org

Sapolsky, R. M. (2004). *Why zebras don't get ulcers: The acclaimed guide to stress, stress-related diseases, and coping—Now revised and updated.* New York, NY: Henry Holt and Company.

Schleicher, A. (2018). *Valuing our teachers and raising their status: How communities can help.* Paris, France: International Summit on the Teaching Profession, OECD Publishing. https://doi.org/10.1787/9789264292697-en

Schnellert, L. M., Butler, D. L., & Higginson, S. K. (2008). Co-constructors of data, co-constructors of meaning: Teacher professional development in an age of accountability. *Teaching and Teacher Education, 24,* 725–750. https://doi.org/10.1016/j.tate.2007.04 .001

Schroeder, S., Curcio, R., & Lundgren, L. (2019). Expanding the learning network: How teachers use Pinterest. *Journal of Research on Technology in Education, 51,* 166–186. https://doi.org/10.1080/15391523.2019.1573354

Schultz, K. (2010). *Being wrong: Adventures in the margin of error.* New York, NY: Harper-Collins.

Sebastian, J., Herman, K. C., & Reinke, M. Do organizational conditions influence teacher implementation of effective classroom management practices: Findings from a randomized trial. *Journal of School Psychology, 72,* 134–149. https://doi.org/10.1016/j.jsp.2018.12.008

Seaward B. L. (2018). *Managing stress: Principles and strategies for health and well-being.* Burlington, MA; Jones & Bartlett Learning.

Shaw, G. B. (1903). *Man and superman: A comedy and a philosophy.* New York, NY: Penguin Classics.

Schonert-Reichl, K. (2017). Social and Emotional Learning and Teachers. *The Future of Children, 27*(1), 137–155.

Shogren, K. A., Kennedy, W., Dowsett, C., Villarreal, M. G., & Little, T. D. (2014). Exploring essential characteristics of self-determination for diverse students using data from NLTS2. *Career Development and Transition for Exceptional Individuals, 37,* 168–176. https://doi.org/10.1177/2165143413486927

Shulman, L. S. (2004). *The wisdom of practice: Essays on teaching, learning, and learning to teach.* San Francisco, CA: Jossey-Bass.

Skaalvik, E. M., & Skaalvik, S. (2016). Teacher stress and teacher self-efficacy as predictors of engagement, emotional exhaustion, and motivation to leave the teaching profession. *Creative Education, 7,* 1785–1799. https://doi.org/10.4236/ce.2016.713182

Smith, M. (2017). *Genius hour in elementary school.* Retrieved from https://www.edutopia.org/article/genius-hour-elementary-school

Snowden, D. (1999). Liberating knowledge. In CBI Business Guide, *Liberating knowledge* (pp. 9–19). London, England: Caspian Publishing.

Snowden, D. J., & Boone, M. E. (2007). A leader's framework for decision making. *Harvard Business Review, 85*(11), 68–76.

Spencer, J., & Juliani, A. J. (2016. *LAUNCH: Using design thinking to boost creativity and bring out the maker in every student.* San Diego, CA: Dave Burgess Consulting, Inc.

Spencer, J., & Juliani, A. J. (2017). *Empower: What happens when student own their learning.* San Diego, CA: Dave Burgess Consulting, Inc.

Spillane, J. P. (2006). *Distributed leadership.* San Francisco, CA: Josey-Bass.

Spillane, J. P. (2012). *Distributed leadership* (4th ed.). New York, NY: Wiley.

Stedman, L. C. (1994). The Sandia report and U.S. achievement: An assessment. *The Journal of Educational Research, 87,* 133–146. https://doi.org/10.1080/00220671.1994.9941235

Strauss, V. (2014, October 24). Teacher spends two days as a student and is shocked at what she learns. *The Washington Post.* Retrieved from https://www.washingtonpost.com/news/answer-sheet/wp/2014/10/24/teacher-spends-two-days-as-a-student-and-is-shocked-at-what-she-learned/

Strauss, V. (2018, January 9). Teacher handcuffed, arrested after questioning school board about superintendent's contract. Here's the riveting video. *The Washington Post.* Retrieved from https://www.washingtonpost.com/news/answer-sheet/wp/2018/01/09/

teacher-forced-out-of-school-board-meeting-for-asking-tough-questions-is-handcuffed-arrested-heres-the-riveting-video/

Sutcher, L., Darling-Hammond, L., & Carver-Thomas, D. (2019). Understanding teacher shortages: An analysis of teacher supply and demand in the United States. *Education Policy Analysis Archives, 27.* https://doi.org/10.14507/epaa.27.3696

Tabibnia, G., & Lieberman, M. D. (2007). Fairness and cooperation are rewarding: Evidence from social cognitive neuroscience. *Annals of the New York Academy of Sciences, 1118,* 90–101. https://doi.org/10.1196/annals.1412.001

Taylor, R. D., Oberle, E., Durlak, J. A., & Weissberg, R. P. (2017). Promoting positive youth development through school-based social and emotional learning interventions: A meta-analysis of follow-up effects. *Child Development, 88,* 1156–1171. https://doi.org/10.1111/cdev.12864

Teach Engineering: STEM curriculum for K-12. (2020). *Maker challenges.* Retrieved from https://www.teachengineering.org/k12engineering/makerchallenges

Teacher Collaborative and Education First. (2017). *Building a sustainable structure to elevate teacher voices: A guide for school and district leaders.* Retrieved from https://education-first.com/wp-content/uploads/2017/11/Education-First_Teacher-Leadership-Sustainable-Structure-December-2017.pdf

Teacher Leadership Exploratory Consortium. (2011). *Teacher leader model standards.* Retrieved from http://www.nea.org/assets/docs/TeacherLeaderModelStandards2011.pdf

Teach to Lead. (2020a). *Lifting up educators in rural Mississippi.* Retrieved from http://teachtolead.org/stories/lifting-educators-rural-mississippi/?back=%2Fstories%2F

Teach to Lead. (2020b). *Transforming teacher retention through mentorship.* Retrieved from http://teachtolead.org/stories/transforming-teacher-retention-mentorship/?back=%2Fstories%2F

Urban, W. J., Wagoner, J. L., & Gaither, M. (2019). *American education: A history* (6th ed.). New York, NY: Routledge.

U.S. Bureau of Labor Statistics. (2017, April 27). *Employment in families with children in 2016.* Retrieved from https://www.bls.gov/opub/ted/2017/employment-in-families-with-children-in-2016.htm

U.S. Department of Energy. (n.d.). *Do it yourself: Home energy audits.* Retrieved from https://www.energy.gov/energysaver/home-energy-audits/do-it-yourself-home-energy-audits

U.S. Environmental Protection Agency. (1990). *Clean Air Act Title IV - Subchapter A: Acid Deposition Control.* Retrieved from https://www.epa.gov/clean-air-act-overview/clean-air-act-title-iv-subchapter-acid-deposition-control

U.S. National Commission on Excellence in Education. (1983). A nation at risk: The imperative for educational reform: April 1983. Washington, DC: The National Commission on Excellence in Education.

Van Dam, A. (2019, February 14). Teacher strikes made 2018 the biggest year for worker protest in a generation. *The Washington Post.* Retrieved from https://www.washingtonpost.com/us-policy/2019/02/14/with-teachers-lead-more-workers-went-strike-than-any-year-since/

Vanthournout, G., Noyens, D., Gijbels, D., & Van den Bossche, P. (2014). The relationship between workplace climate, motivation and learning approaches for knowledge workers. *Vocations and Learning, 7,* 191–214. https://doi.org/10.1007/s12186-014-9112-1

Vélez-Ibáñez, C. G., & Greenberg, J. B. (1992). Formation and transformation of funds of knowledge among U.S.–Mexican households. *Anthropology & Education Quarterly, 23*(4), 313–335.

Voiles, D. (2018, September 18). *Want to improve schools? Look to teacher leaders.* Retrieved from http://blogs.edweek.org/teachers/teacher_leader_voices/2018/09/_want_to_improve_schools_look_.html

Wenner, J. A., & Campbell, T. (2017). The theoretical and empirical basis of teacher leadership: A review of the literature. *Review of Educational Research, 87,* 134–171. https://doi.org/10.3102/0034654316653478

White, F. (2014). *The overview effect: Space exploration and human evolution.* Reston, VA: American Institute of Aeronautics and Astronautics, Inc.

Williams, J. D., Wallace, T. L., & Sung, H. C. (2016). Providing choice in middle grade classrooms: An exploratory study of enactment variability and student reflection. *Journal of Early Adolescence, 36,* 527–550. https://doi.org/10.1177/0272431615570057

Wolk, S. (2008). Joy in School. *Educational Leadership, 66*(1), 8–15.

York-Barr, J., & Duke, K. (2004). What do we know about teacher leadership? Findings from two decades of scholarship. *Review of Educational Research, 74,* 255–316. https://doi.org/10.3102/00346543074003255

Index

In this index, *f* denotes figure and *n* denotes footnote.

About the Author

Patricia (Tish) Jennings is an internationally recognized leader in the fields of social and emotional learning and mindfulness in education and Professor of Education at the Curry School of Education and Human Development at the University of Virginia. Her research places a specific emphasis on teacher stress and how it impacts the social and emotional context of the classroom, as articulated in her highly cited theoretical article "The Prosocial Classroom." Jennings led the team that developed CARE, a mindfulness-based professional development program shown to significantly improve teacher well-being, classroom interactions, and student engagement in the largest randomized controlled trial of a mindfulness-based intervention designed specifically to address teacher occupational stress. She is a co-author of Flourish: The Compassionate Schools Project curriculum, an integrated health and physical education program and is co-investigator on a large randomized controlled trial to evaluate the curriculum's efficacy. She was recently awarded an Education Innovation Research grant from the U.S. Department of Education to conduct a study that will examine whether CARE may enhance the effectiveness of a social and emotional learning curriculum. A member of the National Academy of Sciences Committee on Fostering Healthy Mental, Emotional, and Behavioral Development among Children and Youth, she was awarded the Cathy Kerr Award for Courageous and Compassionate Science by the Mind & Life Institute in 2018 and recently recognized by Mindful Magazine as one of "Ten Mindfulness Researchers You Should Know." Earlier in her career, Jennings spent more than 22 years as a teacher, school director, and teacher educator. She is the author numerous peer-reviewed journal articles and chapters, as well as several books: *Mindfulness for Teachers: Simple Skills for Peace and Productivity in the Classroom*, *The Trauma-Sensitive School: Building Resilience with Compassionate Teaching*, and *Mindfulness in the Pre-K–5 Classroom: Helping Students Stress Less and Learn More* (part of the Social and Emotional Learning Solutions series by Norton Professional Books of which she is editor).